Made with Words

Made with Words

HOBBES ON LANGUAGE, MIND, AND POLITICS

Philip Pettit

PRINCETON UNIVERSITY PRESS

PRINCETON AND OXFORD

Copyright © 2008 by Princeton University Press

Published by Princeton University Press, 41 William Street, Princeton,
New Jersey 08540

In the United Kingdom: Princeton University Press, 3 Market Place, Woodstock,
Oxfordshire OX20 1SY

Library of Congress Cataloging-in-Publication Data

Pettit, Philip, 1945–
  Made with words : Hobbes on language, mind, and politics / Philip Pettit.
    p. cm.
  Includes bibliographical references and index.
  ISBN 978-0-691-12929-7 (hardcover : alk. paper) 1. Hobbes, Thomas, 1588–1679. I.
Title.
  B1247. P48 2008
  192—dc22   2007017230

British Library Cataloging-in-Publication Data is available

This book has been composed in Palatino

Printed on acid-free paper.∞

press.princeton.edu

Printed in the United States of America

10 9 8 7 6 5 4 3 2

For Tori

Contents

Introduction

I ARGUED IN A PREVIOUS BOOK that Thomas Hobbes was one of the earliest critics, and perhaps the most significant opponent, of the republican way of thinking about freedom and government (Pettit 1997). His ideas about freedom, although fashioned to fit with an absolutist view of the state, were entirely original and played a crucial part in the development of classical liberalism—a later, nonabsolutist alternative to republican theory—in the nineteenth century. It was that fact about his views that led me to become interested in Hobbes's thought. And it is a good reason for being interested, since he sponsored a radical, conceptual innovation in thinking about liberty.

But there are many, many other reasons for taking an interest in Hobbes, as I have discovered since writing my earlier book. That discovery came about as a result of two graduate seminars on Hobbes that I taught at Princeton University with Dan Garber, first in 2003 and then in 2005. We set out to develop a picture of Hobbes in the round, taking account of his writings in the many different areas where he worked. I cannot overstate my gratitude to Dan for exposing me to the riches of Hobbes's thought and the wealth of connections between his thinking in different domains. Nor can I overstate my appreciation for the contributions of our students to the seminars in which we found our way through the Hobbesian texts. They were sparkling, memorable events.

Unsurprisingly, I came to refine the details of my views about Hobbes on liberty, as will be clear from the discussion in chapter 8 (Pettit 2005). But more surprisingly, I came to think that Hobbes is one of the most significant and least appreciated of modern thinkers. I like to move between different areas of philosophical inquiry, building on the analogues and connections that bubble up in that exercise, and seeking out the bigger picture that such shuttle research makes possible. I found that in this respect, if not in his political views, Hobbes is about as congenial a master as I could wish for. He is the very model of a thinker who ranges over many topics, searching out commonalities and connections across the many domains he covers.

But it is not just the broad, webbed quality of his work that struck me in this recent reading. I was even more forcibly impressed by the way his thought develops around a single idea that was quite original to him.

This is the idea, in the title of my book, that human minds are made by words.[1] More specifically, it is the idea that by nature human beings are more or less as other animals, and that what makes them different, giving them the capacity for thought, is the impact of a cultural development: the invention of speech at some distant time in the past. Language is an invented technology, not a natural inheritance, according to Hobbes, and it is a technology that transformed our kind, introducing a deep cleavage between us and otherwise comparable animals.

This idea now has wide currency, of course. It often surfaces in scientific discussions of cultural evolution and the great break that appears to have occurred among anatomically modern human beings over fifty thousand years ago (Tattersall 2002).[2] And it is a recurrent motif in eighteenth- and nineteenth-century romantic thought, receiving typical expression in Percy Bysshe Shelley's line from *Prometheus Unbound*: "He gave man speech and speech created thought."[3] But the idea appeared first in Hobbes and may ultimately derive from him. He is the inventor of the invention of language. He is the inventor of the idea that language is a transformative technology that has shaped our species, accounting for our characteristic features on both the positive and negative side of the ledger.

Hobbes's thesis about the transformative part played by speech shapes every aspect of his theory. It enables him to be a materialist about the human mind, giving him an account of what makes us special that he could invoke in place of a Cartesian dualism; it is no accident that he aired the thesis within three years of René Descartes' first excursion into these topics. It makes it possible for him to develop a theory of reasoning that equates it with the manipulation of words or symbols; a theory of personhood according to which persons are essentially spokespersons who can give their word to others and thereby "personate" themselves; and a theory of group agency that equates incorporation with rallying behind the words of a collective representative or spokesperson. The thesis allows Hobbes to analyze the predicament that makes peace and polity so hard to attain, tracing this to the effect on people's passions of having the words that enable them to worry about the future and fret about their standing relative to one other. And finally, it provides the materials with which he develops his story about the role that sovereign and commonwealth play as they marshal people's speech-derived capacities—their ability to reason, personate, and incorporate—in order to rescue them from their speech-derived predicament. So at any rate I try to show.

How many of these ideas remain worthy of attention in their own right? The idea that language is a transformative technology that provides a naturalistic explanation of what makes us special has not yet been mined, I suspect, for its full riches; this idea certainly retains contemporary significance. But so does the idea that reasoning is an exercise that presupposes access to language (Pettit 2007a). So does the claim that persons are marked by the role they can play in committing themselves to one another and, more broadly, proving themselves fit to be held mutually responsible (Pettit 2001). And so does the theory of incorporation, which rightly emphasizes the crucial role of representation in the formation and maintenance of a group agent (Pettit 2003).[4]

What about the idea that the capacity for speech, enabling us to worry about the future and our standing relative to others, has a warping effect on our desires? Hobbes thinks that access to speech introduced amour propre, in Jean-Jacques Rousseau's famous phrase—roughly, the desire for enduring preeminence—as distinct from the *amour de soi* that we share with simple animals, the natural concern for our day-to-day welfare. The role of such a concern for relative standing, whether in the relation between individuals or groups, is of first importance (Brennan and Pettit 2004). It appears in the resentment associated with relative dispossession, and the rage that disrespect and humiliation—even disrespect for others in one's ethnic, religious, or cultural reference group—can foster. Those who cherish the utterly implausible idea that our rational self-interest will generally block any otherwise unproductive concern with position and status sometimes describe themselves as Hobbesians. Their self-description couldn't be further off the mark. Hobbes would have regarded their psychology as shallow, and the policies it suggests as silly and dangerous.

This observation argues strongly for the continuing importance of Hobbes's ideas about human appetite and passion, though in his thinking about this topic he consciously or unconsciously makes an implausible move. While he rightly marks the concern that we human beings feel for our standing relative to others, he proceeds on the assumption that this always takes the form of a desire for superior standing; he ignores the fact that often we are content with the standing of equals. We may take pleasure in our power over others, as he contends, and the acknowledgment of that power—the honor, as he calls it—that usually follows. But we also take pleasure in not being under the power of others—in having a basis of protection and redress against them—and in its being a matter of general awareness that we enjoy that undominated standing; this enables us to command their respect and not have to live at their mercy. We crave the sort of nondomination that republicans have long equated with freedom—an equation that Hobbes roundly rejected—and the recognition or status that goes with this being a matter of common awareness (Pettit 1997, 2007c).

There is a crucial difference between the desire to be superior to others and the desire not to be inferior. It is not possible for everyone to be superior to others, since everyone cannot be top dog or even be above average. But things can be arranged, at least within certain domains, so that everyone can have the satisfaction of not being inferior to others. Hobbes asserts that people are locked in inevitable conflict, as each seeks superiority in resources and reputation, and many are vain enough to think they can attain it. And it is that alleged fact—that state of nature—that enables him to present the absolute state, notoriously, as the only practicable or indeed legitimate regime. Yet things will look very different, even from within an otherwise Hobbesian perspective, if people are acknowledged to find a high degree of satisfaction in having equal standing with others. Let that be granted, and it is possible to be much more sanguine about what people can achieve on the basis of the Hobbesian resources of ratiocination, personation, and incorporation. The mixed constitution of the republican tradition that Hobbes mocked so relentlessly begins to look like a real political possibility—as indeed it has proved to be, with the successes of constitutional democracy.

I have written this short book in the hopes of persuading others of the originality and unity that the invention-of-language theme gives Hobbes's work. The line of argument is straightforward. Human beings are distinguished from other animals by the transformation that occurred as a result of the invention of language. This gave people three positive capacities, associated with ratiocination, personation, and incorporation, but it also had a dark side: it warped their appetites, focusing their attention on the future as well as the present, and on their standing relative to others as well as their private welfare. The dark side means that by nature—by the second nature that they share in the wake of language—human beings are put in a situation of inescapable competition. But their positive capacities show them a way out: that of incorporating under a sovereign to whom they ascribe more or less absolute authority.

This line of argument is reflected in the eight main chapters of the book. The first chapter presents Hobbes's view of the simple mind that human beings share with other animals, and the second shows the difference that words make to that mind. Chapters 3 to 5 then explore the bright side of that difference, looking at ratiocination, personation, and incorporation, and chapter 6 explores the dark side, looking at the warping effect that words have on desires. Chapter 7 presents Hobbes's view of the state-of-nature predicament to which their warped desires lead human beings, and chapter 8 outlines the solution that absolute sovereignty is supposed to provide.

The book, I should add, might well have had a ninth chapter. This would have explored the dark side of words in warping human beliefs as distinct from human desires. It would have investigated the effects of words in leading people to profess parroted beliefs that they do not understand; to snare themselves in confused and incoherent commitments; and to let doctrines diversify and generate conflict under the pressure of amour propre. All of these themes get an airing in the book, but I decided against a separate treatment of the effects of words on belief because this would have required an investigation of Hobbes's views on religion. That investigation would have stretched my resources of scholarship as well as shifted the focus from issues of continuing philosophical concern to questions of a somewhat more arcane kind.

Not only is the book selective in abstracting from Hobbes's views on religious belief. It is also selective in the attention given to issues of interpretation. The book offers a brisk reading of the Hobbesian corpus, using footnotes to remark on where that reading departs from the views of a selection of commentators. The best argument for the controversial points in my interpretation may be that they hang together in a reading of Hobbes that makes him substantially more interesting and significant than he often appears—certainly more interesting and significant than he previously appeared to me. In order to highlight the unity of his thought, as that appears under this reading, I have provided a proposition-by-proposition summary of the chapters at the end of the book.

Following the approach associated with historians of thought like John Pocock, John Dunn, and Quentin Skinner, I am fully persuaded that "the history of thought should be viewed not as a series of attempts to answer a canonical set of questions, but as a sequence of episodes in which the questions as well as the answers have frequently changed" (Skinner 1988, 234). I have paid some service to this principle, indicating a number of striking occasions when Hobbes was focused on issues and pressures specific to the world in which he lived. Inevitably in a book of this short compass, however, I have often had to abstract from such contextual matters in order to concentrate on the unifying argument that I find in his work.

In referring to contemporary pressures on his thought, I often mention episodes in Hobbes's life, and it may be useful to recall the high points. These include his lifelong association with the Cavendishes from when he became a family tutor in 1608, as a young Oxford graduate of twenty; his early expertise in humanist learning and rhetoric; his brief period as secretary to Francis Bacon in the 1620s; the publication of his translation of Thucydides' *History of the Peloponnesian War* in 1629; his exposure to the new sciences in the 1630s; the period he spent in Paris, associating with leading French thinkers, between 1640 and

1651; the exchanges, after his return to England, with contemporary scientists like Robert Boyle and John Wallis; and his retirement in a Cavendish country residence from 1675 to his death in 1679, at the age of ninety-one. This life pattern is worth keeping in mind as we look at Hobbes's ideas (for background and biography, see Schuhmann 1998; Martinich 1999; Malcolm 2003, chapter 1).

The ideas relevant to the concerns of this book had more or less stabilized from about 1640, when Hobbes circulated *The Elements of Law*. I shall try to vindicate this claim by using a wide range of Hobbesian sources in support of my interpretation and by occasionally commenting on apparent signs of second thought. There is some development in his views, of course, as I indicate at various points, but on the whole I find it remarkable how stable and unchanged the basic ideas remain throughout the texts I use (see also Tuck 1988a, 1988b; Schuhmann 2004).

The main texts on which I draw, with the English editions I use, and the abbreviations I employ in citations are as follows:

EL   *The Elements of Law*, circulated in 1640, published in 1651 (Hobbes 1994a)

DCv   *De Cive*, published in 1642, second edition in 1647, in Latin (Hobbes 1998b)

L   *Leviathan*, published in 1651, translated into Latin in 1668 (Hobbes 1994b)

DCr   *De Corpore*, published in 1655, in Latin, translated into English in 1656 (Hobbes 1839a)

DH   *De Homine*, published in 1658, in Latin (Hobbes 1998a)

B   *Behemoth*, written by 1670, published in 1679 (Hobbes 1990)

D   *A Dialogue between a Philosopher, and a Student of the Common Laws of England*, written between 1668 and 1675, published posthumously in 1681 (Hobbes 2005)

I have incurred a number of serious debts in the course of writing this book. I have already recorded my gratitude to Dan Garber and our students in the Princeton seminars that we taught together. I also owe a debt to Kinch Hoekstra, Quentin Skinner, and Richard Tuck for many exchanges on Hobbesian and related matters. And I owe a special debt to the three of them, as I do to Dan Garber and Duncan Ivison, for their detailed comments on an earlier draft. These friends and colleagues are outstandingly generous citizens in our frail and sometimes frazzled republic of letters. Had I acknowledged their influence point by point, I would have had to add hundreds of footnotes.

I completed the final draft of the book at the Edmond J. Safra Foundation Center for Ethics at Harvard University, where I was Senior Scholar in Ethics, 2006–7, and I would like to express my appreciation for the support of the faculty and staff there. I also owe many debts of gratitude to the various friends and colleagues whom I have interrogated or regaled on specific issues. They include Charles Beitz, Annabel Brett, Victor Caston, Joy Connolly, Ed Curley, John Ferejohn, Moira Gatens, Bernie Gert, Tony Grafton, Jonathan Israel, Susan James, Melissa Lane, Steven Lukes, Steve Macedo, Jim Moor, Jim Murphy, Sankar Muthu, Christian Nadeau, Eric Nelson, Josh Ober, Pasquale Pasquino, Alan Patten, Jennifer Pitts, David Plunkett, David Runciman, Tamsin Shaw, Paul Sigmund, Walter Sinnott-Armstrong, and Maurizio Viroli. I am also grateful to Owen Pettit for some work he did in cleaning up the manuscript; to Chris Karpowicz, who provided invaluable research assistance; to Ian Malcolm, my editor at Princeton University Press; and to Cindy Milstein, my copy editor. Finally I must thank Tori McGeer, with whom I am fortunate enough to be able to share a life of conversation, both on Hobbes and other matters. I dedicate the book to her.

CHAPTER ONE

Mind in Nature

THE MEDIEVAL BACKGROUND

The theory of mind and nature that came down to philosophers of the seventeenth century from medieval scholasticism, and ultimately from Aristotle, depicted the mind of animal and human as a hierarchical system of faculties. At the base, there were the faculties of the senses whereby, so it was thought, sensory properties and objects were grasped and reproduced, brought to life in the mind in much the way a television set brings to life the pictures and sounds produced by a broadcasting station. The color and texture of things, their smell, taste, and sound, were given an intentional existence in the mind, it was said, which faithfully tracked the real existence that they were assumed to have in the world. The different senses combined to reproduce a perceptual counterpart to the external unity of the object seen and touched, tasted, smelled, and heard, and they did so in reliable if not entirely unfailing fidelity to its character.

Beyond the faculties of sense, and superior to them, was the faculty of intelligence or understanding, which according to the received picture was found in humans only, not in other animals. This faculty served the same reproducing or broadcasting function as the sensory faculties, but in relation to the real nature of things, not their accidental, sensory trappings; it was the source of judgment, in which human beings give internal or external expression to their understanding of the essence of things. My senses may serve in a given instance to make salient an object of iridescent color and fantastic form, but it is only by virtue of intelligence and understanding that I can make the judgment that the object in view is a peacock. In such understanding and judgment, so the received view went, I grasp the essence or nature of the object, an abstract entity that is shared universally with other items of the same kind. That essence is revealed in my understanding of the object, just as its sensory character is reproduced in my perceptual appreciation. It is given an intentional existence in my mind, in addition to the real existence that it has in different peacocks.

The faculties of sense and understanding, perception and judgment, were not left isolated in the medieval story but were situated in a rich chorus that also included the voices of imagination and memory, inference and reasoning. One further faculty was given particular prominence, though there were differences on whether it should be cast as the master or servant of judgment. This is the faculty of will in which the mind freely decides on what any situation requires in the way of action and proceeds to enact its decision. The faculty was not to be found in nonhuman animals, mere creatures of instinct and habit—not at least by standard accounts—but it had a central place in the human soul, created, as this soul was taken to be, in the image of God.

The medieval picture of the mind serves as the backdrop for understanding the radically different image that was developed by Hobbes and other thinkers who identified with the revolution created by the emerging, scientific account of the universe. The signal effect of that revolution was to indict as innocent and naive the belief in appearances that was built into the foundations of the received picture. The very earth moved, under the account that science now gave of how things are. If our senses and intelligence did not spontaneously register such a basic fact about the world we inhabit, then it began to seem that they could be mistaken on just about any question.[1]

Those in tune with the new developments thought in particular that the sensory impressions of color and sound, texture, taste, and smell, were not really properties of those objects but rather effects wrought on us, without our realizing it, by perceived objects. This theme is powerfully taken up in Hobbes, who speaks of "the great deception of sense": namely, that "whatsoever accidents or qualities our senses make us think there be in the world, they are not there, but are seemings and apparitions only" (EL 2.10). For Hobbes, all that there was to be found in the world itself, as distinct from the world as it appeared within our senses, was the motion of matter; and to such motion, transmitted invisibly through the air, he traced the effects in us with which he identified color, sound, and sensation in general. "The things that really are in the world without us, are those motions by which these seemings are caused" (EL 2.10). Thus there is no color in things. Rather, we mistakenly ascribe color when light has certain effects on us, as when it comes "to the eyes by reflection from uneven, rough, and coarse bodies" (EL 2.8).

The matter of which everything is composed, according to this picture, is parceled out in bodies, where "a body is that, which having no dependance upon our thought, is coincident or coextended with some part of space" (DCr 8.1).[2] All change in the world boils down to the motions of such matter, he says; "all mutation consists in motion," where motion is "a continual relinquishing of one place, and acquiring of another," (DCr 8.10).[3] There are some properties that truly belong in the external world, according to this account, being aspects of matter in motion; for Hobbes, examples include the extent of matter and the magnitude of motion. But by contrast with such primary qualities, as they came to be called, the secondary qualities associated with sense have no place in the world, and neither have the tertiary, evaluative properties that scholastics would also have taken to be objective. Hobbes adopts a consistently hard line on "colour, heat, odour, virtue, vice, and the like" (DCr 8.3).

But Hobbes's iconoclasm did not stop at denying the reality of secondary and tertiary qualities or properties. Like many others, he also went on to deny the reality of those universals that had been posited as the proper objects of understanding and judgment. As he thought that the external world was colorless and soundless, without texture, taste, or smell, so he thought that it was a patchwork of particular bodies, each entirely unique to itself (L 4.6). Such objects might have similar effects on us, but there was no literal sense, he held, in which they instantiated the abstract commonalities or universals that were hailed in the medieval picture. Where he traced the belief in the reality of colors and other sensory qualities to a natural deception of sense, he thought that the belief in universals was due to our mistaking the universality displayed by common nouns and other words for a universality in the world itself; more on this in the next chapter.

THE NEW THEORY OF MIND

The world revealed by science was bereft of homely features like color and texture, then, and no longer ordered on the lines of manifest essence or nature. It was a bleak, alien place that operated according to its own laws—laws that Hobbes took to be deterministic and inexorable (DCr 9.3)—in sublime indifference to the expectations of common intuition. But if this was how "the world itself, as distinct from the world as it appeared within our senses," was constituted, then could it make any room for mind, in particular for the sort of mind of which we are aware in ourselves? Could it make room for sensation, feeling, and experience, deliberation and reasoning, agency and free will?

In his widely read and much celebrated investigations, Descartes had come to the conclusion that no, the external world—the world of spatial, material, or extended things—did not itself provide the makings of mind. Some results of his inquiries appeared in his *Discourse on Method* of 1637 and, more substantively, his *Meditations* of 1641. Descartes claimed that apart and separate from matter or extension, there was also thought and mind; that among things in the material, spatially extended world, thought was present only in human beings;

and that each human being was a composite, therefore, of matter and mind: a thinking thing, or *res cogitans*, lodged within a spatially extended thing, or *res extensa*. He thereby inaugurated the view that came to be known as dualism, after the duality of matter and mind that it postulated. The medieval picture had seen a hierarchy of being in the material world, encompassing the purely physical, the vegetative, the sentient, and the rational, and had posited a distinct soul, a distinct unifying principle, at each new level of organization; plants had vegetative souls, animals had sentient souls, and humans had rational souls. Descartes now replaced that hierarchy with a duality, expelling everything but the rational soul of human beings into the bleak, dark world of matter. Even nonhuman, quite complex animals were cataloged as mere machines in the dichotomous, Cartesian bookkeeping.

Hobbes knew Descartes' views well and had thought critically about them (Tuck 1988a). By courtesy of his friend, the French priest and scientist Marin Mersenne, he was invited to contribute to the set of anonymous objections to the *Meditations* that Descartes reviewed in a reprinting of the book; this took place in 1642, one year after the original publication. Although this only appears indirectly in the objections that he posed for Descartes, Hobbes was a fervent opponent of dualism. His response to the scientific image of the world—he had become familiar with the new science from the early 1630s on—was to embrace monism as distinct from dualism, and argue that everything in the world, our own mind included, was entirely material in nature. Such a radical view might be expected to go with a rejection of the appearances of introspection, as it went with a rejection of the appearances of sense; it might be expected to encourage a denial that the mind, as we know it, is real. But Hobbes never flirted with such a view. Like Descartes, he thought that there really were minds, as we know or seem to know them; indeed, unlike Descartes, he thought that minds could be found in animals as well as humans. Where he broke with his eminent contemporary was in denying that the reality of mind meant that mind could not be material. He believed that mind amounted to nothing more than a complex mode in which matter is organized and the motions of matter are channeled to systematic effect.

In making this move, Hobbes identified a challenge that continues to figure as one of the main tasks recognized among contemporary philosophers.[4] How can mind as we know it—mind in all its flexibility and rationality—emerge out of the bare mechanisms supplied by material nature? Hobbes took up that challenge squarely, arguing that the rich fabric of mental appearances can be fully explained on the hypothesis that the mind is material. He undertook the task of showing how matter, suitably organized, can implement processes that deserve to be described as experience, imagination, and memory, episodes that warrant characterization as acts of deliberating and choosing, accomplishments that rank as instances of reasoning and judging.

Not only was Hobbes one of the first to undertake the task of locating mind in the motions of matter, as any mind-friendly materialist will have to do. He was totally original in adopting a two-stage approach to the challenge. He first of all attempts to explain the way in which those features of mind that are common to human and nonhuman animals can arise out of material motions. And then he tries to account for the distinguishing marks of the human mind by an appeal to the bootstrapping effects on the natural, animal mind of having access to language. He thinks of speech as a human invention, culturally transmitted across the generations, whereby people are enabled to go beyond other animals and achieve a novel level of mentality. This monistic account of human beings was just as novel as the dualistic alternative provided by Descartes, though it has only rarely been given the same attention. The striking, even outrageous character of Hobbes's political theory has generally had the effect of eclipsing the psychological theory that lay behind it.

In the following sections, I will look briefly at how Hobbes accounts in material terms for the workings of the natural mind common to human and animal. And then in the five chapters following I will turn to the effects whereby, as Hobbes thought, speech transforms the natural mind, enabling people to reason, perform as persons, and incorporate in groups, and furnishing them with desires of a reach and kind unknown in other species. It is this transformation that creates the circumstances of politics, according to Hobbes, and in the last two chapters I will explore the political problem to which the transformation gives rise and then the political solution that it makes possible.

THE NATURAL MIND: COGNITIVE POWERS

In a number of different places, Hobbes gives an account of the mind that is shared between human beings and at least some animals, most notably in *Elements of Law* (2–4, 7, 12), *Leviathan* (1–3, 6), and *De Corpore* (25). I propose here to give a brief sketch of the view that he defends, as this is all that is required for the present purposes. What Hobbes claims about the natural mind belongs to that area of natural philosophy or science that he describes as physics, and treats as more or less speculative. For reasons I will discuss at the end of the chapter, he thinks that with these phenomena, we can only identify "some ways and means by which they may be (I do not say they are) generated" (DCr 25.1; see also DH 10.5).

Hobbes distinguishes in this theory of the natural mind between powers cognitive and powers motive (EL 1.7). The cognitive powers are those whereby we gain a knowledge of the world. As a good empiricist, he says that these all involve the organs of sense, not any innate sources of knowledge (L 1.2); he thinks, indeed, that we cannot even conceive of the mind in the absence of an external world that provides sensory inputs (DCr 8.1). The organs of sense register motions that have their origin in an external object, and sensation is an "internal motion in the sentient, generated by some internal motion of the parts of the object, and propagated through all the media to the innermost part of the organ" (DCr 25.2).

But what is the internal motion—ultimately, as he assumes, the motion of sense organs, nerves, and the brain—in which sensation consists? We naturally characterize it differently, depending on whether vision or hearing, touch, taste, or smell, is involved, says Hobbes. But in each instance, it remains essentially the same sort of process—one that he describes either as a conception or image of the object, or an object-related thought, idea, or phantasm; these words he uses more or less indifferently (Gaskin 1994, 265). So far as the motion originates in the effect of external bodies on the senses, it is "a representation or appearance, of some quality or other accident, of a body without us" (L 1.2). Hobbes says nothing on what makes it fit to count as a representation of an object, but we might well construe him as if he meant only to say that it covaries with the object's presence.

The internal motion that we describe as a sensation when its object is present will usually continue for some time after the object is removed, in which case Hobbes speaks of it as an imagination rather than a sensation. So far as the imagination involved is taken to be related to the past sensation, he thinks of it more specifically still as a memory or remembrance. His picture is that one and the same sort of internal motion deserves to be described as a sensation in one context, and an imagination in another, and that whether it is construed as a mere imagination or a memory depends on the function we take it to be serving: the one thing "for divers considerations hath diverse names" (L 2.3). Although the details need not concern us, he also extends this parsimonious accountancy further, arguing that internal motions may have still other names, depending on background assumptions; they may count as figments, dreams, or fancies, and so on.

Internal motions must come in numbers, according to Hobbes. If there is to be sensory representation, there must be a retention of what was past as well as a registering of what is present; sense "hath necessarily some memory adhering to it" (DCr 25.5). And if humans and animals are to be sensitive to perceptual similarity and difference, then again there must be some interaction between memory and sensation.[5] Won't the number of internal motions present in a mind at once tend to generate confusion? They would do so, observes Hobbes, were it not for the fact that attention, as we would call it, organizes the mind: "an earnest studying of one object, takes away the sense of all other objects for the present" (DCr 25.6). Despite the hurly-burly of motions produced under current input, surviving from past input, and produced by the mixing of conceptions into novel fictions, the natural mind can rely on "the vehement motion made by some one object in the organs of sense" to ensure that at any moment it can attain focus, and not be lost to a miasma of impressions.

Apart from the concurrent association of different internal motions—different images, conceptions, or ideas—there is also an association across time, as conceptions succeed one another in this or that pattern. Conceptions sometimes bubble around in the mind in an unruly succession, and some of the conceptions that do this may not be subject to current sensory prompts, as in dreaming or mere imagining. But the normal, orderly pattern of mental life involves the recruitment and marshaling of conceptions in the service of one or another goal. Assume that someone has a desire for a certain goal. "From desire ariseth the thought of some means we have seen produce the like of that which we aim at; and from the thought of that, the thought of means to that mean; and so continually, till we come to some beginning within our own power" (L 3.4).

Hobbes describes this orderly "succession of conceptions" as a discourse of the mind, but by his lights, it is important that we do not think of the process as one that is voluntarily directed in the manner of reasoning with words. It involves a passive association of ideas, even when it is instrumentally useful and rational; the rationality appears by the grace of nature, not by the dint of voluntary effort. Driven by the desire to check my views, I may set out voluntarily to reason about things in words—and I may do this out loud, *sotto voce*, or entirely silently. But I don't do anything of the kind when, like a nonhuman animal, I instantiate a train of thought of the kind envisaged here. In order to mark this point, Hobbes proposes a terminological safeguard in *Elements of Law* (4.1): "because the word discourse is commonly taken for the coherence and consequences of words, I will (to avoid equivocation) call it discursion."

The human or nonhuman mind that has lived through a life of sensory input will develop what Hobbes calls experience, by which he means a memory of what gives rise to what: "remembrance of what antecedents have been followed with what consequents" (EL 4.6). Such experience gives rise, more or less spontaneously, to expectation: "after a man hath been accustomed to see like antecedents followed by like consequents, whensoever he seeth the like come to pass to any thing he had seen before, he looks there should follow it the same that followed then" (El 4.7).[6] Those humans or beasts who employ experience well in the formation of expectation are possessed of what Hobbes calls prudence. Such prudence will appear in the fact that without any effort on their parts, they will form more or less reliable expectations.

So much for the cognitive powers of the natural mind, as Hobbes conceives of it. It is based in internal motions of the mind that serve, depending on their origin, as sensory representations, memories, and imaginings. These motions are organized at any time by the object of the agent's attention, while they succeed one another over time in an irregular, daydreaming fashion or a regular manner that serves in the pursuit of goals. And the upshot of many such motions is the development of experience, and if experience is well used in forming expectations, prudence. But what now of the motive powers of the mind? How is the natural mind led to act?

THE NATURAL MIND: MOTIVE POWERS

Hobbes's story is continuous with that which I have sketched so far. Here is how he tells it in the fullest treatment he offers, in *De Corpore* (25.12). The internal motions of the mind do not just stop in the brain but are transmitted naturally to the heart, the organ that Hobbes treats as "the original of life." When an internal motion is transmitted to the heart, however, it is bound to have some effect on the vital motion associated with the flow of blood; it "must necessarily make some alteration or diversion of vital motion, namely, by quickening or slackening, helping or hindering the same." And it is at this point that the motion assumes a pleasing or painful aspect: "when it helpeth, it is pleasure; and when it hindereth, it is pain, trouble, grief, &c."

But pleasure and pain are not phenomena to materialize, be savored, and die. They give rise to animal motion, which is driven by desire and will, as distinct from the vital, unwilled motions that I have been describing so far. The creature who registers pleasure will try to sustain and repeat it, and the creature who registers pain will try to reduce and remove it. "And in animal motion this is the very first endeavour, and found even in the embryo; which while it is in the womb, moveth its limbs with voluntary motion, for the avoiding of whatsoever troubleth it, or for the pursuing of what pleaseth it." This first endeavor may consist in blind trial and error, but in Hobbes's picture, all creatures will experiment so that "by accustoming themselves by little and little, they come to know readily what is to be pursued and what to be avoided." This point made, he can introduce the notion of desire: "endeavour, when it tends towards such things as are known by experience to be pleasant, is called *appetite*, that is, an approaching; and when it shuns what is troublesome, *aversion*, or flying from it."

This portrait of how internal motions affect the heart, generate pleasure or pain, and lead to appetite or aversion may suggest that the normal state of the natural creature is one of rest, and that animal motion is only an occasional disturbance. But that is not at all what Hobbes thinks. He dismisses the search among "the ancient philosophers" for the final end, "felicity," on the grounds that "there is no such thing in the world, nor way to it, more than to Utopia: for while we live, we have desires" (EL 7.6). He associates the point with his scientific commitment to motion as the natural state of things: "life itself is but motion, and can never be without desire" (L 6.58).

The animal motion that occurs as a result of desire is distinct from the vital motion not just by its origin in desire but also by the role played by thought in channeling it. The picture painted by Hobbes is the now-familiar one in which desire furnishes the agent with a goal, and thought or belief directs the agent to the means by which to achieve that goal; desire provides the motor engine, as we might say, and belief the steering device. He depicts this most vividly in *Leviathan* (8.16): "thoughts are to the desires, as scouts, and spies, to range abroad, and find the way to the things desired: all steadiness of the mind's motion and all quickness of the same, proceeding from thence." Where such a concordance of desire and belief fails, according to Hobbes, there are more or less serious breakdowns of agency. Just "as to have no desire, is to be dead: so to have weak passions, is dullness; and to have passions indifferently for every thing, giddiness, and distraction; and to have stronger and more vehement passions for any thing, than is ordinarily seen in others, is that which men call madness."

Hobbes adds one further, important element to this story of desire and belief. In the normal run of things, humans and animals will find themselves with many different candidates for the desire or desires, or the belief or beliefs, on which to act. And so a process is necessary in which their desires and beliefs resolve themselves. The process whereby appetites and aversions do battle with one another until one desire wins out is described by Hobbes as deliberation; the process whereby rival thoughts or opinions alternate until one becomes fixed is called doubt. The desire that emerges as the winner in deliberation is the agent's will, and the opinion that emerges as the winner in doubt is the agent's judgment: "as the last appetite in deliberation is called the will, so the last opinion in the search for the truth of past and future is called the judgment" (L 7.2). Whenever an action is performed on the basis of belief and desire, then, it will be the issue of will, and being the issue of will, it will count as a voluntary action: "voluntary actions and omissions are such as have beginning in the will" (EL 12.3).

This final addition to his psychological story marks nicely the enormous contrast between Hobbes's mind-friendly monism and the dualism that he opposed in Descartes. Where Descartes saw will or *volonté* as something belonging essentially to the nonmaterial soul, the thinking thing, Hobbes casts it as nothing more than the final desire formed in a natural process in which appetites and aversions contend with one another for the control of action. And where Descartes saw will as the expression of an irreducible power of self-determination in the soul, free of all necessitating antecedents, Hobbes sees it as the deterministic product of a material process—something so unmysterious, indeed, that it is found in beasts as well as humans. Thus, he thinks that while we may call action that naturally issues from the will voluntary, the will cannot issue from itself in that way, and so is essentially involuntary. In a wonderful, wicked play on words, he says that "a man can no more say he will will, than he will will will, and so make an infinite repetition of the word will" (EL 12.5).

The story about the motive powers of the natural mind is similar in spirit, then, to the story Hobbes tells about its cognitive powers. Like the cognitive story, it gives center place to the internal motions of the mind. These move from the brain to the heart, help or hinder the flow of the blood, and thereby generate organic pleasure or pain. They provide the basis on which the bearers of natural minds adjust their responses or endeavors so as to preserve pleasure or remove pain, and thereby come to form desires or appetites. And these desires combine with beliefs to generate animal motion or action, as distinct from the simple vital motions considered so far. The process in which beliefs condense in fixed judgment is described by Hobbes as doubt, and the process in which desires condense in fixed will is depicted by him as deliberation. This completes the picture that Hobbes paints of the natural mind that he takes to be common to both human beings and animals.

Hobbes's Method

It may be useful to say something at this stage about Hobbes's view of the method that he follows in his philosophizing. This will help us to understand the overall structure of his vision and argument; I take a more positive view on that issue than many commentators (Strauss

1952; Warrender 1957; Sorell 1986; Malcolm 2003, chapter 5). Those who are not interested in the methodology, however, may go straight to the next chapter without serious loss; the material is relevant only at a few points later in the text, mainly in the opening to the final chapter.

As mentioned earlier, Hobbes thinks that the story just told about the natural mind belongs to the more speculative end of science. He would surely maintain that in broad profile something along the lines sketched must be true, but he would admit that at the level of detail, it is a story of "such causes and generations as may be" (DCr 25.1), not an account of the only imaginable way in which things can transpire within the natural frame of animals and humans. In this respect, he thinks that the theory of mind—like astronomy, music, and other parts of what he calls physics—is at a relative disadvantage by comparison with the other areas of philosophy in which he works.

In those other areas, Hobbes thinks that an a priori demonstration of results is possible—that is, a demonstration of their truth that is grounded in the definition of the terms used, as in Euclidean geometry, and that does not require confirmation by empirical or experiential tests (DH 10.5). In the psychology of the natural mind, he thinks that the results are not confirmable without reference to at least a certain amount of empirical knowledge, such as the knowledge about the motion of the blood that Hobbes took from the English physician William Harvey; the results are a posteriori to experience, in the sense of coming after it, not prior to experience or a priori.

There are two areas, in particular, where Hobbes thinks of himself as working in a demonstrative or a priori mode (DH 10.4–5). The one is in the most basic account of bodies, especially natural bodies. And the other is in the account of social bodies, where this can be taken to include the study of all matters conventional, ranging from speech to morals to politics. By contrast with the study of psychological bodies, these accounts can be pursued, he thinks, on an a priori basis—that is, on the basis of understanding what we mean by the names that we give to things; on the basis of understanding the definitions of our words, and the implications of those definitions.

The difference between the psychology just sketched and theorizing about the natural and the social is that in these latter areas, unlike the psychological, we human beings can bring about the phenomena ourselves. The general line, in Hobbes's words, is this: "science is allowed to men through . . . a priori demonstration only of those things whose generation depends on the will of men themselves" (DH 10.4). But when, as in the natural psychological case, "the causes of natural things are not in our power . . . we that do not see them, cannot deduce their qualities <that is, the qualities of those things> from their causes." We can only achieve a second-best guess, speculating "that such and such could have been their causes. This kind of demonstration is called a posteriori, and its science, physics" (DH 10.5).

It is reasonably clear how Hobbes can think that we human beings are capable of constructing social bodies, creating the conventions required: "we ourselves make the principles—that is, the causes of justice (namely laws and covenants)" (DH 10.5); we put such rules in place when "making, and maintaining commonwealths" (L 20.19). But how can he say that we can construct natural as distinct from artificial, social bodies?

The explanation derives from his view that the basic theory of natural bodies is geometry. This is not the study of abstract and unreal objects, he thinks—points without extension, lines without latitude, and surfaces without thickness, as it is represented in standard accounts (Hobbes 1839b, 210). Rather, it is the abstractive study of regular objects—a study that is ready, as appropriate, to abstract from a consideration of their extension, latitude, or thickness—and in particular, an abstractive study of the motions of regular bodies. As the study of such "ways of motion" (DCr 6.6), indeed, it is "the mother of all natural science" (L 46.11). The reason why we human beings can be said to be able to bring about natural bodies is that we can construct the figures studied in geometry; we can draw points and lines, circles and squares, and the like. "Since . . . the generation of the figures depends on our will," he says, "nothing more is required to know the phenomenon peculiar to any figure whatsoever, than that we consider everything that follows from the construction that we ourselves make" (DH 10.5; see also DCr 18.4).

In adopting this line Hobbes embraces a version of the so-called *verum factum* principle, made famous some decades after Hobbes's death by the Italian thinker Giambattista Vico (1982, 50–56). According to that principle, we can properly understand and know only the sort of thing that we can and do make; in Hobbes's version, it is only things of that kind that we can know a priori or demonstrably. While we may be able to speculate about the causes of appetite or aversion in the motions of the heart, we will never be able to confirm our speculations by seeing if such desires can indeed be brought about by such and such causes. But we will not have to rely on speculation with the causes of geometric figures or social conventions, for we will ourselves be able to test any claims as to how they may be brought about (Tuck 1988b). "Geometry therefore is demonstrable; for the lines and figures from which we reason are drawn and described by ourselves; and civil philosophy is demonstrable, because we make the commonwealth ourselves" (Hobbes 1839b, epistle dedicatory).

It is one thing to say that we can resort to our own constructive capacities to confirm various causal claims, however; it is quite another to say that they are a priori demonstrable—demonstrable just on the basis of the meanings of the words used in the claims. Why does Hobbes think that the two go together? The explanation has to do with the fact that he takes geometry as his exemplar of how science is done, and casts geometry as the a priori study of what is implied in notions like those of line and point, square and circle.

When we find that a compass provides a reliable way of making what counts at first pass as a circle, we dignify that mode of construction by defining a circle so that there is an a priori linkage between using a compass suitably and drawing a circular figure. We define it, in Hobbes's words, as "a figure, from whose one middle point all the extreme points are reached unto by equal radii" (DCr 1.5). Take this definition as given and there will be an a priori connection with the figure that would be produced in normal usage by a compass—that is, by "the circumduction of a body whereof one end remained unmoved" (DCr 6.5).[7]

There are two aspects to the a priori knowledge that Hobbes takes to be available in such a case, and this knowledge will be grounded in the definition of the circle together with the definitions of basic elements like points and lines.[8] Let the geometric elements involved in the use of the compass be posited and suitably defined, and it will follow a priori that a circle is present. Let the circle be posited and suitably defined, and it will follow a priori that it was made, or at least can be reliably made, by the use of the compass; "by knowing first what figure is set before us, we may come by ratiocination to some generation of the same, though perhaps not that by which it was made, yet that by which it might have been made" (DCr 1.5).[9]

Hobbes describes the knowledge of the maker-to-made connection as synthetic or compositive, and the knowledge of the made-to-maker connection as analytic or resolutive. Demonstrative science should ideally set out a body of knowledge in the first, synthetic manner, though the order of discovery as distinct from demonstration often has the second, analytic form. "The whole method, therefore, of demonstration, is *synthetical*, consisting of that order of speech which begins from primary or most universal propositions, which are manifest of themselves, and proceeds by a perpetual composition of propositions into syllogisms, till at last the learner understand the truth of the conclusion sought after" (DCr 6.12).[10]

As things stand with the knowledge of geometry and natural bodies, so Hobbes thinks that they can stand also in the study of convention and society. This is his great project: to develop for the first time what he calls a civil science, not just to contribute—as he thought he did also contribute—to the science of nature.[11] He believes, as we have just seen, that we can isolate basic and derived factors in geometry, test our knowledge of how things are made there by actually making them, give expression to this knowledge in suitable definitions, and thereby underwrite a system of a priori demonstration. He holds that we can do exactly the same sort of thing in the social area, and this is what his new civil science is meant to achieve.

In the full ideal of civil science that he embraces, he thinks of it emerging as the third section in a three-part study of nature, mind, and society. That is how he planned to present his work in, respectively, *De Corpore*, *De Homine*, and *De Cive*. But under the pressure of political events he published *De Cive* first, in 1642, leaving the other works until 1655 and 1658; in that earlier period, he also wrote *The Elements of Law* (circulated in 1640, and published in 1651) and *Leviathan* (1651). Did this order of presentation offend against his own methodological precepts? He did not think so, arguing that even those who have not built up from first principles a demonstrative knowledge of motion, in particular a knowledge of the motions of the mind, can still pursue the study of politics, starting from "the experience of every man that takes the pains to observe those motions within himself" (DCr 6.7). This is his excuse for writing *De Cive* (see preface) without any discussion of the natural mind or the mind that materializes under the influence of words.

This brief discursus may help to provide some insight into how Hobbes would have viewed what he was doing. It is time now to turn to the substantive parts of Hobbes's theory that are of interest here. I shall be examining what he holds on a range of topics, starting with language, and moving through human reasoning, personation, incorporation, and passion to his view of the problem of politics as well as his famous solution to that problem. In this exercise, Hobbes would have seen himself as generally exploring issues in the domain where humans make or can make things thus and so, and in a domain therefore where there is no block to the method of definition and demonstration whereby proper, a priori science can be established.

Appendix: Hobbes's Use of Cause

In this account of Hobbes's method I have not introduced the word *cause*, because while Hobbes uses the word frequently, his usage is apt to be misleading. In contemporary usage, a cause is a contingent antecedent of an event, and the elements of geometric figures do not look like causes. But Hobbes's causes include components as well as antecedents of phenomena, and so may include the points and lines that make up geometric figures (DCr 1.8), as they include even the parts that make up a watch (DCv preface). Hobbesian causes may be factors that go into the constitution of something, like the component waves that make up a tsunami, the constitutive antibodies that confer immunity to a disease, or the vibrating molecules that make water boil. Or they may be factors that are antecedent to its appearance, such as the earthquake at the origin of the tsunami, the exposure that gives rise to the immunity, or the fire that starts the boiling.

That Hobbes uses the word *cause* in this encompassing way is clear from the fact that by his account, "the entire cause" of a change in a body includes not just the external, "agent" factors inducing the effect but the changes in the parts of the "patient" object that are involved in that effect. "The cause therefore of all effects consists in certain accidents both in the agents and in the patient; which when they are all present, the effect is produced, but if any one of them be wanting it is not produced" (DCr 9.3).

The entire cause in this sense is an aggregate of all the different necessary causes, and those will include both antecedents and components of the phenomenon in question; each is likely in the circumstances to be a sine qua non of the phenomenon, which is what it takes according to Hobbes to be a necessary cause (DCr 9.3). Given that the entire cause includes all the necessary components and antecedents, it is no surprise to find that for Hobbes there is no time lag between the presence of the entire cause of a phenomenon and that phenomenon itself; "in whatsoever instant the cause is entire, in the same instant the effect is produced" (DCr 9.5). Once the earthquake has occurred and the waves have materialized, then the tsunami exists; once the exposure has taken place and the antibodies have appeared, then the immunity is established; once the fire is lit and the molecules attain a certain mean motion, then the boiling has begun. There is no room for a time lag between cause and effect when the cause is taken to include components as well as antecedents; if we think that there must be, then we are restricting the use of cause, contrary to Hobbes's own usage, to antecedents alone.

CHAPTER TWO

Minds with Words

Two Limitations

This picture of the mental life with which nature furnishes human beings, according to Hobbes, has two striking features. The first is that every process that takes place within the mind, cognitive or appetitive, is entirely particularistic. People will see and remember, represent and desire, only concrete things and situations. They will have no capacity to hold by general claims about how things are, or by general policies or principles for the direction of action. They will be prisoners of the imagined particular. Presented with a triangle, they will register just the individual figure contemplated, not any general aspect of the triangle (DCr 6.11; L 4.9). They will see the triangle before them, but will not register it as a triangle, a closed figure, or a drawing; not having access to such classes, they will not have the capacity to register it as anything more general than this particular thing: they will not be able, however implicitly, to classify it.

The second aspect of Hobbes's picture is that all that happens in the natural mind does precisely that: it happens. The succession of conceptions in which mental life consists is a form of vital motion, not of animal or voluntary motion; "one conception followeth not another, according to our election, and the need we have of them, but as it chanceth us to hear or see such things as shall bring them to our mind" (EL 5.1). The process does not evolve under the prompting or guidance of the agent's desire to have those conceptions assume a certain pattern—say, constitute correct and consistent representations—but only as a by-product of a desire to act in one or another concrete fashion. If the subject is well constructed, then the succession of conceptions will lead rationally to action; the action will satisfy the subject's desires according to evidentially sensitive representations. But no matter how rational the process or result, this succession of conceptions will not be prompted or guided by the agent's desires in the manner of an active, intentional performance. The natural agent, animal or human, may be rational, instantiating a certain model of *homo rationalis*. Yet no one in this natural state will exemplify *homo ratiocinans*. No one will display the sort of active reflection that we naturally ascribe to Auguste Rodin's sculpture of the thinker, bent over in concentrated thought.

But while the natural mind is particularistic and passive in Hobbes's portrait, he had no doubt that is not how our minds are. We adult, articulate human beings have words and concepts, not just for particular things, but for classes and categories of things, and we use them to classify, cross-check, and pursue interconnections. More specifically, we do this actively or intentionally, asking ourselves questions about how the words and concepts go together, and seeking to determine the answers. We may do this publicly in speaking with one another, but we may also do it silently, as in reflecting and taking counsel with ourselves. In these two respects, then, we reveal a mind that is decidedly different from the natural mind that Hobbes finds in the animal kingdom.

The Linguistic Way Beyond

How do human beings escape the constraints of the natural mind? How do they achieve the capacity to represent and desire things under general aspects, and think about them in an active, voluntary way? Hobbes's answer is the most startling and original claim that he makes in the whole of his philosophy.

The claim is that language or speech is a historical invention, and that it is language that makes possible the general, active form of thinking that we human beings display; it enables us to classify as well as register particulars, and seek out the implications of those classifications in a voluntary or active manner. Language, in Hobbes's story, provides the magic that enables us to jump the limitations of the natural, animal mind. The claim is most vividly expressed in *Leviathan*. Having reviewed the capacities of the natural mind that human beings share with animals, Hobbes directs us to other human capacities or faculties that "proceed all from the invention of words, and speech. For besides sense, and thoughts, and the train of thoughts, the mind of man has no other motion; though by the help of speech, and method, the same faculties may be improved to such a height, as to distinguish men from all other living creatures."(L 3.11).

Hobbes compares the transformative invention of language to the invention of printing, of which his contemporaries would have been keenly aware, and the even more important, if undated, invention of letters. The discovery of language was a similar sort of event, though of much greater significance; "the most noble invention of all other was that of speech, consisting of names and appellations, and their connection, whereby men register their thoughts, recall them when they are past, and also declare them one to another for mutual utility and conversation" (L 4.1). This invention is greater than either of the other two, because without it "there had been amongst men, neither common-wealth, nor society, nor contract, nor peace, no more than amongst lions, bears, and wolves."

Hobbes says little or nothing on how the invention of speech may have come about. He admits that it would be incredible to imagine people coming together to establish speech among themselves; presumably his thought is that they could not have done this without already having access to speech. But he is content to say that no such incredibility attaches to the idea that a single person introduced a few words, as indeed Adam is said to have done, and that "these names, having been accepted, were handed down from fathers to their sons, who also devised others" (DH 10.2). He is not interested in the details of how all this could have happened but is quite certain that something of the kind must have happened: "speech could not have had a natural origin except by the will of man himself."[1]

Why is Hobbes so sure that language must be an invention, and in particular, a transformative invention: a technology that changed the minded nature of those among whom it spread? I believe he must be thinking along the following lines; we might describe the train of thought as the master argument for his position.

- Those who are able to speak, and only those who are able to speak, have a capacity for active, classificatory thought—in short, for "thinking"; this is a plausible assumption that Hobbes does not explicitly defend.
- The ability to think in this sense is not sourced in the natural mind, since that mind is common to human beings and unthinking animals; this is the upshot of Hobbes's psychology of the natural mind.
- The correlation between speech and thinking can only be explained, then, by the fact that speech itself is at the origin of people's capacity to think; this is the one possibility that is left in place by the foregoing premises.
- But where can transformative speech come from? The only plausible, naturalistic explanation, and so the only explanation that would have made sense for Hobbes, is that it is the product of an invention by natural minds.

If speech is the source of active, classificatory thought, however, and if speech is an invention of the natural mind, why is it that only humans ever developed speech? Hobbes's answer to this challenge is to say that there is one natural appetite, curiosity, that distinguishes human beings from other animals, and that it was necessary for the invention of language.[2] "As in the discerning faculties, man leaveth all community with beasts at the faculty of imposing names; so also doth he surmount their nature at this passion of curiosity" (EL 9.18; see also L 3.5). And "this passion," he says, has given rise to "the invention of names" (EL 9.18).

Hobbes admits that animals may look for the immediate causes of things, as the curious cat looks for the source of the scratching noise or the play of light. But he suggests that this desire is not powerful within animals "in whom the appetite of food, and other pleasures of sense, by predominance, take away the care of knowing causes" (L 6.35). In human beings, by contrast, curiosity is—or at least can be (L 8.25)—"a lust of the mind, that by a perseverance of delight in the continual and indefatigable generation of knowledge, exceedeth the short vehemence of any carnal pleasure." And not only are human beings more curious than beasts, they are also curious in an extra dimension. We seek out causes, as other animals do, but we also seek out the effects that a cause has or is likely to have; "we imagine what we can do with it, when we have it" (L 3.5). Hobbes claims of this sort of curiosity that he has "not at any time seen any sign, but in man only."

While Hobbes suggests that this desire to explain and explore must have driven human beings to words, he doesn't ever give an account of how it can have done so. It is certainly true that access to words facilitates causal knowledge, as we shall see, but it remains obscure how a desire to know causes or effects might have prompted the appearance of words in the first place. His idea may be that words appeared initially on the basis of accident or fortuity, and that the fact that they could facilitate causal knowledge, and thereby satisfy the natural curiosity of human beings, ensured their tenure and increase. Perhaps his view is that they were generated by a process of cultural evolution in which the satisfaction of curiosity played a crucial, selection role.

SOME HISTORICAL OBSERVATIONS

In order to understand Hobbes's view of language as an invented, transformative technology, we need to see how it is supposed to serve as the source of active, classificatory thought. But before moving on to that question, there are a few historical observations that are worth putting in place.

A first is that Hobbes was certainly aware of at least one contemporary who championed a rather different explanation of the correlation between speech and thinking. This was Descartes, the absent darling of the Paris circles in which Hobbes moved in the 1640s; the absence, in Holland, was self-imposed. Descartes thought of the mind as a thinking thing, a *res cogitans*, and took its capacity for thought to be the source of speech, not the other way around. He could do this since, unlike Hobbes, he held that the mind was nonmaterial in nature and denied that it was present in nonhuman, unspeaking animals.

Hobbes first put forward his views on speech in *The Elements of Law*, which he circulated among his friends in 1640. But in 1637, in the *Discourse on Method*, Descartes had argued precisely the opposite, and Hobbes would certainly have been well aware of that fact. Richard Tuck (1988a, 37–39) has shown that Hobbes's account of perception in *The Elements* was outlined in response to some claims in the *Discourse*. There can be little doubt, given the chronology established by Tuck, that what Hobbes maintains about speech was also developed in conscious response to that text.

In the *Discourse*, Descartes (1985a, 139) considered the possibility that there might be "machines" that "bore a resemblance to our bodies and imitated our actions as closely as possible." But, so he argued, we would be able to determine that they did not possess the capacity to think, just by the fact that they would not have the capacity to speak; in particular, they would not have the capacity, later celebrated by Noam Chomsky (1965), to understand a more or less indefinite range of utterances.

> For we can certainly conceive of a machine so constructed that it utters words, and even utters words which correspond to bodily actions causing a change in its organs (e.g. if you touch it in one spot it asks what you want of it, if you touch it in another it cries out that you are hurting it, and so on). But it is not conceivable that such a machine should produce different arrangements of words so as to give an appropriately meaningful answer to whatever is said in its presence, as the dullest of men can do. (Descartes 1985a, 140)

Hobbes's claim about language is all the more striking for the fact that it was first made within three years of Descartes having put forward that argument, and it was made, moreover, in a book circulated in Parisian circles where Cartesian thought was an object of great interest. Descartes asserted, as a later, well-known parody put it, that there had to be a ghost in the machine of the human body—a ghostly center of thinking that was the source of speech. Hobbes must have been quite clear, and must have expected others to be quite clear, that he was taking on his celebrated contemporary on precisely this point. For him, there is no ghost in the machine. Human beings are machinelike the whole way through.

The difference between Descartes and Hobbes comes out nicely in the exchange between them on one of Hobbes's objections to the *Meditations*. Hobbes hypothesizes that "as well may be the case," "reasoning is simply the joining together and linking of names or labels by means of the verb 'is,'" so that all we really make inferences about is "whether or not we are combining the names of things in accordance with the arbitrary conventions which we have laid down in respect of their meaning." He thinks that determining whether combinations are rightly made is a matter of imaginatively recalling and exploring the conventional extensions of our words. And so he presents the hypothesis as a route to materialism: "reasoning will depend on names, names will depend on the imagination, and imagination will depend (as I believe it does) merely on the motions of our bodily organs; and so the mind will be nothing more than motion occurring in various parts of an organic body" (Descartes 1985b, 125–26). Descartes' terse response is to deny the hypothesis, insisting that reasoning "is not a linking of names but of the things that are signified by the names," and that it "deals with this something which is signified, rather than merely with the words" (Descartes 1985b, 126). The divide is clear and turns clearly on the role of language in relation to thought.

Not only was Hobbes taking on Descartes in claiming that language transformed the very minds that invented it, ushering into existence an active, general mode of thinking unknown to animals. He was also taking on the broad sweep of Western thought down to his time. For Platonists and Aristotelians alike, and the medieval thinkers who followed them, language was the sign of a capacity to think, as indeed Hobbes was well aware (L 4.14), and not its source. The received idea was that the intellect was naturally capable of thinking, having concepts that could be actively or voluntarily deployed to the purpose of general classification; words served to give expression to those concepts, not to make them possible. As Saint Thomas Aquinas puts it, "In us this intellectual concept is properly called a word, because this is what the spoken word signifies" (Clark 1972, 254).

But though Hobbes was breaking quite new ground in suggesting that speech was the source of the capacity to think, there was one precedent of which he would certainly have been conscious as a student and teacher of rhetoric. This is a famous account given by Marcus Tullius Cicero in *De Inventione* of the origin of eloquence: in effect, public, persuasive speech. That account begins with the remark, suggestive of Hobbes's own picture of things, "There was a time when men wandered at random over the fields, after the fashion of beasts, and supported life on the food of beasts; nor did they do anything by means of the reasoning powers of the mind; but almost everything by bodily strength." But Cicero goes on to make it clear that while "a great and wise man . . . collected men, who were previously dispersed over the fields and hidden in habitations in the woods into one place," that individual relied on a preexisting mastery of speech. As he says, "No wisdom which was silent and destitute of skill in speaking could have had such power as to turn men on a sudden from their previous customs, and to lead them to the adoption of a different system of life" (Cicero 1888, book 1.2).

The Ciceronian account may have provided a model for Hobbes, but it did not come near to matching the radicalism of his own proposal. And the same is true of the earlier traditions on which Cicero was drawing. While Sophists and the Stoics made much of the fact that words were conventional, not natural, and that the use of common words was essential for the development of human society, they invariably took language to presuppose thought, not to be a prerequisite of thought.[3] They assumed that words were expressive of an independent capacity to think, not that they lay at the origin of that capacity (Kerferd 1981, chapter 7; Cole 1990, chapter 4; Frede and Inwood 2005).[4]

While we are making some historical observations on the novelty of Hobbes's view of language and thought, it is worth adding that this view must have been influential in the development of romanticism in the eighteenth century—a development that Hobbes himself would have viewed with dismay. The core romantic idea is that language is the source of thinking, and that as languages vary in character from culture to culture, as indeed Locke (1975, book 2, 22.6) already noted, so we should expect to find the corresponding forms of thought and mentality varying across those divides. In each culture we should expect to find its own *conscience collective*, its own *Volksgeist*.

Hobbes would have found romanticism objectionable, believing in "the similitude of the thoughts and passions of one man to the thoughts and passions of another" (L introduction 3), and believing, as we shall see, in the desirability of purging natural languages of their various imperfections.[5] But the idea that speech is the source of thinking is his idea, and wittingly or unwittingly, the romantics must surely have been in his debt for that proposal. One possible conduit from Hobbes to the romantics is via the debate about the origin of language that began in the late seventeenth century in France—a debate in which Rousseau, one of the inspirers of romanticism, was later to take an active part (Wells 1987). It is surely plausible that since the Hobbesian oeuvre was well known in France, his idea about the invention of language may have been a stimulus for the rise of the origins debate, though this possibility is not routinely registered among historians (Aarsleff 1976).

Speech and Classificatory Thought

According to the master argument outlined earlier, Hobbes's naturalistic philosophy drove him to the conclusion that speech must be the source of active, classificatory thought. But it is not easy to see how speech alone is supposed to transform the passive, particularistic mind that humans are said to share with animals into the active, classificatory mind. In this subsection, I address the question as to how speech was meant to move human beings from thinking wholly particular thoughts to thinking at a more general or classificatory level. And in the next, I go on to consider how it was supposed to make the mind capable of active rather than just passive thought. Hobbes's rather sparse comments on these issues leave a lot of room for interpretation, but we can reconstruct an account of how the job is done that fits quite well with what he says.[6]

The big transition that Hobbes associates with the appearance of words is an ability not just to have a conception of something in its particularity but to have different conceptions of one and the same thing, each "signified" by a different word; those words each "denote" that to which the conceptions refer.[7] I will have a particularistic conception of something insofar as I contemplate it wordlessly or under a proper name. I will have a general conception of something insofar as I contemplate it as the bearer, referent, or *denotatum* of a general or common name, whether this be a simple name like *man* or a compound one like *bachelor* (DCr 2.4). For anyone capable of using such a name, it will be "a mark to bring to his mind some conception concerning the thing on which it is imposed" (EL 5.2).

Common names and the general conceptions that they bring to mind enable people to think about collections of items, then, not just about particular things. The items about which people are enabled to think in this general way come in many varieties. They may be bodies, like men or triangles, or the qualities of bodies, like squareness or redness, or the senses whereby qualities are discerned, like sight or hearing, or indeed names or the uses of names—say, a common name or the affirmative use of a common name (L 4.15–19). And not only are people enabled to think positive thoughts by virtue of having such names at their disposal. The existence of negative words like *nothing* or *infinite* makes it possible for them to think negative thoughts as well. These words are "not names of anything" but signs of refusing to use a name in a given instance; they enable speakers to take the name of a property—say, being a unicorn—and to say and think that there is no particular thing that bears that property (L 4.19).

At one level, Hobbes's idea is fairly straightforward. With common names available, we can address ourselves to an object, not in its particularity, but under its general aspect as the bearer of one or another general name. We are enabled "to think not only of the thing, but also by turns to remember the divers names, which for divers considerations

thereof are applied to the same" (DCr 4.8). We can form "many conceptions of one and the same thing, and for every several conception give it
a several name" (EL 5.5). Taking "the conception of man," he explicates
the idea as follows.

> First, he is conceived to be something that has extension, which is
> marked by the word *body*. *Body*, therefore, is a *simple name*, being put
> for that first single conception; afterwards, upon the sight of such
> and such motion, another conception arises, for which he is called an
> *animated body*; and this I here call a *compounded name*, as I do also the
> name *animal*, which is equivalent to an *animated body*. And, in the
> same manner, an *animated rational body*, as also a *man*, which is equiv-
> alent to it, is a more compounded name. And by this we see how the
> composition of conceptions in the mind is answerable to the compo-
> sition of names; for, as in the mind one idea or phantasm succeeds
> to another, and to this a third; so to one name is added another and
> another successively, and of them all is made one *compounded name*
> (DCr 2.14).

There is an enormous leap associated, according to this story, with
the appearance of words. Prior to access to words, the natural mind can
only register particulars and can have only one particularistic conception of each thing it registers. Or at least this is so for something seen
at a given time, from a given perspective and distance (DCr 1.3). After
words become available, this all changes. The articulate or worded mind
can register particulars—now under this name, now under that; now
under one conception, now under another—and so it can register things
as belonging to different classes. It does not merely see, it sees as. It does
not merely register things, it also classifies them.

The import of the difference made is illustrated by Hobbes with reference to a triangle. He suggests that without words, it is impossible to
see in a triangle presented for observation anything other than that
particular triangle, and so it is impossible to carry any lessons of
understanding—he has a surprising view of how much particularistic
understanding can yield—from one case to another.

> For example, if any man, by considering a triangle set before him,
> should find that all its angles together taken are equal to two right
> angles, and that by thinking of the same tacitly, without any use of
> words either understood or expressed; and it should happen after-
> wards that another triangle, unlike the former, or the same in a dif-
> ferent situation, should be offered to his consideration, he would not
> know readily whether the same property were in this last or no, but
> would be forced, as often as a different triangle were brought before

him (and the difference of triangles is infinite) to begin his contemplation anew (DCr 6.11; see L 4.9).[8]

So much by way of showing the difference that names are supposed to make in making general, classificatory thought possible. Yet the story is problematic in one salient respect: it is exposed to an obvious objection of circularity. If access to words, in particular to common names, has a truly transformative effect on natural minds, then prior to that access, natural minds must not be aware of the general aspects of things by virtue of which they can be assigned to different classes. But if they are not aware of the general aspects of things, then it is not clear how they can learn the use of general words. They are said to use different words for one thing, after all, on the basis of the thing's various aspects—the "divers considerations" (DCr 4.8) it calls to mind. And that suggests that far from general words making the general aspects of things accessible, it is an awareness of those general aspects that enables people to master the words in the first place.

The problem can be stated as a dilemma. Either people are independently aware of the general aspects of things that cue their use of words or they are not. If they are aware of such general aspects, then the mastery of words is not necessary for classificatory thought. If they are not aware of those aspects, then the mastery of words is impossible. This problem need not be destructive, however, of the Hobbesian proposal. It presupposes that the aspects that things present can cue people's use of words only if people are explicitly aware of those aspects, prior to the mastery of the words. That presupposition is unsupported, and it turns out that by rejecting it—as Hobbes may have implicitly rejected it—we can see our way to a plausible reading of the proposal.

When I associate a name with a thing, at least in the case of naming perceptually registered things, then I do so on the basis of its affecting me in a certain way. This is the central claim in Hobbes's account: "because the same things may enter into account for divers accidents, their names are (to show that diversity) diversly wrested and diversified" (L 4.14). Thus, to consider the names of objects, "a thing may enter into account for matter or body, as living, sensible, rational, hot, cold, moved, quiet"; we give different names to the same thing, as he puts it elsewhere, when "diverse considerations thereof are applied to the same" (DCr 4.8; see also 1.3).

This account certainly invites the circularity objection. Yet it does so only on the assumption that in order to be primed by this or that aspect of something into applying a certain name, I must be aware of that aspect as such. The priming effect of the object must not operate below the level of my awareness; it must not be subliminal. There is absolutely no need, however, to endorse this assumption. Introduced to a name that is meant to apply to many things, and presented with some putative examples, I may find it natural to extend the name to things in a certain range and deny it to others. But this may be natural because of an unnoticed effect of the things to which I apply the name, not because of any factor that enters my awareness. That effect may play the required, priming role without my being aware of the source of the effect—the common aspect of the things in question—or even of the effect itself. There is now considerable neuroscientific evidence that this indeed is how most priming occurs; in this respect, the brain generally works behind the back of the mind (Gazzaniga, Ivry, and Mangun 1998; Pettit 2007b).

It is quite natural to read Hobbes in a way that allows for the subliminal priming of words. We confer different names on the same thing as a result of the different effects that the thing has on us, he says. But for all he adds, we may do this without being aware of the different effects or considerations by virtue of which we apply the various names to that one thing. Equally, we confer the same name on different things, but for all he says, we may do this without any sense of the common effects or considerations on the basis of which we apply the same name to all those entities. In each case we find it natural, we know not why, to use names as we do. Provided with some basic training in suitable names and examples, we find ourselves disposed, without having any exact sense of why, to apply different names to one thing, and the same name to different things.

If we interpret the Hobbesian idea on these lines, then it is easy to explain the sense in which language is meant to support general, classificatory thought. Suppose that we learn to apply common names across a certain domain of entities, and that this mastery of general words is subliminally primed, not guided by aspects of which we are explicitly aware. Such names will enable us for the first time to think or conceive of a given entity as something deserving of one name and belonging to one class, or as deserving of another name and belonging to that other class. Each name will provide a reference class within which to place the item. And this will be so, even though we may have little or no awareness of the common effects that members of that class have on us, when they prompt us to use the relevant name. I see a given person, and depending on which feature or aspect moves me, and moves me without my necessarily being aware of the fact, I use the name *body, animal, man,* or *carpenter* of him. But by virtue of being disposed to do this, I can now take the person under any one of those names, and since each name applies to many things, I can place him in any one of the corresponding classes. Scaffolded by the habits of naming that language gives me, I can think of the person at one time under any one of a number of general concepts, not just in a single, particularistic representation.

Think of the sort of change that takes place when you learn to apply a term like *art deco* to the heterogeneous set of buildings, furniture, and objets d'art of which it is generally used. With the common term as an organizing principle, it becomes possible to see a surprising unity in that rather mixed bunch of things, and to think about them, not just one by one, but as a general, perspicuous class. Previously, the members of the category may have seemed entirely disparate; now, with the word in hand, they display an unmissable commonality. Hobbes's claim is that the introduction of words to the natural mind has the same sort of effect across the full spectrum of awareness, bringing to light patterns that were previously accessible only at a level of subliminal sensitivity.

This account of Hobbes's views not only saves him from the circularity objection raised earlier. It also helps to make sense of his claims on two distinct fronts.

First of all, it enables us to make sense of the way in which he thinks that experience can accumulate and give rise to prudence, as we saw him claim in the last chapter. He thinks of experience as "remembrance of what antecedents have been followed by what consequents" (EL 4.6), and holds that it gives rise in the prudent or well-trained mind to a reliable expectation. When a person "seeth the like to come to pass to any thing he had seen before, he looks there should follow it the same that followed then" (EL 4.7; see also L 5.5.). Hobbes does not think that the natural mind sees that there is a likeness between what happened previously and what is likely to happen now; that would require the general thinking he associates with language. The idea is simply that the likeness registers with the subject and engenders the appropriate expectation. But how is the likeness to register, under the particularistic image of the natural mind? I can now provide an answer: because it registers in a subliminal way that cues the subject's expectations about what will happen in the later case.

Not only does this story make sense of the role of prudence in the natural mind. It enables me, second, to explain the rather curious things Hobbes says about nominalism. He endorses the doctrine when he says that there is "nothing in the world universal but names; for the things named, are every one of them individual and singular" (L 4.6). But he makes his commitment obscure when he goes on to remark that "one universal name is imposed on many things for their similitude in some quality or other accident." And the obscurity intensifies when he describes the imposition of a universal name in the absence of such a similarity as a case of equivocation or ambiguity (EL 5.7). By most accounts, accepting that there are similitudes in quality or accident means believing in universals and rejecting nominalism. And so there is a problem about explaining what Hobbes believes (Watkins 1973, 107). How can he claim to be a nominalist and admit such properties into his ontology?

The problem disappears when we take him to allow for the existence of similarities and differences to which natural minds are subliminally sensitive. For now we can take his nominalism as the claim not that there are no properties in the world—no classes organized on the basis of the similarities and differences between particulars—but that there are none there that natural minds can consult in the way in which traditional realism about universals thought they could be consulted. When a similarity operates on us in a subliminal way, after the fashion of natural minds, it does not enable us to form a conception of the background property and does not put us in a position to consult it. The property has an effect on us, to be sure, but it does not itself come into view. Hence our world is a world of particulars, as nominalists claim. That changes only when we gain access to words and can bring to light the properties that were previously hidden. Thus, to take one of Hobbes's own examples, the property of whiteness has no salience for us as natural minds, but becomes an object of attention once we have a word for it; "the appellation white bringeth to remembrance the quality of such objects as produce that colour or conception in us" (EL 5.2).

To conclude, then, Hobbes's claim that the natural mind is wholly particularistic, and that language is required for general thought, can be given quite a plausible interpretation. Not only is the claim proof against the circularity objection under that interpretation. It also fits quite well with his story about the capacity of the natural mind to form prudent expectations and the support he gives to a brand of nominalism.

The interpretation is true to the spirit of Hobbesian psychology insofar as it leaves in place the great divide that he alleges between nonhuman and human mentality. Not being able to pull away from the hold of current, particular stimuli, not having access to general categories in which to cast them, nonhuman animals will still be captives of the temporal and spatial present. They may respond rationally to the objects that command their attention, acting on the basis of reliable conditioning— acting, as Hobbes would say, with prudence—so as to satisfy their appetites. And they may display a sensitivity to general similarities and differences in doing so. But the phenomenology of their perceptual world will remain one of immersion in particularity. They will be lost in the hurly-burly of minute-to-minute stimulation and response, unable to gain any distance on what they register and know what they think about it—unable indeed to think about it at all.

Speech and Active Thought

Prearticulate, particularistic thinking involves the involuntary succession of conception after conception, whether in an unorderly fashion or one that is regulated by some organizing desire. In either event, it is a case of vital or organic motion, akin to the beating of the heart or the adjustment of posture to kinesthetic cues. It is not a case, in Hobbes's language, of animal motion that is driven, as in a voluntary act, by the desire for a certain goal and the representation of that motion as the way to that goal.

According to the Hobbesian story, however, access to words means that thought can become not just general or classificatory in character; it can also assume an active, voluntary profile. People will no longer just undergo thought processes, as when this or that strikes them, or they are swept along in this or that train of associative or even regulative thought. They can now set themselves questions, identify the information they need in order to answer those questions, and undertake to consider what is true, as well as what follows from what, in a voluntary or intentional search for the answers to their questions. They can think in the active fashion represented in Rodin's sculpture.

This aspect of the transformation that language is supposed to occasion becomes clear as Hobbes elaborates on what we do with names or words. We may each use them for marks designed to serve memory, and in this use, so he suggests, we will find that we can access classificatory as well as wholly particularistic thoughts. As "marks, or notes of remembrance," names will serve for "registering of the consequences of our thoughts; which being apt to slip out of our memory, and put us to a new labour, may again be recalled, by such words as they were marked by" (L 4.3). But using words as marks may not yet make room for active or voluntary thinking; after all, they might confer the classificatory benefit, while leaving the mind wholly passive in character. Words do not only serve as marks, though, in Hobbes's view; they also serve as signs—specifically, as "signs of our conceptions" (DCr 2.5). And it is because of serving in this role that they can facilitate voluntary thinking.

Words serve as signs when they are used to communicate our thoughts to others. As marks, they help me to recall at a later time something about an earlier conception of an object; thinking of the thing under a distinctive mark or name, I can recall the aspect under which it engaged my interests. As signs, words serve in the interpersonal communication of thought as distinct from its intertemporal, intrapersonal transmission. Hobbes captures both roles in his definition of names. "A name is a word taken at pleasure to serve for a mark, which may raise in our mind a thought like to some thought we had before, and which being pronounced to others, may be to them a sign of what thought the speaker had, or had not before in his mind" (DCr 2.4).

Hobbes insists that when words serve in communicating one person's thought to another, they do so through being connected with one another in sentences. In using words as signs, not just as marks, people "use the same words to signify (by their connection and order) one to another, what they conceive or think of each matter, and also what they desire, fear, or have any other passion for" (L 4.3). The emphasis on the need to connect up words is not surprising. If I utter a single referring expression like "human being," then it is unclear what thought I want to communicate. The phrase on its own may serve me in memory as I recall a particular man—say, John Smith—and so classify him as human. But it will not serve to communicate that thought to another unless I chain words together sententially, as in saying, "John Smith is a human being." In the intrapersonal usage, I may have implicitly and passively classified John Smith as a human being, though Hobbes does not actually put things this way. In interpersonal usage, I will have to spell out my classification actively and explicitly.

The fact that words are used in active, explicit classification lets us see how they make it possible for thought to become voluntary and active. For just as speaking with others is a voluntary activity, undertaken out of a desire to communicate interpersonally (EL 5.13), so speaking with oneself can be a voluntary activity, undertaken out of a corresponding, intrapersonal desire. Once I am inducted into language, others can ask me questions and I can ponder the answers to give, as I can ask them questions and invite them to ponder the answers. But this being so, I can also ask myself questions, invite myself to ponder the answers, and take up that invitation in an intentional effort to deal with the questions. And doing this, plausibly, is precisely what active thinking requires.

Hobbes recognizes that there are many ways in which we use words, from keeping a record, to communicating the knowledge recorded, to making commitments, to entertaining our hearers (L 4.3). The use of speech to keep a record—in particular a personal, mental record—illustrates the sort of voluntary activity in which we speak with ourselves and think out things in this active, voluntary way. It requires "repeating orally, or mentally, the words" that are relevant (EL 5.4). It involves an activity in which the aim, for example, may be "to register, what by cogitation, we find to be the cause of any thing, present or past, and what we find things present or past may produce, or effect; which in sum, is acquiring of arts" (L 4.3).[9]

What will be the general desire that drives such active, intrapersonal thought? Hobbes clearly thinks that it is checking oneself with a view to attaining truth. Someone will want to check his thoughts when "he seeketh precise truth," for "truth consisteth in the right ordering of names in our affirmations" (L 4.11). This goal of attaining truth—the goal ultimately of method and science—becomes available with speech, and only with speech. Without language we may be said to be in error when, for example, "we expect that which shall not be." But truth and falsehood presuppose the chaining of marks in affirmation, and so "where speech is not, there is neither truth nor falsehood."

In summary, then, Hobbes asserts the dependence of thought on language, both for its classificatory and its voluntary character. The relationship between the two, he suggests, is like the relationship between numbering and numerals. As numerals make counting possible, so language makes thinking possible:

> The use of words in registering our thoughts is in nothing so evident as in numbering. A natural fool that could never learn by heart the order of numeral words, as *one, two,* and *three,* may observe every stroke of the clock, and nod to it, or say *one, one, one,* but can never know what hour it strikes. . . . Much less will he be able to add, and subtract, and perform all other operations of arithmetic. So that without words there is no possibility of reckoning of numbers. (L 4.10)

Imagine how difficult it would be to multiply if, like the Romans, we did not have a zero and used numerals in the following pattern: i, ii, iii, iv, v, and so on. There would be no way of telling quickly what was the product of ten and five, x and v, in such a notation. What Hobbes invites us to imagine, even more radically, is how difficult it would be to count at all if we did not use numerals of any kind. The difficulty is easy to envisage and is borne out by evidence of the limited numerical capacities among peoples and children who lack a system of numerals (Gordon 2004; Carey 2007). It gives us a nice instance of the claim that in the absence of words, thinking of any kind, numerical or otherwise, would be impossible.

The upshot is clear. By grace of the invention of language, human beings are transformed utterly, becoming capable of general, classificatory thought, particularly thought of an intentionally direct, active character. As the access to numerals may be expected to transform the capacity to number, so the access to words may be expected to transform the capacity to think. As people master words, then, and learn to perform the active, classificatory exercises that they make possible, their "faculties may be improved to such a height as to distinguish men from all other living creatures" (L 3.11).

Common Meanings

Hobbes is hostile to any suggestion that it might be reasonable for people to use words according to their own idiosyncratic and so idiolectical definition. Thus, he rebukes the Oxford "Professors of the Mathematics" for lapsing into a language of their own in their proof of a certain result. "If you had demonstrated it in Irish or Welsh, though I had not read it, yet I should not have blamed you, because you had written to a considerable number of mankind, which now you do not" (Hobbes 1839b, 263). But how do common meanings get established?

Hobbes suggests that words have their meanings fixed across different individuals, and for the same individual across times, by a sort of contract or agreement. Assuming that human beings are fundamentally alike (L introduction, 3), he almost certainly supposes that they will naturally form the same conceptions in response to the same stimuli. And so he proposes that short of falling into equivocation—more on the sources of equivocation later—they will cooperate in employing the same "voluntary signs" to elicit the same conceptions and give them what he calls the same "understanding" of the words (L 2.10). The cooperation envisaged here is supported by people "from their own will and agreement" (DCr 5.1), though this does not mean "that men once came together to take counsel to constitute by decree what all words and all connections of words would mean" (DH 10.2). It consists in the fact that the meanings of words are "determined by the common consent of speakers of the same language (as by a kind of agreement necessary for human society)" (DCv 18.4); words "have their signification by agreement and the constitution of men" (L 31.38).[10]

Hobbes allows, admittedly, that "it must be extreme hard to find out the opinions and meanings of those men that are gone from us long ago" (EL 13.8), recommending that we take due account of their circumstances in order to interpret what they mean. And equally he allows that people may sometimes misspeak, as when a king gives expression to a state of mind—say, a permissive attitude—that is not consistent with the authority that he must be assumed to claim for himself (L 22.5; EL 21.13; D 20; B 118). But still he insists that language is inherently shared, not idiolectical, and that for each term there is a conception "for which the name was ordained": a "true meaning" that is "derived from the custom and common use of speech" (EL 5.8). There are specific, identifiable thoughts, he says, that certain words "and their connection, were ordained and constituted to signify" (L 4.22; see also Hoekstra 2005, 32).

This belief in the availability of common, more or less fixed meanings means that Hobbes sees great potential in the exercise of classificatory reasoning, to which I turn in the next chapter; it can deliver results that will hold for everyone who uses words according to those meanings. But the belief does not sit easily with the fact, as we shall see, that Hobbes continually innovates in the definitions of his own crucial terms, much to the chagrin of his contemporaries, and that he regularly claims novelty for the definitions he puts forward. In order to take him seriously, we must suppose that while he recognizes that his definitions are often new, he still thinks of them as cleaving more carefully to patterns of common usage. Or if not to actual common usage, at least to the patterns that common usage would assume in the absence of any influence from the mistaken definitions he rejects. This attitude is in evidence when he writes in *De Cive* (18.3), "It sometimes happens that though words have fixed meanings defined by decision, they are so distorted in popular usage from their proper meanings by a particular passion for ornament or even deception, that it is very difficult to recall to memory the concepts for the sake of which they were attached to things, and it needs a keen judgment and intense labour to overcome the difficulty."[11]

CHAPTER THREE

Using Words to Ratiocinate

THE NATURE OF REASON

The word *reasoning*, both in Hobbes or more generally, refers to a particular variety of active, general thought: that in which our thinking leads us, not to recognize one or another truth, as for example in classifying objects of perception, memory, or imagination, but to recognize the connection that ties different truths together. The exercise of reason in this usage is inherently inferential. It consists in seeing that one proposition entails another, and on that ground, in moving from an acceptance of the first proposition to an acceptance of the second, or from a rejection of the second to a rejection of the first.

Hobbes's classificatory view of thought is important to his understanding of how such inferential reasoning is possible. On his view, every unequivocal, universal term has an extension or class of things associated with it—the same class for different speakers—so that we can think of those terms as being connected with the domain of referents on a pattern like that illustrated in figure 1. Terms a to e may be the names of objects, such as the names of animals or collections of such animals; or the names of accidents, such as the names of colors or collections of such colors; or whatever. In any area, the pattern of connections between universal names and things will be as in figure 1.

Given this pattern of association between terms and referents, it is possible to take the extension of a given term, add or subtract the extension of another term, and identify the result—in particular, see whether the result is the extension of any further term. Take term b, for example, and subtract term a from it; strictly, take the extension of term b and subtract the extension of term a from it. That means taking (1, 2, 3, 4, 5) and removing (1, 2, 3), which leaves (4, 5), which is the extension of term e. Or take term c (2, 3, 5) and subtract term d (2, 5), and this will leave one object, 3—the object that we can refer to by the proper name 3. Again, take term a (1, 2, 3) and add term e (4, 5), and this will give us term b (1, 2, 3, 4, 5). The pattern is straightforward.

These patterns, as Hobbes observes, answer to patterns of inference. To take one term, subtract another, and then get a third term as a result

Terms:

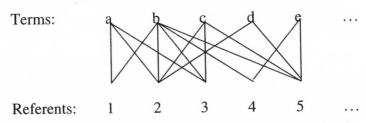

Referents: 1   2   3   4   5   ...

Fig. 1. The term a has as its associated class referents 1, 2, and 3; the term b has referents 1, 2, 3, 4, and 5; the term c has referents 2, 3, and 5, and so on.

will be to argue on the following lines: for any x, if x falls under the first term but not under the second, then it falls under the third. We might say, along these lines, that if any object is b but not a, then it is e, or if it is c but not d, then it is 3. Again, to take one term, add another, and get a third term as a result will be to argue like this: for any x, if x falls under the first term and under the second, then it falls under the third term. And along these lines we might say that if any object is both a and e, then it is b.

On this account, then, reasoning requires human beings to form beliefs not just about the things that nonhuman animals can form beliefs about but also about the words and sentences they use. People's mentality goes metalinguistic, as they pay attention to words and sentences, notice patterns in the relationships between the extensions of the words and presumably the truth conditions of sentences, and then let their observations shape their overall view. Noticing that if something is a and e, as they believe it is, then it is also b, they come to form the belief that it is b, or perhaps to reject the belief that is it a and e. And so on in other cases.

Hobbes is not particularly original in his account of the sorts of relationships or patterns that are registered in reasoning; his views conform broadly to received Aristotelian theory.[1] But he gives an interesting twist to his account when he sums it up by saying that all reasoning is a matter, ultimately, of addition and subtraction.

> By RATIOCINATION, I mean *computation*. Now to compute, is either to collect the sum of many things that are added together, or to know what remains when one thing is taken out of another. *Ratiocination*, therefore, is the same with *addition* and *subtraction*; and if any man add *multiplication* and *division*, I will not be against it, seeing multiplication is nothing but addition of equals one to another, and division nothing but a subtraction of equals one from another, as often as is

possible. So that all ratiocination is comprehended in these two oper-
ations of the mind, addition and subtraction. (DCr 1.2; see also L 5.1)

By casting reasoning as a matter of addition and subtraction, Hobbes
achieves three ends, each attractive to him in a different way. First of all,
he demystifies reasoning, depicting it as a pedestrian exercise analo-
gous to keeping accounts. Second, he connects it with science and what
he sees as a model of how reasoning should be conducted. And third,
he represents it as a skill, not as an innate faculty; it is a skill developed
from childhood on the basis of an induction in the use of words, not a
capacity that comes on stream when the child reaches the age of reason.

Hobbes emphasizes the common aspect of reasoning when he says
that "reason, in this sense, is nothing but reckoning (that is, adding and
subtracting)" (L 5.2). For reckoning is something that regular folk do
whenever they take out their counters and try to keep their accounts in
order. All that reasoning involves is a reckoning in which counters are
replaced with words; as he says, "Words are wise men's counters, they
do but reckon by them" (L 4.13).

The connection between reasoning and working with numbers, however, also gives Hobbes a basis for underscoring the high pitch to which
the art can be taken, as evidenced in the successes of science. Thus
geometry, by which he means the general science of motions, "proceeds
from the addition, multiplication, subtraction, and division, of these
motions, and what effects, what figures, and what properties, they produce" (DCr 1.6). And by being careful about how the sums are done,
geometry, as he observes elsewhere, reaches conclusions that "have
thereby been made indisputable" (L 5.7). There is a high ideal signaled
by the equation of reasoning, even run-of-the-mill reasoning, with the
art of addition and subtraction. It shows that the consummation of reasoning is in science—"the knowledge of consequences, and dependence of one fact upon another" (L 5.17). Hobbes has an idealized picture of scientists, noting that "they proceed from most low and humble
principles, evident even to the meanest capacity; going on slowly, and
with most scrupulous ratiocination (viz.) from the imposition of names
they infer the truth of their first propositions; and from two of the first,
a third; and from any two of the three a fourth; and so on, according to
the steps of science" (EL 13.3).

But the equation between reasoning and numerical computation
serves a third purpose for Hobbes as well. For by stressing the fact that
reasoning depends on the availability of words, as more explicit forms
of adding and subtracting depend on the availability of numerals, he
breaks the spell of the traditional idea that reason is an innate faculty
that is simply switched on at a certain stage of development (DCv 2.1n).

Thus he says, "Reason is not, as sense and memory, born with us" (L 5.17; cf. D 18). Nor is it, he adds, something that comes naturally to us in the way that prudence—a habit of forming reliable expectations—develops spontaneously in human and nonhuman animals, on the basis of experience; it is not "gotten by experience only." Reason, on the contrary, is a skill in the proper employment of words and their exploitation for the purposes of discovering truths; he calls the skill "sapience," as distinct from mere "prudence" (EL 6.4; L 5.21). Such sapience, such reason, is like the capacity to play the piano; however dependent on native ability, it consists in a facility at a certain cultural task and presupposes individual training. Reason is "attained by industry; first in apt imposing of names; and secondly by getting a good and orderly method in proceeding from the elements, which are names, to assertions made by connection of one of them to another; and so to syllogisms, which are the connections of one assertion to another" (L 5.17).

The net effect of all this is to dethrone reason. In Hobbes, it ceases to be a divine spark lodged in the human heart—a source of light and inspiration—as it had been in almost all earlier, Western thought. It becomes a skill in the use of an artifact: something useful and precious, for sure, but also something entirely unmysterious and at base mechanical. For Hobbes as for a fellow revolutionary like Descartes, the human body was nothing more than a complex machine. But where reason for Descartes appeared by grace of a ghost in that machine, it appeared for Hobbes by grace of another machine—this time, a machine made of invented, artificial materials.

Hobbes's views on the artificial, mechanical character of human reason have led some to identify him as an adherent of the computational model under which the mind functions like a computer and is purely mechanical in its operation (Dascal 1996).[2] This is perfectly reasonable, and it highlights another aspect of his originality, though it is doubtful whether Hobbes—unlike, for example, Gottfried Wilhelm Leibniz—fully appreciated the line of thought that he was opening up.[3]

The computational model assumes a simple form in Hobbes's story. Take the capacity to add and subtract, multiply and divide, which he takes to be exemplified both in numbering and other forms of reasoning. Think of this, in the computational idiom, as a capacity at the neurophysical, personally inaccessible level to manipulate an uninterpreted terminology—a language of thought (Fodor 1975)—according to a certain pattern. We can model Hobbesian numbering as an exercise in which that manipulative capacity is put to use with terms that have been given an interpretation as numerals. And we can think of Hobbesian reasoning more generally as the employment of that capacity with terms that have been given an interpretation as ordinary names.

Hobbes never addresses the question as to whether animals might be able to reason, if they had access to language. It is worth noting, however, that his adherence to this computational model would enable him to deny that language alone could induce other animals to reason; for all that he says, they may lack the required computational ability. Although prelinguistic human beings have a mental life like that of other animals, they may be the only species to have the potential to be transformed by language. Reason may be a developing skill, not an innate faculty that comes on stream at a certain age or under certain prompts. But it may still presuppose an innate faculty or capacity of the kind postulated in the computational model; it may not be capable of appearing and developing in the absence of such a faculty.

REASON, THEORETICAL AND PRACTICAL

The account offered so far may suggest that reasoning is always going to be theoretical in character: a matter of connecting truths with truths, and deciding what to believe. But it is important to realize that many truths will have a practical bearing, in Hobbes's view. One crucial example is the truths of natural law, which I shall be discussing later. These are "dictates of reason" for how people should lead their lives; "conclusions or theorems concerning what conduceth to the conservation and defence of themselves" (L 15.41).[4] Hobbes thinks of these theorems as derivable only for creatures who have terms in which to spell out axiomatic notions like those of self-preservation, contract, and obligation, and who can see connections such as that between contracting with others for peace, setting up obligations to stick by those contracts, and thereby promoting the chances of their own self-preservation.[5] Another example where reasoning is critical for working out truths that are primarily of practical import is provided by civil science. "The skill of making, and maintaining commonwealths, consisteth in certain rules, as doth arithmetic and geometry; not (as tennis-play) on practice only: which rules, neither poor men have the leisure, nor men that have had the leisure, have hitherto had the curiosity, or the method to find out" (L 20.19).

But natural law and civil science are still relatively theoretical disciplines. How can reasoning as characterized by Hobbes be relevant in more distinctively practical matters—say, in decisions about what to do? He does not address the question explicitly, but the only position that coheres with his practice is the view that the distinction between the two sorts of reasoning turns on the use to which they are put.

Think of reasoning, based on Hobbes's picture, as an exercise in which we explore the connections between truths. That exercise will constitute theoretical reasoning when the exploration is designed to impact on the beliefs we form, thereby aiding the formation of judgment, and an exercise in practical reasoning when it is designed to impact on our desires and actions, thereby aiding the formation of will; "the last appetite in deliberation is called the will," as we saw, and "the last opinion in the search for the truth . . . is called the judgment" (L 7.2). Seeing that p implies q may lead in the context of theoretical, belief-forming interests to believing q or not believing p, whereas it may lead in a practical, intention-forming context to deciding to make p true in order to make q true. Depending on whether it helps in the formation of judgment or will, it will constitute a theoretical or practical exercise.

But while reasoning may take a theoretical or practical form, it should be noticed that Hobbes is not committed to thinking that whenever human beings form beliefs or intentions, whenever judgment or will materializes in them, there is reasoning. We know that from his perspective, nonhuman animals form beliefs and desires, judgment and will, as well as human beings; this is one great point of contrast with Descartes, for whom only human beings have mental states. The difference between human and other animals is that human beings can reason or ratiocinate, and other animals cannot. Yet the fact that human beings can reason does not mean that they reason whenever their judgment or will forms. For all we have been told, they may only call on reason in special cases, as when there is some reason to worry about the spontaneous process in which such attitudes form, not "according to our election," but as chance happens to "bring them to our mind" (EL 5.1).

Using Reason Well

Given this account, it should be clear that reason will work well only under certain specific conditions. A first is that words are used constantly across times and persons, so that a word like a universal name continues in all uses to refer to the same class. Let the linkages between words and their referents wobble or shift, and any attempt to reason will be jeopardized. When Hobbes makes this point, he is at one with a long logical tradition, according to which the term common to two sentences, by virtue of which the corresponding propositions appear to entail a third, must have the same meaning in each occurrence. *Bank*, the common or middle term, must mean the same in "This institution is a bank" and "Every bank is on the water's edge" if the propositions are to entail that this institution is on the water's edge.

While Hobbes does mark his agreement with the tradition on this point, however (DCr 4.3–6), he is true to form in turning the message into something quite distinctive. The lesson he derives is that the first and most important moment in any sort of reasoning or science is that of definition, when words are fixed firmly on their proper referents and the user is enabled to remember those semantic values.

> Seeing then that *truth* consisteth in the right ordering of names in our affirmations, a man that seeketh precise *truth* had need to remember what every name he uses stands for, and to place it accordingly; or else he will find himself entangled in words, as a bird in lime twigs, the more he struggles the more belimed. And therefore in geometry, (which is the only science that it hath pleased God hitherto to bestow on mankind,) men begin at settling the significations of their words; which settling of significations they call *definitions,* and place them in the beginning of their reckoning. (L 4.11)

The second condition for using words well is that not only are they disciplined by strict definition but they are also linked with one another in a manner that makes sense; the usage is not only constant but also coherent. For Hobbes words may refer, as we know, to bodies, accidents of bodies, or modes of sensory registering of accidents, or to other words or uses of words; words may also be negative as distinct from positive, registering the refusal to confer a name, as in saying "nothing" rather than "thing" (L 4.15–19). Since these referents go together only in specific ways, then, he thinks it is essential for reasoning that words be put together only in patterns that answer to the ways things in the world go together. Hobbes thinks there are many varieties of incoherence, of which one example would be using a word that names an accident of other words—say, the word universal—to bodies; thus, he can say that the belief in objective universals is not only false but incoherent (L 5.10–13).

The third condition for reasoning well concerns the mode in which reasoning is carried out, rather than the ways in which the words used connect with things or one another. This is that the reasoning is followed through with care, exposed to the correction of others. He thinks the crucial conditions are to avoid inconstancy and incoherence, but admits that even if they are absent, the length and difficulty of a piece of ratiocination may lead a person astray. "To him that can avoid these things it is not easy to fall into any absurdity, unless it be by the length of an account; wherein he may perhaps forget what went before. For all men by nature reason alike, and well, when they have good principles. For who is so stupid, as both to mistake in geometry, and also to persist in it, when another detects his error to him?" (L 5.16).

Guarding against Abuse

The fact that there are preconditions that must be satisfied for reasoning well means that they can be breached, and it raises the question as to whether there are strategies for avoiding such breaches, such abuses of reason. There is not much to be said, of course, about carelessness in reasoning and how to avoid it. Hobbes passes over the topic with suggestions to the effect that its rectification requires "going on slowly, and with most scrupulous ratiocination" (EL 13.3), especially with "long deductions" (EL 8.14). He has more interesting things to say, however, about the breaches associated with inconstancy and incoherence, and about what is needed to avoid them. The lessons he teaches here are reminiscent of those taught by Francis Bacon (2000), with whom Hobbes worked for a short time as a secretary, probably in the mid-1620s.

The problem of incoherence arises, according to Hobbes's account, because of a lack of attention to what words designate, and in particular to whether they designate bodies, accidents, sensory modes, or other words. But what might lead someone not to take account of the referents of their terms in this way? Doesn't the nature of speech and reckoning require the very attention to referents that ought to rule out the possibility or likelihood of incoherence?

Not for Hobbes. As a parrot may use words, without any contact with their referents, so the same can be true of human beings. It is possible, Hobbes says, that "a man reasoneth with his lips only" (EL 6.3). In this case, "the mind suggesteth only the first word, the rest follow habitually, and are not followed by the mind," and so speakers have "no images or conceptions in their minds answering to the words they speak" (EL 5.14). This is possible, in particular, with words and word combinations that are constructed out of foreign roots that the speaker does not understand. "And therefore you shall hardly meet with a senseless and insignificant word, that is not made up of some Latin or Greek names" (L 4.21). An example would be the use of a name like "incorporeal body, or (which is all one) an incorporeal substance"— that is, as Hobbes sees it, a body that is not a body.

The great offenders against coherence, of course, are the Scholastic philosophers who rely so heavily on "vain Latin words" (L 36.19). Hobbes decries the resort to names "taken up, and learned by rote from the schools, as *hypostatical, transubstantiate, consubstantiate, eternal-now,* and the like canting of schoolmen" (L 5.15). The schoolmen specialize in "names that signify nothing," and the result, unsurprisingly, is nonsense. "The natural philosophy of those schools, was rather a dream than science, and set forth in senseless and insignificant language" (L 46.11).

What is the cure for the danger of parroting, and being led into insignificant or incoherent speech and reasoning? For Hobbes, it is the formation of those conceptions that words, assuming they are well-defined, should raise in the mind; if you like, it is an avoidance of empty speech. Incoherent words are terms "making nothing understood," and so the cure is to assure yourself that with every expression you hear, read, or use, you are able to understand it; you have access to "the imagination that is raised in man . . . by words or other voluntary signs"—in particular, to the sort of imagination or conception that is occasioned "by the sequel and contexture of the names of things into affirmations, negations, and other forms of speech" (L 2.9).

The important thing, as we might put it, is never to let words lead you on without thinking through exactly what they are supposed to bring to mind. This is particularly important in reading past authors, Hobbes thinks, since one can easily be carried along without thought, taking "absurd speeches" on "credit" (L 3.12). And so he recommends "instead of books, reading over orderly one's own conceptions" (EL 5.14), and denounces "they that trusting only to the authority of books, follow the blind blindly" (L 5.21). Although John Aubrey's short biography of Hobbes insists that he had read much, it suggests that he took his own lesson to heart. "He was wont to say that if he had read as much as other men, he should have known no more than other men" (Aubrey 1994, 240).

An even greater problem than that of incoherence, according to Hobbes, is inconstancy or equivocation in the use of words. This can come about in various ways. The main source is the simple failure to define—the lack of method—which he thinks is characteristic of the work of philosophers down to the rise of science and, as he described it, the geometry of motion. In his view, "there can be nothing so absurd, but may be found in the books of philosophers." "And," as he says, "the reason is manifest. For there is not one of them that begins his ratiocination from the definitions, or explications of the names they are to use; which is a method that hath been used only in geometry" (L 5.7).

But apart from a lack of method, there are at least three other sources of equivocation and inconstancy that Hobbes identifies. One is the use of metaphor, which he also thinks dangerous for the possibility of encouraging incoherence (L 5.14). Metaphor involves the use of terms, not according to their literal meaning, and so not in accord with the definition of those words. And this is clearly an instance of using words inconstantly. Yet he admits that "metaphors are (by profession) equivocal" (EL 5.7) and suggests that in comparison with other forms of equivocation, they "are less dangerous, because they profess their inconstancy" (L 4.24; but see 8.8). This supports the excuse he offers at the end of *Leviathan* for having resorted himself, as he so adeptly does, to the use of metaphor and associated flourishes of eloquence: "wheresoever there is place for adorning and preferring of error, there is much more place for adorning and preferring of truth" (L Review, 4).

A further source of equivocation that is closely related to the use of metaphor is the rhetorical use of speech to invert proper usage in the attempt, driven by emotional investment and partiality, to persuade and move an audience. Words may be used, he says, not according to their definition but their significance for "the nature, disposition, and interest of the speaker," as when "one man calleth *wisdom*, what another calleth *fear*; and one *cruelty*, what another *justice*; one *prodigality*, what another *magnanimity*; and one *gravity*, what another *stupidity*"; "such names," he says, "can never be true grounds of any ratiocination" (L 4.24).

Hobbes is referring here to the rhetorical figure of speech known as "paradiastole," or more simply, "redescription." And it is a signal of his rejection of the tradition of rhetoric in which he had been raised—and which he taught his pupils in the Cavendish family—that he selects this favored rhetorical tactic for specific indictment (Skinner 1996). The terms that are particularly vulnerable to redescription are those thick evaluative terms, as they are often called, that have a normal descriptive meaning, as with the words Hobbes mentions in illustration, but also have an evaluative or affective valence; laced with a "tincture of our passions" (L 4.24), they indicate approval, as with a word like "magnanimity," or disapproval, as with "prodigality." What Hobbes recognizes is that the passion of speakers may lead them to use such terms against the grain of descriptive meaning, describing reckless behavior as courageous, cowardly behavior as cautious, and so on. He sees a sharp contrast between the way in which the passions can warp our speech in this area, and the situation in "the doctrine of lines and figures" where people don't flinch from admitting the truth, whatever it may be, since it "crosses no man's ambition, profit or lust" (L 11.21); here it was "never heard of, that there was any controversy concerning any conclusion" (EL 13.3).

A third source of equivocation to which Hobbes gives importance, though not under any single name, might be described as evaluative indexicality. An indexical word is a term, like *mine, here,* or *now,* that has a different reference at different contexts or indexes of usage, even if it has the same character across those contexts. Thus, *mine* refers to me when I use it, and to you when you use it; *here* refers to Princeton when I am speaking in Princeton, and to Canberra when I am speaking in Canberra. Hobbes is not worried by indexicality in general, only by the sort of indexicality that, leading to controversy, "must either come to blows or be undecided" (L 5.3). And he suggests that the indexicality of evaluative terms such as *good* and *bad* is like this.

These are thin evaluative terms that have no descriptive meaning, unlike their thicker counterparts, but only an evaluative or affective valence. The problem they raise is that while people use them to commend or condemn courses of action, and so may use them in a way that leads to controversy about what to do, they each use them according to a personal rule. I call good whatever raises warm feelings in me, and you call good whatever raises warm feelings in you. As Hobbes puts it, "Whatsoever is the object of any man's appetite or desire, that is it which he for his part calleth *good:* and the object of his hate and aversion, *evil*; and of his contempt, *vile* and *inconsiderable*" (L 6.7). And as he explains it, the problem is broadly one of indexicality. "For these words of good, evil, and contemptible, are ever used with relation to the person that useth them" (L 6.7). Worse again, indeed, they are used with relation not just to the person using them but to the state of that person's appetites at any time (L 6.6).

Why should people come to blows over indexical, evaluative terms, but not over ordinary indexical terms like *here* and *now*, or *I* and *you*— except where these are used to make inconsistent claims like "It's not yours, it's mine"? If *good* and *bad* are indexical in the way Hobbes thinks, then strictly there is no inconsistency between my saying something is good and your saying it is bad; I am expressing or reporting my approval, and you are expressing or reporting your disapproval. Hobbes may have the view that though evaluative words are used as indexicals, still my saying a plan or proposal is good is meant to express a disposition to act in a certain way, and an expectation that others will help or at least not hinder. Thus, if you respond by saying that the plan or proposal is bad, then you register a practical clash: you are disposed to stand in my way. Or alternatively, he may have the view that though the words should be seen as indexicals, ordinary people see them mistakenly as expressing the objective character of plans and proposals, and think of themselves as being in theoretical as well as practical conflict with one another (Tuck 1996, 181). We do not need to resolve this issue, but my inclination is to think that Hobbes posits a practical clash only. He does not generally depict people as mistaken about the objectivity of value in the way he certainly thinks they are mistaken, say, about the objectivity of color.

The resort to strict method is the solution suggested by Hobbes for equivocation resulting from the problems of metaphor, redescription, and indexicality, as it is the solution for the failure of definition. "Seeing then that *truth* consisteth in the right ordering of names in our affirmations, a man that seeketh precise *truth* had need to remember what every name he uses stands for, and to place it accordingly" (L 4.24). While continuing to use metaphor—justified as the adorning of truth—Hobbes takes a hard line on "rhetorical figures" in the body of *Leviathan*, arguing that "in reckoning and seeking of truth such speeches are not to be admitted" (L 5.14).[6] All is to be done, it appears, by strict method. With self-conscious irony—and surely, personal amusement—Hobbes puts the message in a powerfully metaphoric way: "The light of human minds is perspicuous words, but by exact definitions first snuffed, and purged from ambiguity; *reason* is the *pace*; increase of *science*, the *way*; and the benefit of mankind, the *end*. And on the contrary, metaphors, and senseless and ambiguous words, are like *ignes fatui*; and reasoning upon them is wandering amongst innumerable absurdities; and their end, contention and sedition, or contempt" (L 5.20).

Strict definition can be straightforwardly invoked as the cure for the dangers of rhetoric, but how is it supposed to apply to the indexicality problem? Hobbes's suggestion is that those who employ emotional, evaluative words like *good* and *bad* should not use them from the index provided by their personal feelings, or their feelings at any time, but rather from an index to which they can defer in common. He points to such a solution when he says that the words might not be used "with relation to the person that useth them" but rather from the viewpoint of "an arbitrator or judge whom men disagreeing shall by consent set up, and make his sentence the rule thereof" (L 6.7). I will return to this theme when discussing the passions.

REDEFINITION AND REDESCRIPTION

Hobbes (1994c, 250) always claimed to have written "in prose that was simple and direct, not in rhetoric." But apart from the adornment of truth that he actually tried to justify in the conclusion to *Leviathan*, there is one area in which he remained faithful, however covertly, to rhetorical practice.

This is, ironically, in his employment of the principle according to which it is necessary "for any man that aspires to true knowledge, to examine the definitions of former authors, and either to correct them where they are negligently set down, or to make them himself" (L 4.13). More than almost any author before him, Hobbes finds the definitions of former authors to be negligently set down and continually proposes novel definitions of his own. This is strikingly true, for example, when it comes to his redefinition of liberty, where he claims with characteristic assurance, even arrogance, that "no writer has explained what liberty and servitude are" (DCv 9.9).

The strategy of redefinition is not very different from rhetorical para-diastole or redescription of the kind that Hobbes so expressly con-demned. For he used it, again and again, to outmaneuver his oppo-nents by switching from the meanings they gave their terms to the meanings that suited his purposes better. The embrace of method and science did not seriously hamper Hobbes's polemical and political projects. He could claim the high methodological ground, while prac-ticing the well-honed skills of an orator in doing battle with his many enemies. He could denounce rhetoric, and often denounce the resort to rhetoric in his opponents, while using one of the most powerful tools of rhetoric under the guise of scientific orthodoxy.

Of course, the tactic was not lost on those opponents. His account of liberty prompted his republican adversary, James Harrington (1992, 20), to remark, "The mountain hath brought forth and we have a little equivocation!" And his general strategy led his mathematical adver-sary, John Wallis, into something approaching apoplexy. Thus, on learning that Robert Boyle had been challenged by Hobbes about his claim to have created a vacuum, Wallis wrote to him in sympathy. "Mr Hobs is very dexterous in confuting others by putting a new sense on their words rehearsed by himself: different from what the words signi-fie with other men. And therefore if you shall have occasion to speak of chalk, he'll tell you that by chalk he means cheese: and then if he can prove that what you say of chalk is not true of cheese, he reckons him-self to have gotten a great victory" (quoted in Shapin and Schaffer 1985, 118). As our discussion evolves, we may begin to understand the exas-peration that Harrington and Wallis must have felt in trying to deal with Hobbes.

CHAPTER FOUR

Using Words to Personate

I HAVE DOCUMENTED one way in which speech expands the horizons of human beings, giving them a capacity for thinking and reasoning. But there is quite a distinct capacity that it also underpins, according to Hobbes. This is the ability to assume the mutual commitments and contracts that mark them not just as centers of reasoning but as persons—in Hobbes's terminology, as centers of personation (L 16.3). This second benefit is just as dramatic in its implications as the first, though it receives less explicit attention in his work; it is brought to the fore only late in the story, when he begins to consider how the state or commonwealth might emerge on a contractual basis.[1]

BEYOND BOETHIUS

The standard definition of a person within the philosophical tradition with which Hobbes was familiar went back to Anicius Manlius Severinus Boethius, a Christian philosopher writing about A.D. 500 who was described by Dante as the last of the Romans and the first of the Scholastics. In a definition later endorsed by Aquinas, and given almost authoritative standing, Boethius had said that a person is an individual substance of rational nature—*naturae rationalis individua substantia*. Hobbes could not accept this, of course, since he did not think that any animal, humans included, had a rational nature, at least not in the sense that this implied the capacity to reason, independently of the availability of language. Unsurprisingly, then, he adopted quite a novel line on personhood, arguing that persons are distinguished not by their metaphysical nature but by the things they can do, the roles they can play.

Boethius's approach to defining what it is to be a person was shaped by metaphysical and theological concerns. But the notion of a person or *persona* had come to have a life outside such contexts with the adoption of Roman law in medieval times and the development of the notion of a corporation, a legal person.[2] A legal person was an entity that could enter into standard legal relations, owning property, forming contracts, bringing charges, and being exposed to the charges brought by others. It was a role-based concept that laid no demands on the character of the entity that played the role. Thus, it was possible for medieval legal theory to recognize not just an individual but also a corporate entity as a person—a *persona ficta* or fictive person, if not a *persona naturalis* or natural person (Canning 1980; Kantorowicz 1997). The guild, the monastic order, or indeed the church itself could be regarded as a legal person insofar as it was able to make many of the legal claims and incur many of the legal duties associated with individual persons. It had standing before the law and the culture in general.

Hobbes brought this legal way of thinking into philosophy, defining a person as an entity that could play what he took to be a characteristic role. He didn't define the role in straightforwardly legal terms, however, but at a more abstract level. And at this level speech figures essentially. Persons, he said, are individuals who speak or act—or presumably can speak or act—in their own name or the name of a principal, and who are accepted by others as having this capacity. "A person, is he, whose words or actions are considered, either as his own, or as representing the words or actions of another man, or of any other thing to whom they are attributed" (L 16.1).

Hobbes's view, to put it in a slogan, is that there are no persons but spokespersons. Natural persons are spokespersons for themselves, acting and speaking in their own name, and artificial persons are spokespersons for another. When the words or actions "are considered as his own, then is he called a natural person; and when they are considered as representing the words and actions of another, then is he a feigned or artificial person" (L 16.2). I will look at artificial persons in the next chapter; here I shall concentrate on natural persons.[3]

Hobbes's notion of the natural person is deeply social, since one can adopt the role of a spokesperson only if there is a possible audience that one conceives of oneself, rightly or wrongly, as engaging. Could Hobbes allow that the individual might be a person in relation to earlier or later selves, operating as an intertemporal, intrapersonal spokesperson? Not in the full sense in which this can be true with other individuals; the crucial factor, as we shall see, is that one cannot owe an obligation to oneself. According to his theory, then, one can be a person only if one can play a role in relation to a real or imagined audience: one can speak to that audience for oneself. One can be a person only insofar as one can conceive of oneself in interaction with others.

This idea of a natural person will go down badly in many quarters, since it means that only those in more or less full possession of their faculties can count as persons, being able to communicate and authorize their attitudes; thus "children, fools, and madmen" are clearly excluded (L 16.10). Hobbes might say that those who are not fully possessed of their faculties can count as persons in a broader sense: in the sense of being of the same human kind with actual, proper persons. But it is not clear what he would actually have said on the point. And it is worth mentioning that when it comes to the question of whether "some strange or deformed birth" "be a man or no"—and so of the same human kind with actual, proper persons—he holds that this is to be decided "by the laws," on the grounds that here "right reason is not existent" and "some man, or men, must supply the place thereof" (EL 29.8). He thinks there is no fact of the matter, not at least in this extreme case, as to whether the deformed birth is human or not, and he is content to allow the convention of the local sovereign to rule.

NATURAL PERSONS

What is it for others to consider one's words or actions as one's own, as they do with natural persons? The answer is: they take one to own the actions and words in an active sense in which owning means authorizing or endorsing—seeing oneself as bound by them. In particular, so the assumption appears to go, they take one to do this as a matter of common awareness.

Speaking of the case where representatives act or speak in the name of other natural persons, Hobbes says that they must have their "words and actions owned by those whom they represent" (L 16.4); they act or speak with "authority," "commission," or "licence," so that the represented person is really the "author" of what is said or done. The same lesson applies to the natural person. When he "beareth his own natural person" (L 19.4), acting or speaking in his own name, that individual will own what is said or done in the sense of authorizing it. That person will treat it as said or done with his imprimatur or authority; "there being no author but himself" (L 16.8), that individual will relate to it as a principal, not just as a hired hand. Others consider the natural person's actions and words as his or her own precisely insofar as they take that person, as a matter of common awareness, to give those signs this authority.

There are two aspects to being a natural person that this account underlines. The first is that the natural person voluntarily or intentionally communicates their state of mind, or more plausibly, is capable of such communication. Unthinking reflexes or actions might reveal what someone wants or believes without the agent's seeking this effect, and without the agent's even being aware that it is occurring; such involuntary or unintended symptoms may even be "the best signs of passions present" (L 6.56). But speech and speech-related activities are exercises in which the individual tries, if sincere, to reveal their wants or beliefs—they are "voluntary significations"—and in normal cases it is a matter of common or public awareness that that is the goal: everyone is in a position to see that if sincere, this is what the speaker is doing; everyone is in a position to see that everyone is in this position; and so on.

Such intentional communication may not successfully reveal a person's mind, according to Hobbes. Words may be used insincerely; they may be employed to express passions, for example, "whether they that use them have such passions or not" (L 6.56). And those who use words sincerely to express their minds may still misspeak, as when a king says something that, if taken literally, would be inconsistent with his role; "the consequences of words are not the signs of his will, when other consequences are signs of the contrary" (L 22.5; EL 21.13). But intentional communication is certainly reliable in the general run, and in any case, it is the sort of communication in play when natural persons speak for themselves.

The second important aspect of Hobbes's account of personhood is that being a natural person means communicating or being able to communicate in such a way that one's words and actions have a certain authority, and others can "consider" them as one's "own." One speaks or acts in the guise of a licensed spokesperson, not a mere reporter, inviting the relevant audience to rely in certain contextually salient ways on what one says or does.

Here, the contrast is with the sort of communication in which one might report on one's state of mind in the role of a journalist or social scientist, a patient in psychotherapy or a diarist. Suppose I tell you in a confessional mode that I seem to be fixed in the belief that Aunt Sally is an alien or in the feeling that I am bound to do anything you request; suppose I tell you this with the attitude I would have in reporting it to my psychoanalyst or recording it in my diary. So far as you understood the attitude behind my words, you would not consider them my own in the appropriate sense. You would realize that I did not think that I ought to believe that Aunt Sally is an alien or that I was obliged to honor your every request. And you would realize, then, that I was not authorizing you in any way to hold me to those words. You would not claim any license to complain against me later, for example, if it turned out that I was not treating Aunt Sally like an alien or was not acknowledging an obligation to fulfill your requests.

When I authorize my words and address you as a self-spokesperson, not as a self-reporter, then I do two things. First, I present the words—"Aunt Sally is an alien" or "Your wish is my command"—as expressions of an attitude that I take to be formed under appropriate constraints, evidential or otherwise—that is, as expressions of an attitude

I do well to form. And second, I present them as expressions of an attitude that I intend to enact in future performance, on pain of exposing myself to rebuke from you—this, at any rate, insofar as nothing unforeseen happens in the meantime to make the attitude inappropriate.[4]

PERSONATION

Summing up the general theme, then, persons in Hobbes's sense are agents who relate in a certain way toward others—in effect, toward one another—authorizing their own words and actions as signs of their minds, and inevitably, taking others to authorize their words and actions in the same way. They do not relate just as agents who are pretty good at reading one another's minds and giving off cues that make such mutual reading possible; brute animals may well do this, as Hobbes suggests (L 6.56), when they take stock of each other as prey or predator, competitor or mate. Persons relate in a quite different manner. They intentionally communicate their attitudes to one another, presenting those attitudes as well-formed commitments and inviting the audience to rely on their faithfully enacting them.

This mode of relating to others is described by Hobbes, from the time of *Leviathan*, as personating or representing oneself (L 16.3). The word persona comes from the Latin term for a theatrical mask, as Hobbes mentions, deriving from the verb *sonare*, to sound, and *per*, through. As the theatrical figure sounds or speaks for a character through a mask, so human beings can speak for themselves, manifesting in an authoritative way the judgments and wills that may be ascribed to them— licensing the attribution of such states.

Hobbes obviously sees personation, like ratiocination, as an enormous benefit conferred by language. By virtue of being able to personate, human beings achieve a way of predicting one another's behavior and knowing when they can rely on one another, which is not merely rooted in their ability to read minds. They can underwrite mutual reliance by using words and actions, not just as a reporter's indication of their judgment and will, but as a guarantor's warranty or assurance.

In a situation of purely reportive self-representation, people could hope to have an influence on others only insofar as the profile they presented in word and action, like the profile presented by a natural scenario or a brute animal, would lead others to revise their view of the opportunities and incentives available, and ideally, would lead others to behave in a congenial manner. But given that people are capable of authoritative self-representation, this all changes. They can now hope to influence others not just by inducing such responses in a more or less passive manner but by actively inviting the responses: by licensing expectations of fidelity to the mind they make and manifest, and by proving themselves capable of being held to those expectations. They will prove themselves capable of being held to such expectations by generally conforming to them, and when they fail to do so, by accepting that they can be held to account in one or another manner; more on this later.

The developments that personation makes possible are of the utmost importance for Hobbes. Unlike dumb animals (L 14.22), persons can explicitly or implicitly give their word that they will do such and such in the event of others doing so and so, they can have that word accepted, and they can combine thereby to improve their collective lot. It is only by the power of personation, and the giving and taking of words, so he thinks, that people are able to escape the horrors of war and enjoy the fruits of "commodious living" (L 13.14); these range from transport to trade and towns and buildings, to culture and knowledge and the arts (L 13.9). I shall return to that theme in later chapters.

Side by side with ratiocination, then, personation represents the second great break with animal life that speech makes possible. It gives an extra resonance to Hobbes's claim that "man leaveth all community with beasts at the faculty of imposing names" (EL 9.18). As language liberates us from the hold of the concrete and particular in our mental processing, so it releases us from the world of merely mechanical forms of interpersonal influence, opening up the space in which mutual contract becomes possible.

COMMITMENT AND CONTRACT

But though personation and contract hold out this great potential for human life, they are deeply problematic. The problem is that they require that people are not just willing to give their word—with the actions that accompany it—but are each willing to keep any word they give and accept one another's word in turn (EL 15.4). In particular, personation and contract require people to be willing to accept one another's word even in circumstances where it might appear that there is an incentive for the other person to defect. But it is a "necessity of nature," according to Hobbes, that people "choose that which appeareth best for themselves" (L 27.8; EL 14.6; DCv 1.7).[5] And doesn't this mean that people might not keep a word they have given, if that proves to be in their best interest? If each knows that this is so, knowing human nature, how in general can anyone have confidence that others will stick to the word they give in representation of themselves?

There are two different problems here, each associated with a different sense in which people may give their word and represent their minds to others. They may represent themselves as judging or willing something, and therefore as required to act accordingly, so long as they maintain that judgment or will. This self-representation involves a commitment on people's part to live up to how they represent themselves, so long as no element in the self-representation is disowned. And in addition to such commitments, they may make contracts or more particularly covenants—that is, contracts that depend on one party trusting in the future performance of another, or as Hobbes puts it, that involve "promises . . . upon consideration of reciprocal benefit" (EL 15.9). In a simple commitment, the person who commits does so only conditionally on not disowning the self-representation in question. In the contract, something stronger is involved: not just a commitment to be faithful to a self-representation that has not been withdrawn but a commitment not to withdraw that self-representation—not at least without the agreement of the other party or parties to the contract (L 15.13). In order to take personation to its fullest flowering, people will need to be reliable not just in making simple commitments but also in making the double commitments involved in contracts or covenants.

Why would people keep and be expected to keep the simple commitments they make in authorizing their words? Why would they keep and be expected to keep the commitments involved in giving expression to a judgment or a noncontractual will—a will they express without renouncing the possibility of changing it unilaterally (L 6.55)? Hobbes has an intriguing line on this issue. He suggests that to announce a judgment that such and such is the case, tacitly authorizing the words used to express the judgment, is to expose oneself to the penalty of manifest self-contradiction or absurdity in the event of then going on to announce an inconsistent judgment, and he clearly believes that the same holds of announcing a noncontractual will.

Suppose, to take the theoretical case, that a person asserts one thing and then without withdrawing that assertion, goes on to assert something inconsistent or, as it presumably might be, act in a way that displays a rejection of the assertion that is on record. Such an agent, says Hobbes, "is driven to contradict an assertion by him before maintained" (EL 16.2). Suppose, to go to the practical case, that someone manifests a will to perform a certain action "by some voluntary and sufficient sign or signs" (L 14.7)—as a person may do without actually making a promise or contract—and then goes on to do something else instead. Such a person, Hobbes notes, "willeth the doing and the not doing of the same thing, at the same time; which is a plain contradiction" (EL 16.2). Just as people are tied on pain of self-contradiction to assertions that are not withdrawn, so they are tied on the same basis to expressions of will that are not renounced.

This line of thought is perfectly intelligible if we assume, as Hobbes clearly does, that when judging an agent for a contradiction of opinion or will, we look at the agent over time, and take the public assertions and contracts—the public manifestations of the agent's mind—as unquestioned. But it is one thing to say that people who fail to live up to simple or conditional commitments contradict themselves in this way. It is quite another to say that this gives them an incentive to guard against such a failure of commitment, and gives others a reason to expect them to do this. Does Hobbes have anything to say on this question?

He doesn't say anything explicit but it is fairly clear what he would say. The requirement to be consistent in one's thoughts and intentions, one's judgment and will, is a requirement of rationality (Broome 2004). It spells out what is involved in being a psychological subject that functions properly, reasoning successfully in the manner characterized in the last chapter: reckoning properly on the basis of the definitions of one's words. To be in self-contradiction is to fail to be a subject of that kind. And to represent oneself in such a malfunctioning guise is to invite dismissal by others: "he, that is driven to contradict an assertion by him before maintained, is said to be reduced to an absurdity" (EL 16.2). Hobbes takes it for granted, I think, that such absurdity or self-contradiction, in particular the public reduction to absurdity, is its own penalty. No one who is involved in self-contradiction can perform properly. And no one who appears self-contradictory to others, being reduced to absurdity, can command serious acceptance. Thus, there is no problem as to why people should be willing to keep simple, conditional commitments of the kind in question; and, assuming that these facts are available to all, there is no problem as to why people should expect others to be ready to do so as well.

But now we come to the really serious problem. Why would people keep and be expected to keep the double commitments they make when they enter contracts or covenants? We may grant that the aversion to self-contradiction gives them reason, and reason that is manifest on all sides, to stick by self-representations that they have not withdrawn or disowned. But why should they commit themselves never to withdraw words or actions that have a contractual cast? And why should they be expected by others not to withdraw them? Why, in short, should they be obliged by such acts of signification?

To be obliged or obligated to do something is to be bound or tied to another person to act in that way, as the etymological connection with *ligare*, the Latin term for binding, suggests. Obligations to others are never inherited, Hobbes thinks, rejecting the feudal picture of the obligations of children to parents, servants to masters, vassals to lords, and of course subjects to sovereigns; they are always voluntarily incurred. We each come into the world free of social bonds and become tied to others in different ways only insofar as we acquiesce, however tacitly, in being bound to them—only insofar as we implicitly or explicitly enter contracts with them. There is "no obligation on any man which ariseth not from some act of his own; for all men equally are by nature free" (L 21.10).

The acts that give rise to obligations, however, cannot involve contracting with oneself. One cannot be "be obligated to oneself" (DCv 6.14), for "he that can bind, can release" (L 26.6), and one could always release oneself from any pretended contract with or promise to oneself. The acts to which Hobbes traces obligations are promises that are made not to oneself but to other persons.

The obligations generated by contracts with others have two aspects. Having made a promise, one will be tied *by* a contract in the same way that one will be tied by an expression of judgment or will that one has not withdrawn; this is the element common to simple and dual commitments. But one will also be tied *to* a contract in a way in which one is not tied to any casual expression of judgment or will; this tie goes with the extra commitment that a contract involves. The by-contract bond is unproblematic insofar as we accept what Hobbes says about the penalty of absurdity and reduction to absurdity that attends acting against a manifestation of one's mind that remains on record. The problem that has to be explained bears on the to-contract bond. Why would people not break to-contract ties, just as it suits them, disowning any inconvenient promises? And why would others not expect people to break those bonds on such an opportunistic basis?

In order to understand Hobbes's line on this central question, it is important to appreciate the viewpoint from which he addresses it. He thinks it is obvious, I believe, that human beings will be much better off if they can reach out to one another in contract, sharing the capacity to tie themselves to others by the words they utter. To be able to tie, bind, or obligate oneself to another sounds like a dubious ability, but from Hobbes's perspective it matches reasoning as one of the great capacities of human beings. It enables human beings to empower their words as tokens of obligation and open up all the prospects of commodious living in which we know he rejoices. For reasons to be rehearsed in discussing the passions, he thinks that human beings are not naturally fitted for society; unlike many other animals, such as the bee, they are not naturally sociable (DCv 1.2). But they can overcome this problem and reach out to one another, even achieve what he calls union, insofar as they can give one another their word on how they will conduct themselves and then make that word stick—that is, prove themselves worthy of this credence and trust, this "acceptation" (EL 15.4).

Given his perspective, Hobbes does not see the primary problem raised by a contract as one of ensuring that people are enabled to resist the temptation to defect opportunistically on contracts that were initially made in the hope of either contractual benefit or a benefit from opportunistic defection. There may be occasions when there is a local advantage attached to defecting in this way—to free riding—but Hobbes maintains that only a fool would think that it was the rational thing, at least in general, to grasp at that advantage (B 44, 155). Someone "that breaketh his covenant . . . consequently declareth that he may with reason do so" (L 15.5); he manifests a will to defect, presumably because defection is so likely to be detected.[6] Breaking a covenant, then, amounts to renouncing the obligations generally associated with covenants; it amounts to an explicit rejection of the covenant (Hoekstra 1997). And so, Hobbes argues, the person who breaks a covenant "can in reason expect no other means of safety than what can be had from his own single power" (L 15.5); even one defection is liable to alienate potential allies. To risk such isolation, Hobbes believes, is complete folly. For even "in the natural condition, where each one is an enemy to each one, no one can live securely without the aid of allies" (L 15.5n7).[7]

But if there is no rational temptation for people to defect on initially sincere contracts or make contracts with an eye to later defection, then what is the difficulty with a contract? Why is there any problem raised by the way people are bound to stick to their contracts over and beyond the problem, already solved, as to why they are tied by the contracts to which they stick? If it is rational for people to keep the contracts they have already made—and presumably made for good reason—then won't they generally keep them? And if this is a matter accessible to all, as it surely will be, then won't others also expect them to keep the contracts? So why is there any difficulty?

There is still a difficulty for reasons to do not with why people should comply with contracts but with why people should expect others to comply. It may be clear to all that rational parties will keep the contracts they make, assuming that rational parties will only enter rational contracts. But it may not be clear to all that others will always be rational. Hobbes thinks that a weakness of will, mind, or soul (*impotentia animi*) can strike just about anyone, so that he "does or fails to do what he had previously promised by agreement not to do or not to fail to do" (DCv 3.3). And so he thinks that people will want an assurance on that point. There might be good reason to enter and comply with a certain contract were one assured that the other parties would prove to be rational, but there may be no such assurance available.

This lack of assurance is a serious obstacle for the possibility of having binding contracts and associated obligations. Hobbes thinks that it goes against a rational concern with one's own preservation and prosperity to enter a contract where there is "just cause of distrust" (L 22.29). And this means for him that it does against the laws of nature, as he calls the maxims of self-preservation and more broadly self-concern. Contracts are not validly or legitimately undertaken, according to the laws of nature, if there is even a "reasonable suspicion" (L 14.18) that others will defect. Thus, it is possible that "covenants be effectual" only if "he that performeth first shall have no reasonable cause to doubt of the performance of the other" (EL 15.10).

How, then, can assurance be provided for the different sides in any potential contract (EL 15.4)? How can people make their contractual overtures credible, substantiating the claim to give their word sincerely and reliably?

A necessary but not sufficient requirement of credibility is that certain formal conditions are met (cf. Grotius 2005, book 2, chapters 11–12). People must manifest their will clearly; manifest it in a domain where they have control over what they do; and manifest it on a matter where they are currently uncommitted. The first condition requires that the words used in a contract should reveal a current will to perform as promised (L 14.13–16; cf. EL 15; DCv 2.7–13), not just a prediction, and that they should be used in more than a casual manner (DCv 2.8).[8] The second condition means that the courses of action that people contract to perform must be ones that they are capable of enacting (EL 16.18); since I cannot abjure my right to preserve my life, for example, a "covenant not to defend myself from force by force is always void" (L 14.29). And the third condition implies that the matter in which people claim to make a contract must not be one on which they have already made a commitment to others; earlier contracts have precedence over later ones that are inconsistent with them (EL 15.14).

But while such conditions have to be satisfied for assurance in a contract, Hobbes does not think that their satisfaction is sufficient to make the words of would-be contractors credible. A would-be contractor might fulfill these conditions and still, for all we know, be subject to irrational impulses. There is an extra, more substantive condition that also has to be fulfilled, if that person is going to prove credible, and if it is going to be rational for us—and so permissible under the law of nature—to accept their word.

This substantive requirement is that contractors be able to stake something on any words they purport to give, showing that there will be an extra incentive available—the loss of the stake—to remind them of their commitments and regulate their performance (DCv 13.15–17). That people give their word, just on its own, is not enough for assurance, "the force of words being . . . too weak to hold men to the performance of their covenants" (L 14.31). They have to put something more in the hands of a promisee, then, in order to generate an assurance that their word will stick and there is no danger of defection (L 14.18). In effect, they have to give up something that might be used in order to recall them to the contract—in order to save them from the danger of their own irrational whim or weakness.

People in a contract cannot avoid putting their reputation in the hands of a promisee, of course, since they will want to win the esteem of being found true to their word—and avoid the disesteem of being found to be duplicitous (Pettit 2002, part 3, essay 2). But even the concern with reputation is not going to be enough to assure the promisee properly, being "a generosity too rarely to be found to be presumed on" (L 14.31). Hobbes thinks that what people will have to do in order to provide real assurance is to expose themselves to the prospect of a sanction, a feared penalty, in the event of not performing appropriately. "The passion to be reckoned upon is fear," he says (L 14.31)—in particular, "the fear of some coercive power" (L 14.18). Let those who would contract with others accept a sanction that will be inescapable in the event of defection, and their word will be credible. They will be able to gain access to others in a contract and win for themselves the great benefits that such alliances make possible.[9]

The upshot is an elegant picture of how people may manage, once words have been invented, to bind themselves to one another and make possible the fruits of such commitment. People are rationally bound, on pain of self-contradiction, to act in fidelity to words they have given and not withdrawn. And people are rationally bound, on pain of losing out on great potential returns, not to withdraw any words that they have given in contract. But will people be motivated to prove themselves rational, overcoming irrational impulses? Yes, Hobbes contends. They will be faithful to commitments that remain on the record for fear of being shown to be inconsistent and thereby reduced to absurdity. And they will tie themselves to those commitments that amount to promises or contracts—they will put aside the possibility of unilateral defection—by exposing themselves to penalties in the event of not complying. Their tying themselves in this way makes rational sense, moreover, given the great benefits that successful contracts can bring on stream.

THE VOLITIONAL AND THE VOLUNTARY

Even though this picture explains nicely how human beings may avail of words to tie themselves to one another and reap the benefits of union, it is counterintuitive in one important respect. By all accounts, Hobbes's included, a contract has to be voluntarily assumed if it is to generate an obligation. But it doesn't take much for a contract to count as voluntary in Hobbes's reckoning. People will enter a contract voluntarily, according to him, if their conflicting appetites resolve in its favor in the course of the process, common to human and nonhuman animals, that he describes as deliberation. No matter how this process materializes—it may or may not be aided by explicit reasoning—and no matter what appetites it takes as input—these may include fear or anxiety—the product will count as voluntary. So the contract accepted under duress or pressure, even under coercive threat, can be just as binding as a contract that is undertaken with relish.

The position that Hobbes takes here is driven by the psychology of the natural mind that I surveyed in the first chapter. According to that psychology, any act that issues from deliberation accords with the last appetite or will that materializes in deliberation (L 6.53). The fact that it conforms to the agent's will might lead us to describe it as volitional, acknowledging that even the victim of a highwayman who sacrifices money rather than life does so volitionally. Hobbes equates the volitional in this sense with the voluntary, both words deriving from the Latin for will, *voluntas*. He can then insist that two acts may be equally voluntary, even when the one is driven by a mesmerizing fear, and the other by a casual desire for market advantage. As he says, "There appeareth no reason, why that which we do upon fear, should be less firm than that which we do for covetousness. For both the one and the other maketh the action voluntary" (EL 15.13).

This move is a revision of ordinary language, on Hobbes's part, even the language of his time; it offers a nice example of the way his definitions often rework common meanings, as I suggested at the end of the previous chapter. What we generally describe as voluntary rather than merely volitional or intentional are not acts that issue from desires of any old kind but only from desires that are formed under intuitively fair conditions—conditions, for example, in which there is no coercion or duress. Hobbes will have none of this. Under his revised use of language, the fact that someone enters a contract out of fear of what may happen otherwise—"fear of those consequences" (L 6.54)—does not mean that the person enters it involuntarily. It therefore cannot excuse any failure to comply with the contractual terms; "that which could not hinder a man from promising, ought not to be admitted as a hindrance of performing" (L 14.20; cf. DC 2.12n). The hold of contractual obligation is not conditional on the absence of such excuses; it is excuse insensitive, as we might say.

This excuse insensitivity is understood in such a radical manner that, in Hobbes's view, even "prisoners of war, if trusted with the payment of their ransom, are obliged to pay it" (L 14.27).[10] It enables him to argue that when slaves acquiesce in the power of a master, they make a contract that obliges them to comply; there is a "covenant, without which the master had no reason to trust them" (EL 22.3). Equally, it enables him to hold that when the vanquished submit to a conqueror in battle, they become contractually obligated to the conqueror; no one is obliged to a victor "because he is conquered (that is to say, beaten, and taken or put to flight), but because he cometh in, and submitteth to the victor" (L 20.11). The fact that contractual obligation is excuse insensitive in this way is important for Hobbesian political theory. As we shall see later, it makes it possible for him to hold that subjects are bound even to a sovereign whom they accept as a result of conquest and intimidation.

If those with whom someone has made a contract are no longer delivering on their part of the bargain, of course—if the conqueror or the master of the slave is no longer giving what was promised—then the contract is off. But so long as they are providing the contractual return, Hobbes takes it that the contract will be as binding as any promise made between equals. What makes the contract binding will be the agreement at its origin, not the motivational reinforcement provided by the penalty that hangs as a threat over any defection—say, the penalty of the conqueror's or the master's ire. Hobbes makes this particularly clear in *De Cive*, when he discusses the source of obligation attaching to a law, even a law that may have been imposed by a conqueror. "A man is obligated by an agreement, i.e. he ought to perform because of his promise. But he is kept to his obligation by a law, i.e. he is compelled to performance by fear of the penalty laid down in the law" (DCv 14.2n).[11]

Hobbes is often represented as a theorist of fear and force, in whom might is right. But while fear does have a place in his story of how people can contract with one another, and while this is one of the least attractive aspects of the story, the place of fear is subsidiary. It is necessary to guard against the lack of assurance that can keep people isolated and miserable, unable to achieve the benefits of cooperation. What makes those benefits accessible, however, is not the fear itself but the commitments and the contracts—the bonds of words—that it facilitates. The relations achieved between conqueror and conquered, or master and slave, may not illustrate the grander possibilities of personation and contract, yet even they have a positive side to them. Under these relations, the stronger control the weaker by nothing more than the utterance of words, and that is a decidedly gentler form of control than the imposition of chains or shackles. Servants obey "of duty," not "to avoid the cruelty of their task-masters" (L 20.12), and where "trust" is supposed, a master "does not require the continuing exercise of force" (EL 22.3).

CHAPTER FIVE

Using Words to Incorporate

CORPORATE PERSONS

There is a third benefit that speech confers on the mind, apart from the capacity to reason and personate. This is the ability of people to incorporate: to come together and act as a single corporate person. Hobbes thinks that individuals are constituted as natural persons by the role they play in self-personation, giving and taking one another's word. And this role theory allows him to make room for the possibility that groups of people might be constituted as something like corporate persons on a parallel basis.

Medieval legal theory had much to say on the nature of incorporation since, as I noted earlier, it took legal persons to be defined by their role or standing under law. Legal standing means that a person can own, buy, and sell property, enter into contracts and perpetrate injury, incur obligations and be able to make claims, and so on. Corporate bodies like guilds and orders, parishes and towns, came to be accorded such a standing in medieval practice and the medieval reworking of Roman law. For example, they owned property, made contracts, filed claims, and had claims filed against them. Legal theory marked this novel development by distinguishing between the *universitas, collegium*, or corporate entity and the mere gathering of individuals—the *congregatio*—and by describing the universitas as a *persona ficta*, a fictional or perhaps artificial person (Canning 1980; Kantorowicz 1997).

This theory of the corporate person—the corporation or *corporatio*, as it had come to be known (Cowell 1607)—remained familiar in Hobbes's day, and would have been taken to support a number of theses. First, unlike the congregatio, the corporatio exists, in a sense, over and beyond its members; it is capable of surviving the deaths of members, enjoying a sort of immortal—certainly, not necessarily mortal—life. Second, the corporatio needs members to speak and act for it, but when people act in that role they put aside their own identities; they became *universi*, representatives, and cease to perform as *singuli* or individuals. Third, the corporatio has a mind or *mens* of its own—a guiding set of goals and judgments—and the council or *concilium* of representatives through which corporate entities function reveal this mind.

It is because of such representation that the corporate entity is uni-fied. As Albericus de Rosciate could write in 1354: "collegium, licet con-stituatur ex pluribus, est tamen unum per representationem"; "a body corporate, although it is constituted out of many members, is neverthe-less one by virtue of representation" (Eschman 1944, 33n145).

Hobbes builds on this tradition, though in his own distinctive way, when he describes the possibility of incorporation. He acknowledges the place that a council or assembly may have in representing a corpo-ration, as we shall see later, but in his usual account of how people can incorporate he assumes that it is a natural person who is going to func-tion in this representative capacity, and his decided preference in the case of political incorporation is for the individual representation of a monarch. I shall concentrate for the moment on the case of the individ-ually represented corporation, and shall build my account mainly on *Leviathan*, rather than on Hobbes's earlier works. As noted below, his earlier position on the individually represented polity—in particular, the monarchy—is different from his mature view; the earlier view, un-like the later, suggests that monarchy always emerges, like aristocracy, from a democratic regime.[1]

The individual who speaks and acts in their own name, as we know, is a natural person according to Hobbes. But what he now acknowledges is that such a person may also speak and act for others, performing like "a feigned or artificial person" (L 16.1; DH 15.1). According to this way of speaking, it is the person representing who is the artificial person, not anything on the side of the represented; this marks at least a termino-logical break with the medieval approach. The explanation for the break may be that, in Hobbes's view, a natural person may speak or act in this artificial role not just for a set of individuals—those who would incor-porate by virtue of being represented in that way—but for a variety of entities that do not speak in their own name—for those like "children, fools and madmen" who are unable to speak for themselves; for "the gods of the heathen" and "the true God" who are not available to speak for themselves; and for "inanimate things (as a church, an hospital, a bridge)" that cannot speak at all, let alone speak for themselves (L 16.9–11). In each of these cases, the representative person is the actor who acts or speaks for the represented entity. The represented entity will be identical with the actor in the case of natural personation and distinct in the case of artificial personation. And if it is distinct, then it may be a multitude of individuals—the case we are interested in—or another in-dependent individual, a dependent individual like a child or madman, a real or imagined god, or a completely inanimate object.

In self-representation, as we know, the actor authorizes their own words or actions; actor and author, in Hobbes's terms, are one. But who is the author in other cases? The owner will authorize the representer of an inanimate entity, Hobbes says; the state or commonwealth will authorize the representer of an idol as well as the representer of a dependent individual; the true God will author his own representation, and so will the independent individual for whom another speaks. But who will author the representation of a multitude? Here Hobbes strikes an inclusive, participatory note, arguing that all of those involved must give their individual assent to the representation of the multitude (L 16.13). They are the "many authors, of every thing their representative saith, or doth in their name" (L 16.14).

Hobbes's list of items that may be represented or personated is a mixed bunch.[2] The lesson is meant to be instructive, I suspect, about multitudes. Hobbes stresses that like the inanimate object or the idol, for example—a "mere figment of the brain" (L 16.11)—a multitude of human beings is really nothing special, even if it is capable of being personated. The members of a multitude are not one, he says, but legion; "a number of men, each of whom has his own will and his own judgment" (DCv 6.1). And so he can speak of the multitude in quite derogatory and dismissive tones, describing it as an "aggregate" or "heap" of agents (EL 21.11), "a disorganized crowd" (DCv 7.11), a "throng" (L 6.37), and in a typical reference, a disjoined or "dissolute number of individual persons" (L 42.27).

This downbeat motif serves his political purposes well, as we shall see later, because it undermines any suggestion that a multitude prior to personation might be able to make claims against its representative—the sovereign in the case of the multitude of political subjects—or indeed against anyone else; "the heap, or multitude, cannot be said to demand or have a right to anything" (EL 21.11). In taking this position, he joins forces with a common royalist line of opposition in England in the 1640s. Deriding parliamentary pretensions to recognize the sovereignty of the people as a whole, royalist critics had given a suitably unflattering image of the people as a multitude "in continuall alteration and change," just like a heap. As one account had it, this body "never continues one minute the same, being composed of a multitude of parts, whereof divers continually decay and perish, and others renew and succeed in their places" (Morgan 1988, 61).

But though Hobbes insists that the multitude that is personated amounts to nothing interesting in itself, he is adamant that personation changes all of that. Out of the larval multitude there emerges a corporate butterfly. Whereas the personation of other items does not in any way change their character or merit the use of a new name to describe them, the personation of a multitude has a transformative effect. It means in Hobbes's terminology that the multitude ceases to be a heap of separate individuals and becomes capable of being understood "for one" (L 16.14). More particularly, it means that those individuals are "made one person" (L 16.13) or "united as one person" (EL 19.8). With this unity established for the inhabitants of a land, those inhabitants cease to be "a multitude of single persons" and become describable as "the people" (DCv 7.7); "the multitude . . . are the people" (EL 21.11). The personation of a multitude is a transformative act. Unlike the personation of things, it gives rise to a novel creation, at least in the deflationary sense of making it right to describe the multitude for the first time as a people.

Where does the unity of the personated multitude come from, given the plurality of the materials available? From the individual who does the personating, Hobbes says, "It is the unity of the representer, not the unity of the represented, that maketh the person *one*. And it is the representer that beareth the person, and but one person: and unity, cannot otherwise be understood in multitude" (L 16.13). Hobbes often speaks of how an individual can "bear the person" of the multitude, as he "beareth also his own natural person" (L 19.4). The idea is that the many, having consented to common personation, are unified in the personator, embodied in what he or she says or does in their common name. Those individuals will each "own and acknowledge himself to be author of whatsoever he that so beareth their person shall act, or cause to be acted" in matters of concern to the whole (L 17.13).

Given that the multitude deserves to be described as a people when it is represented or personated by an individual, a natural question is whether, as in the medieval usage, it can also be described as a person or *persona*, thereby opening up the possibility of seeing the people in a city or country as constituting a state or *civitas*. Well, the people can certainly be described as a personatee, as we might say, since the people is the multitude qua personated. And Hobbes does recognize that secondary sense of being a person, as when he says, "A person . . . is he that is represented, as often as he is represented" (L 42.3).[3] But as we shall see later, there is a clear contrast between the status that a people has as a passive person in that sense and the status that it gains under democracy as an active person or personator—its own spokesperson. And there is some evidence that Hobbes may be sensitive to the contrast, since he is generally willing to speak of a group as a person, only when the group personates itself actively, as with the people in a democracy, the participants in a small-scale company of merchants, or the members of a parliament; "sovereign assemblies, if they have but one voice, though they be many men, yet are they but one person" (B 156).

Still, even when the multitude is represented by an individual and becomes a people on that passive basis, Hobbes comes close to invoking the standard, medieval terminology. He says that when represented by an individual, the "multitude are united by covenants into one person civil" (EL 20.1)—this, presumably, is the sense in which he thinks that "companies of merchants" count as "civil persons" (DCv 5.10). In the political case he is ready to describe such a civil person, in the language of his earlier work, as a body politic (EL 20.1), or in his more usual terminology, as a commonwealth or state; "the multitude so united . . . is called a commonwealth" (L 17.3). And he is willing to say that not only is the multitude represented by the representer or sovereign who gives them unity; the commonwealth, "the person of the people" (B 120), is represented by the sovereign at one and the same time.

But however far the individually represented people constitutes a person and a commonwealth, they do not exist as such apart from the individual personator who gives them voice, unity, and life. The people exists in and through that personator, according to Hobbes; the personator, as he continually asserts, bears the person of the group. Acknowledging that the people is a body, he denies that "the people is a distinct body from him or them that have the sovereignty over them" (EL 27.9). The sovereign personator will have two bodies, to ring a change on the age-old idea of the king's two bodies, personal and political (Kantorowicz 1997). Hobbes quotes Cicero as saying that in the courtroom, he can bear different persons as he enacts a will and a judgment that bears on a different role—say, his own, that of his adversary, or that of the judge (L 16.4). His image of the personating individual is that this individual will bear two persons: his or her own person as well as that of the group. The individual will be a natural person in the role where the personatee coincides with the personator and an artifical person in the role where the personatee extends to encompass all of those in the represented multitude.

When the personator represents a multitude, then what happens in one traditional image is that the personator is the the head or *caput* that gives direction to the other organs and limbs in the institutional body; the personator is a member of the group, but a member with a particularly important role to play. Interestingly, however, Hobbes does not adopt this image (Skinner 2005). Rather, he casts the personator as the soul that gives life and personality to the multitude of individuals in whose name that personator thinks and speaks, wills and acts. To go to the political case that Hobbes always has in his sights, "the sovereign, is the public soul, giving life and motion to the commonwealth; which expiring, the members are governed by it no more, than the carcass of a man, by his departed (though immortal) soul" (L 29.23). The picture fits nicely with the thesis that the act of personating a multitude transforms the nature of that multitude, so that it becomes one rather than many, and in the most comprehensive case associated with the common-wealth, deserves the name of "people."

Hobbes treats the emergence of the people and commonwealth al-most as if he had an ironic, even wicked parallel in mind with the Ro-man Catholic sacrament in which the bread and wine are said to be transformed into the body and blood of Christ by the priest's utterance of the formula of consecration, "This is my body; this is my blood."[4] He thinks that in the preferred mode of forming a commonwealth, the members of the multitude will each authorize their personation in pro-nouncing the equally formulaic words, "I authorize and give up my right of governing myself, to this man, or to this assembly of men, on this condition, that thou give up thy right to him, and authorize all his actions in like manner" (L 17.13). By the utterance of those words, as by the utterance of a sacramental formula, a sea change is supposed to take place, akin to transubstantiation. After the words are uttered, there is a "real unity of them all, in one and the same person," and "the multi-tude so united in one person, is called a commonwealth." And as if this isn't enough to signal the sacramental parallel, he adds, "This is the generation of that great Leviathan, or rather (to speak more reverently) of that Mortal God to which we owe, under the Immortal God, our peace and defence."[5]

THE RANGE OF INCORPORATION

The discussion so far has abstracted from different ways in which peo-ple may incorporate and form corporate persons. There are two points to register in filling out the story. The first, implicit in earlier discus-sions, is that Hobbes sees a big difference between the way in which people may incorporate to form a political group person—the commonwealth—and the way in which they may incorporate to form a private group person. And the second is that he also distinguishes be-tween two quite different ways in which the political group person—even the individually personated group person—may be formed.

The distinction between the political and the private group, accord-ing to Hobbes, is that the political personator—the sovereign—is au-thorized by individuals with hardly any limitations on what may be done in their name—more on this later—whereas the private person-ator is only given a limited brief. People may own "all the actions the representer doth, in case they give him authority without stint," in which event there is a political personator or sovereign, and a common-wealth is formed, or people may "limit him in what, and how far he shall represent them," in which event there is just a private personator and a private corporation (L 16.14). In the private case, people relate to the personator in such a limited way that "none of them owneth more, than they gave him commission to act."

This account is subject to one qualification mentioned in the previous chapter: that no human beings can authorize a personator, even the political personator, to take away their lives or do them direct harm; no one can try to act against the necessity of nature whereby people pursue their own good. But notwithstanding this qualification, there is a clear contrast in place. Hobbes spells it out particularly sharply in *De Cive* (5.10).

> Although every commonwealth is a civil person, not every civil person (by converse) is a commonwealth. For it may happen that several persons will, with the permission of their commonwealth, unite as one person for the purpose of transacting certain business. These will now be civil persons, as companies of merchants are, and any number of other groups, but they are not commonwealths, because they have not subjected themselves to the will of the group simply and in all things, but only in certain matters defined by the commonwealth.

Hobbes recognizes that there will be many personated groups in a society apart from the people considered as a whole. He thinks that only a few will be able to form, however, in the absence of a commonwealth. Without the comprehensive organization of a commonwealth, there will be too little trust available for the appearance of many private group persons—many "leagues" involving the "connection of men by covenants" (L 22.29). Those corporate groups that do appear in a commonwealth, of course, will naturally be subordinate to the laws of the commonwealth; they will be subsidiary entities. As Hobbes says, "The sovereign, in every commonwealth, is the absolute representative of all the subjects; and therefore no other can be representative of any part of them, but so far forth, as he shall give leave" (L 22.5).

Private corporations may assume many forms, in Hobbes's story, ranging from groups formally recognized in law to groups formally unrecognized, and among the groups that are unrecognized, from those that are actually lawful to those that are unlawful (L 22). His main focus, however, is on the lawful, recognized group like the company of merchants. This is the epitome of what would have been regarded as a body corporate or *universitas* in the tradition deriving from medieval times, and it is Hobbes's model of a "civil person" (DCv 5.10).

In the medieval tradition, the salience of the universitas in commercial and ecclesiastical life had led a number of legal theorists, such as Bartolus of Sassoferrato and Baldus de Ubaldis, to argue that in a city republic the people or *populus* had the form of an universitas, with a more or less widely elected *concilium* or council that spoke and acted in its name (Woolf 1913; Canning 1980, 1983; Ryan 1999). These theorists argued that as a corporate body, the populus was a *persona* or person, and that as a persona it could be a *princeps* or prince. Thus, they maintained that in such a city republic the populus was *sibi princeps*, a prince unto itself. The lesson they derived was important in fourteenth-century Italy since it offered some protection against the Holy Roman emperor's claim to be *dominus mundi*, lord of the world. It was widely accepted that a prince was the emperor in his own lands and hence that the emperor could not interfere in the internal affairs of a princedom; if a city republic was a princedom of a distinctive sort, then it too would enjoy that license.

Hobbes follows the lead of those medieval theorists in taking the notion of a corporation as given, being familiar from private instances of the type, and then carrying it over to the characterization of the commonwealth—not just a republican commonwealth in his case, of course, but a commonwealth of any kind. Wittingly or unwittingly, he makes the false claim to be the first to see the commonality between the two types of group person. "And though in the charters of subordinate corporations, a corporation be declared to be one person in law, yet the same hath not been taken notice of in the body of a commonwealth or city" (EL 27.7).

Apart from recognizing private as well as political corporations, Hobbes argues that there are different ways in which the commonwealth may form, even when it is individually personated. He distinguishes between the case where the personator or sovereign gets identified by "acquisition" or imposition and the case where this happens by "institution" (EL 22.1). These are distinguished by two ways in which sovereign power, or the role of personation, may be attained by the representative:

> One, by natural force; as when a man maketh his children, to submit themselves, and their children to his government, as being able to destroy them if they refuse; or by war subdueth his enemies to his will, giving them their lives on that condition. The other, is when men agree amongst themselves, to submit to some man, or assembly of men, voluntarily, on confidence to be protected by him against all others. (L 17.15)

Hobbes claims that in each of these cases there is a contract. In the case of the commonwealth by institution, the contract is between the members of the political multitude to have a sovereign, and though this may only be determined later, to have this or that sovereign in particular. In the case of the commonwealth by acquisition, the contract is made by each with the would-be sovereign to recognize that person or body as personator of the whole, however large the whole may be. But this latter contract does not involve submission to a private master, since the manifest assumption made by the person who submits is that other members of the whole must acquiesce in the personating arrangement as well, otherwise the would-be sovereign would be "disabled to provide for their safety" (L 21.20).[6]

In taking this line, Hobbes breaks with the medieval tradition in which the commonwealth or state is cast as a political corporation. Whereas the medieval theorists would not generally have recognized monarchy as an instance of such a corporation, Hobbes does so; he thinks that in a political corporation, properly so called, even a single individual may play the required, personating role. And Hobbes thinks that the individual monarch may attain this role not only on the basis of a contract of all with all to recognize them but also on the basis of imposition, or as he says, acquisition. The point applies even when the imposition comes about by military victory. He insists, moreover, that there is no great difference between the two cases. The sovereignty attained by imposition "differeth from sovereignty by institution only in this, that men who choose their sovereign do it for fear of one another, and not of him whom they institute; but in this case they subject themselves to him they are afraid of " (L 20.2).

The key to why imposition may work as well as institution is that for Hobbes, as we saw, fear is just one appetite among many and does nothing to reduce the voluntariness of an act; "he that does anything for fear, though he say truly he was compelled to it, yet we deny not that he had election to do or not to do, and consequently that he was a voluntary and free agent" (Hobbes and Bramhall 1999, 78). Thus, Hobbes has no difficulty in thinking that even as we individually submit to a would-be monarch, we do so voluntarily and enter a contract that will be properly binding, so long as that monarch can provide the service required, getting others to submit as well. The very act of submission to a would-be monarch will announce the contractual intention and the obligation assumed; "from the intention of him that submitteth himself to his power, (which intention is to be understood by the end for which he so submitteth;) the obligation . . . is to be derived" (L 21.10). And this will hold even where a person's submission occurs in the wake of a military defeat, under fear of torture or death. "It is not . . . the victory that giveth the right of dominion of the vanquished, but his own covenant" (L 20.11).

Incorporation in the medieval tradition was always cast in a more or less participatory way, representing the possibility of people coming freely together to constitute a new legal entity: the guild or order, town or parish. Hobbes draws on that theory in his story as to how people may use the resources of speech and personation in order to incorporate. But in allowing a monarch to serve as a personator, even a monarch accepted under imposition, he gives a novel, hardly appealing, twist to the story. The twist comes out most clearly in the way he inverts the more or less received notion of a representative of the people. That notion had played an important role in the case that contemporary writers were making for the standing of a parliament (Skinner 2005). Hobbes turned the tables on those opponents, suggesting that as a matter of manifest truth, it was the king who had the most right to be described as representing the people, not the motley members of parliament. For him it is absurd "that in a monarchy, he that had the sovereignty from a descent of 600 years, was alone called sovereign, had the title of Majesty from every one of his subjects, and was unquestionably taken by them for their king, was notwithstanding never considered as their representative" (L 19.3). His own view, on the contrary, is that "the King himself did . . . ever represent the person of the people of England" (B 120).

Corporate Persons, Active and Passive

I have not yet told the whole story, however, as to how multitudes can be transformed into civil persons. For Hobbes allows for the possibility that pluralities of individuals can figure not just as personatees but also as personators (L 16.5; DH 15.3). He insists that the sovereign in a commonwealth may be an individual or a committee, including the committee-of-the-whole: the assembly that would engage all relevant members of the society—in effect, all propertied males. And that means that he thinks the plurality in such a committee must be able to perform as a personator, not just as a personatee.

This being so, the account I have presented as to how a multitude can come to be a civil person cannot represent the only way in which such a transformation may be achieved. The group that personates a multitude will have to act as a single person, since "the unity of the represented," as we know, has to derive from "the unity of the representer" (L 16.13). Suppose that this personating group were to act as a single person because each of the members authorized one of their number to speak and act for them all, as in the story given so far. In that case, the authorized individual would speak and act not just for that group but for the personated multitude. And then the personating group would play no significant role except as a way station of authorization: the members of the multitude would authorize the group in a personating role, and the group members would in turn authorize an individual to exercise that role for them.

This is not Hobbes's image of what happens when a group plays a personating role. An individual may have to act or speak for the group on occasions when the group engages with a distinct agent. But the same individual need not be involved on each occasion. In any case, the mind of the group will not be formed in the formation of that individual's mind. On the contrary, as Hobbes says, the group will make up its collective mind without assigning that job to any personating authority. They will do so, issue by issue, on the basis of a procedure of majority voting, duly adjusted to take care of problems of fifty-fifty divisions (L 16.15–17; B 156). The idea is that rather than authorizing or standing by a spokesperson, as in the original story of group personation, the members of this group will authorize or stand by whatever emerges on any issue as the majority opinion.

The actively personating group envisaged in this version is a rather different sort of entity from the passively personated group to which we are directed in the earlier discussion. It is a personator, not just a personatee; a spokesperson, not just a person spoken for. Hobbes may give some recognition to the difference this makes; as we saw earlier, he seems to be more willing to describe the actively personating group as a person. But on the whole he does not trumpet the contrast.

This lack of emphasis on the difference may be politically motivated. He thinks that the people in a commonwealth may be organized in the fashion of a monarchy with a single king as personator, an aristocracy with a committee as the personator, or a democracy with the whole population—the committee-of-the-whole—as the personator (EL 21; DCv 7; L 19). Clearly, the personator group associated with democracy would be a different sort of people, a different sort of civil person, from the personatee group envisaged in monarchy; it would have an active, participatory character. But Hobbes, anxious to argue for the superior merits of monarchy, may be disinclined to mark that difference; it would be too likely to give support to democracy. While insisting on the contrast between a multitude and a people, he downplays the difference between the passive mode in which a people comes to be constituted under a monarchy or an aristocracy, and the active form that it achieves under a democracy.[7]

This is particularly true of *Leviathan*, where democracy gets shorter shrift than in earlier works like *The Elements of Law* and *De Cive*. In those earlier works, he defends the view that first, with the commonwealth by institution, a democracy always gets formed as an initial step, and then that this gives way either to an aristocracy, as some few people are recognized as effective authorities, or a monarchy, as one person emerges supreme (EL 21; DCv 7). Thus, "democracy is the beginning both of aristocracy and monarchy" (EL 21.6). In *Leviathan*, by contrast, the three regimes are presented as coequal possibilities and then monarchy is identified as the best by certain more or less plausible criteria, as it is also held to be best in the earlier works (L 19). The shift may well be due to the impact on Hobbes of the claims made in the course of the 1640s by the increasingly self-assured and strident parliamentarians. He may have wished to withdraw any approval that his earlier approach might be taken to have given to their populist claims.[8]

The difference between the works shows up in the fact that whereas in *Leviathan*, the people is said to exist as a single person by virtue of any of the three forms of constitution, Hobbes is more ambivalent in the earlier works. He certainly wants to claim that the people exists under nondemocratic representation: "even in monarchies the people exercises power; for the people wills through the will of one man" (DCv 12.8; EL 21.11). But in the earlier period, he talks of that mode of existence as more attenuated than under democracy. He even suggests at one point in *De Cive* that the multitude ceases to be the locus of the people after the end of a democracy, so that "in a Monarchy the subjects are the crowd, and (paradoxically) the King is the people" (DCv 12.8; cf. DCv 7.8).[9]

The possibility of the actively personating group represents the limit case of the incorporation that language makes possible, according to Hobbes. He describes the incorporation envisaged, whether it be of the active or the passive variety, as a case of achieving union. "When many wills are involved or included in the will of one or more consenting, . . . then is that involving of many wills in one or more called union" (EL 12.8). Such union, achieved by artificial means, Hobbes contrasts with concord. Lacking the conflictual passions of human beings, to which I will be turning in the next chapter, bees and other creatures can achieve a natural concord among themselves (EL 19.5). What human beings achieve when they overcome those passions and make contracts for incorporation "signifieth not the concord, but the union of many men" (EL 27.7).

Still, such union is in many ways more important than concord. It involves not the convergence of people's inclinations but the construction of "a real unity of them all, in one and the same person" (L 17.13). The theme will assume particular significance when we come to consider the unification of people "in one person called a commonwealth" (L 17.13).

APPENDIX: HOBBES'S MISTAKE ABOUT MAJORITY RULE

Before leaving the topic of artificial persons and corporate entities, it is worth drawing attention to one difficulty that Hobbes overlooks. The suggestion that a group might make up its mind and constitute a single person on the basis of majority voting came to Hobbes from a long tradition, and was widely maintained after him; it appears, for example, in both Locke (1960, book 2, chapter 8.96) and Rousseau (1973, book 4, chapter 2). But notwithstanding its acceptance among such authorities, the suggestion is deeply flawed.

The problem is that if a number of people each hold sensible, consistent judgments on a range of logically connected issues, still the collective judgments that would be supported under majority voting may be inconsistent and senseless (Pettit 2001, chapter 5; 2003). Suppose that A, B, and C each have a consistent set of judgments on three issues of government; think of those individuals, if you like, as a council representing the people. Taking the need for a balanced budget as granted, they each make judgments: first, on whether to hold taxes steady; second, on whether to increase military spending; and third, on whether to increase other spending. Imagine now that they take a majority vote on these matters. A and B may support holding taxes steady, while C disagrees; C wants taxes increased. A may vote with C for increasing military spending, while B disagrees; B thinks this should be reduced. And B and C may vote for increasing other spending, while A disagrees; A thinks this should be reduced.

	Increase taxes?	Increase defense?	Increase other spending?
A	No	Yes	No (reduce)
B	No	No (reduce)	Yes
C	Yes	Yes	Yes

If the parties vote on these questions in order to identify the corporate view, majority voting will support holding taxes steady (A and B win), increasing military spending (A and C win), but also increasing other spending (B and C win). From perfectly consistent individual sets of judgments they may generate, as the corporate set of judgments, a set of inconsistent, unenactable commitments. This illustrates the problem that confronts any proposal like Hobbes's, to have an assembly do its business on the basis of majority voting. Insofar as that assembly has to resolve connected issues there is a standing probability, increasing as the record of its judgments grows over time, that majority voting will lead it into inconsistency. And that is a real problem, assuming that it makes judgments on a need-for-action basis, so that inconsistent judgments will recommend inconsistent courses of action.

This problem is quite general, as it turns out. Any method of voting that treats every issue as equal to every other, letting it be determined by individual views, and that treats every individual as equal, allowing no dictatorship or privilege, is liable to generate the same sort of inconsistency—or at least this will be so, if it is supposed to work for any input sets of consistent judgments (List and Pettit 2002, 2004). Group persons who operate on a participatory basis will face a "discursive dilemma": they can be responsive to individuals, in which case they will risk collectively irrationality; or they can ensure collective rationality, in which case they may fail to be responsive to individuals.

Given the problem illustrated by the discursive dilemma, the actively personating group may follow procedures less algorithmic than normal voting processes. It might go about its business, for example, by taking a straw vote on each issue, checking whether this would-be judgment is inconsistent with any other judgment on record, and in the case of inconsistency looking for a resolution by going with the minority, not the majority, on one of the conflicting judgments (Pettit 2007d). Thus our little group might decide to go with C, not with A and B, on the issue of whether to hold taxes steady; that would be one way of giving the corporate body the profile of a sensible agent.

CHAPTER SIX

Words and the Warping of Appetite

BUT WORDS ARE NOT A CERTAIN GOOD. For the linguistic capacity that makes reasoning, personating, and incorporating possible has negative effects as well. It creates havoc in the realm of human passion, making monsters out of the simple animals that human beings might otherwise be. We must now explore this dark side of what language, according to Hobbes, does for human beings.

Speech connects up with the passions in two ways, each of them a source of problem and disorder. First of all, as we saw in chapter 2, it enables people to give expression to their passions, putting evaluative terms at their disposal, and second, it serves to expand the range of the passions, thereby increasing the divide between human beings and other animals. I will look in this chapter at these two connections, dealing first with the expression of passion and then with the way in which speech expands the domains where the passions operate.

THE EXPRESSION OF DESIRE

Speech serves passion or desire in the first place by enabling people to give one another "voluntary significations" (L 6.56) of what they are feeling and wanting, not just the natural signs that are provided by "the countenance, motions of the body, actions, and ends." These voluntary significations make it possible for people to deceive one another, for they can be used "arbitrarily" or at will, and may be used to express certain passions, as we saw, "whether they that use them have such passions or not." But still they are of the greatest importance.

Their importance derives in the first place from the fact that as soon as words appear in expression of passion, then in principle, reasoning about the objects of passion becomes possible. Hobbes thinks that the "language of the passions" lends itself to ratiocination, like language of any kind, or at least like anything that truly deserves to be called language. He clearly thinks that "cursing, swearing, reviling, and the like" may be associated with passion, but denies that these are uses of language proper; they "do not signify as speech," constituting only verbal tics—"the actions of a tongue accustomed" (L 6.55).

But what sort of reasoning or ratiocination does the expression of passion allow? The words that are paradigmatically associated with passion, as we saw in the second chapter, are thin evaluative terms like good or bad. Hobbes's view is that we use positive terms for anything that we desire, and corresponding negative terms for anything to which we are averse. If we are attracted to something we call it good, and call it good only on that account; if we are averse to something we call it bad, and call it bad only on that account. As Hobbes says, "Whatsoever is the object of any man's appetite or desire, that is it which he for his part calleth *good:* and the object of his hate and aversion, *evil*" (L 6.7).

Hobbes thinks that where there is desire for something, there is pleasure in the presence or at least the immediate prospect of the object desired, and where there is aversion, there is pain or displeasure; the attractive is the pleasant, and the aversive the unpleasant. He can take the pleasure to be "the appearance, or sense, of good; and molestation or displeasure, the appearance, or sense, of evil" (L 6.11). Thus, he can say that everyone "calleth that which pleaseth, and is delightful to himself, good; and that evil which displeaseth him" (EL 7.3). As we learn to use words like rough, red, or round on the basis of the effects that things have on our senses, so we learn to use good and bad on the basis of the effects they have in giving or promising us pleasure or displeasure.

The question, then, is how words introduced on that sort of basis can be recruited to a process of reasoning. And the question is troublesome, of course (L 6.7). We naturally use words that name what Hobbes regards as real properties of bodies according to how things "simply and absolutely" are; an example might be a word like round. We naturally use words that do not name real properties of bodies but are guided by the common effects that bodies happen to have on us—words like red and rough—according to "a common rule"; the rule will be common insofar as bodies affect us in more or less the same ways. But what are we to do with evaluative terms? There are two problems with these words, as we already know.

First of all, words like good and bad are used by different people to pick out different things, since people vary in the things they find pleasant or unpleasant; "while every man differeth from other in constitution, they differ also one from another concerning the common distinction of good and evil" (EL 7.3). Words like good and bad "are ever used with relation to the person that useth them, there being nothing simply and absolutely so, nor any common rule of good and evil to be taken from the nature of the objects themselves" (L 6.7). They are used by me to pick out those things I find pleasing or displeasing, and by you to pick out those things that you find pleasing or displeasing.

This makes for a problem, because differences in our judgments of good and evil are likely to lead us into strife with one another; our "controversy must either come to blows or be undecided" (L 5.3). As we saw in chapter 3, that problem may stem from the fact that we each mistakenly take ourselves to be making conflicting, nonindexical judgments, or just from the fact that the judgments, even understood as indexical, support conflicting practical dispositions.

The second problem that arises with evaluative terms, however, is that not only are we each disposed to use them for different things but we are also each liable to use them differently at different times. We are subject to intertemporal as well as interpersonal inconstancy. This arises "because the constitution of a man's body is in continual mutation," so that "it is impossible that all the same things should always cause in him the same appetites and aversions" (L 6.5). What Hobbes has in mind here can hardly be the way we are each likely to change our views about what is attractive and good, or aversive and bad; after all, such a change of mind is likely with any beliefs whatsoever. He seems rather to be thinking of the ways in which things may engage our desires differently, depending on which of their elements or aspects is currently salient, and whether our desire is still alive or satiated.

These problems are both reflections of the indexicality of the terms *good* and *bad*, according to Hobbes's analysis. The terms are used differently, depending on the personal and indeed temporal index given by the speaker. And yet they are used across persons and times to shape what is done, whether done by one person or many, so that they raise a possibility of controversy and strife. We cannot expect any person at different times, or different people at the same time, to "consent in the desire of almost any one and the same object" (L 6.5).

How is talk of good and bad to be subjected to the discipline of reason, then, given these indexicality problems? Inevitably, Hobbes's answer is that the words must be given fixed definitions across times and persons. I first consider this issue in the intrapersonal case and then in the interpersonal.

Hobbes adverts to the need to fix the meaning of *good* and *bad* for a single person when he speaks of the difference between the real and the apparent good. In *Leviathan* (6.57), he notes that it can be difficult in "a long chain of consequences" associated with a choice "to see to the end," and in such a case the person who forms a preference one way or the other may mark the difficulty by speaking of it as apparently good or apparently evil. The suggestion is that whether the chain of likely consequences is really good or really evil can only be determined when it is examined and appreciated in every detail—"when everything associated with it hath been considered" (DH 12.1). Yet such consideration may prove to be difficult. One source of difficulty is that "inexperienced men that do not look closely enough at the long-term consequences of things" are led to "accept what appears to be good, not seeing the evil annexed to it" (DH 11.5). Another is that often "appetite seizeth upon a present good without foreseeing the greater evils that necessarily attach to it," and so "perturbs and impedes the operation of reason" (DH 12.1).

With the problem of intrapersonal indexicality, then, Hobbes seems to say that there is a fact of the matter, presumably reflective of the perspectives of the agent at the different times, as to whether overall something is good or bad. The idea might be expressed as follows. For the agent, what is really good or really bad is what is good or bad for the agent over time, not for the agent at any particular time. This is not always going to be visible from the perspective of the agent at a time, focused as that agent may be on a particular aspect of the extended chain of consequences in question. The solution is to move from specific temporal perspectives to that of the person as a whole—the person over time—to see things from that more encompassing point of view.

If this is right, then it is worth asking what things prove to be really good and what really bad from the perspective of an agent as a whole. There is one real good and one real bad for a person, on which Hobbes insists throughout his life: the good is self-preservation, and the bad is death. Self-preservation is not the only thing that is really good. While "bare preservation" is certainly good and something that the commonwealth should secure, the same is true of various "other contentments of life" (L 30.1). But it is really and not just apparently good, and that claim is central to Hobbes's philosophy. As we shall see, for example, it explains why the natural law—the law of sensible self-concern—starts from "the liberty each man hath to use his own power, as he will himself, for the preservation of his own nature, that is to say, of his own life" (L 14.1).

Why should Hobbes, who links good with pleasure, bad with pain, think that self-preservation is really good—and presumptively, always good? He doesn't ever address this question, presumably because he thinks the answer is obvious. Yet the answer is not obvious, since a hedonist might be expected to think that life is good when it promises a balance of pleasure and bad when it promises a balance of pain.

I think that self-preservation is a real good, indeed a supreme good, in Hobbes's view of things not because of his hedonism but because of his view of the place of desire in human life, and the connection between desiring and living. He holds that the process of desiring things is not something that human beings can opt out of—"while we live we have desires" (EL 7.6). And it may well be that he thinks, as a consequence, that it would be a sort of absurdity to desire not to desire. But if this is an absurdity, then it is an absurdity to want to cease living, since living entails desiring; "life itself is but motion, and can never be without desire" (L 6.58).

If this is right, then it would explain why Hobbes suggests that it always is a mistake to desire one's death: if someone "kill[s] himself, it is to be presumed that he is not *compos mentis* but by some inward torment or apprehension of something worse than death, distracted" (D 85; see also L 25.8).[1] Thus, after distinguishing in *De Homine* between apparent and real good, Hobbes comments that "though death is the greatest of all evils (especially when accompanied by torture) the pains of life can be so great that, unless their quick end is foreseen, they may lead men to number death among the goods" (11.6).[2] Even if suicide is sometimes attractive, then—an apparent good—self-preservation remains really good. It is always rational to shrink from "that terrible enemy of nature, death, from whom we expect both the loss of all power, and also the greatest of bodily pains in the losing" (EL 14.6).

Back to the main line. I have sketched the resolution to which Hobbes points, albeit somewhat indirectly, for the problem of intertemporal, intrapersonal indexicality in the use of good and bad. The solution amounts to saying that the person at this time and the person at that time ought each to defer in the judgment of what is good or what is bad to the perspective represented by the person over time. Each time slice ought to give up its own voice, as it were, and countenance only the voice of the whole.

But if that is a somewhat free interpretation of what Hobbes has in mind on the intrapersonal front, there can be no doubt about the parallel lesson that he wants to teach on the interpersonal. As indicated already, his view is clearly that those in contention over what is good and bad should give up their own judgments in favor of a common arbitrator.

He distinguishes in *Leviathan* (5.3) between the case where, with the definitions of words fixed, there is "a right reason constituted by nature," and the case where there is not. Right reason will be in place, as I read Hobbes, either with words like *round* that refer to a real property of things, or with words like *red* or *rough* that are used on the basis of a common effect that real things have on our senses. But even more clearly, right reason will be in place in a discipline like arithmetic that is "a certain and infallible art" (L 5.3). In any such case, people's reasons may get right reason wrong and "no one man's reason, nor the reason of any one number of men," should be regarded as authoritative; none "makes the certainty."

But right reason will not be in place with words like *good* and *bad*, "for want of a right reason constituted by nature." Therefore, Hobbes says, "The parties must by their own accord set up for right reason the reason of some arbitrator or judge to whose sentence they will both stand" (L 5.3; see also D 26). The picture he has is that just as a common measure is needed to establish shared meanings for purely conventional terms of measurement like pint or quart, foot or yard, so a measure is needed to establish shared meanings for evaluative terms, at least when they are used of matters that engage everyone in the society. It "was necessary that there should be a common measure of all things that might fall in controversy; as for example: of what is to be called right, what good, what virtue, what much, what little, what *meum* and *tuum*, what a pound, what a quart, etc." (EL 29.8).

No one can cease to regard their own death as evil, according to Hobbes, insofar as a natural necessity will lead them each to seek their own good (EL 14.6; DC 1.7; L 27.8). Yet there is no reason, he thinks, why people should not be able to give up many of their self-indexed uses of evaluative terminology in favor of a usage that is tied to someone who speaks for them all equally—someone who relates to them as the agent over time relates to the agent at different times. In envisaging that possibility, of course, he is looking to the possibility of a sovereign who will speak for the commonwealth, fixing the meaning of *good* or *bad* so that it refers to what is attractive or aversive by the sovereign's judgment. More on this in the next chapter.

Is this solution to the problem of interpersonal indexicality likely to be readily available? It might be, were it a purely contingent matter that people desire competing things, and so find themselves only occasionally at loggerheads over what is good or bad. But the access to speech, it turns out, changes this situation completely and makes the problem of interpersonal indexicality particularly acute. It leads people to form desires that are not just contingently but necessarily in conflict. We must turn now to this effect of speech in expanding the domains of human concern.

Desires Common to Humans and Animals

For all that has been said so far, the passions that move human beings and other animals might be more or less similar. The only natural difference that Hobbes recognizes between our kind and the beasts, as we saw, is that we are moved in a higher degree by curiosity. We hunt around for the causes of things, as animals do, if with greater intensity. We also look for the effects that an object or process may be used to achieve, thinking about "what we can do with it, when we have it" (L 3.5). But the degree of curiosity aside, we are by nature of a kind with animals in the things that we desire.

What things do we and other animals desire in common? Hobbes mentions natural appetites like "hunger, thirst, lust, and anger" (L 3.5) in addressing this question. These basic appetites, common to human and beast, are all sensual or corporeal in the sense of promising sensual or corporeal pleasures—or the avoidance of corresponding pains. They are those desires that "affect the corporeal organ of sense, and that I call sensual; the greatest whereof is that, by which we are invited to give continuance to our species; and the next, by which a man is invited to meat, for the preservation of his individual person" (EL 7.9). Such passions of the body are contrasted by Hobbes with a set of passions that, as we shall see, are present only in human beings, and present there by grace of what language makes possible. "The other sort of delight is not particular to any part of the body, and is called the delight of the mind, and is that which we call joy" (EL 7.9). But before coming to those human-specific desires, it will be useful to dwell a little on the passions shared between humans and other animals.

There are two features of these sensual appetites that are worth noting in particular. The first is that they are focused on the present rather than the future. The associated pleasures or pains will come about in the presence of the object of attraction or aversion, or perhaps in the immediate anticipation of its presence, not on the basis of any longer-term predictions as to what is likely to happen.[3] "Of pleasures or delights, some arise from the sense of an object present; and those may be called *pleasures of sense*" (L 6.12). Such pleasures and attractions contrast with the passions of which human beings alone are capable. These "arise from the expectation, that proceeds from foresight of the end, or consequence of things; whether those things in the sense please or displease. And these are *pleasures of the mind*" (L 6.12).

The second feature of the sensual appetites that human beings share with other animals is that not only are they present centered, they are also nonpositional. A positional desire is a desire to be in a certain position in comparison to others, whether others in general or others in some reference class: to be first, near the top, or at the average level, for example, or to have a property like distinction or fame that presupposes a position in relation to others (Brennan and Pettit 2004, chapter 1). The striking thing about all the sensual appetites is that they are insensitive to relative position or standing. The desire for food or sex may drive animals or human beings into conflict with one another, but that will only be because their desires happen to focus on the same object; the conflict will be contingent, not inevitable. In general, "living creatures irrational" can manage to live in perfect peace and "good order" among themselves (EL 19.5). Whereas the passions of the body lend themselves to this result, we shall see later that the passions of the mind do not. As they leap beyond a concern with the present, so too do they jump beyond a concern with private, nonpositional satisfaction.

Speech expands the passions available to human beings because it releases people from the animal regime of sensual, organically manifested desire. First, it enables human beings to anticipate the future and focus their desires on what may come to be as well as what is present there before them. Second, it enables them to compare themselves with others, and become concerned with whether they are more or less powerful and more or less honored than others. I will look at these effects in turn.

Beyond Life in the Present

Although other animals can be prudent about the immediate future, in the sense of being in the habit of forming reliable expectations on the basis of past experience, and adjusting accordingly, this falls well short of being able to reason about what is or is not likely to occur in this or that sort of situation. The ability to reason in this way about the future requires a "knowledge of consequences, and dependance of one fact upon another" (L 5.17). It is only by virtue of this knowledge of dependence, this sapience, that we can know what is likely to happen in the future, on another like occasion, when on a given occasion "we see how any thing comes about, upon what causes, and by what manner." Hobbesian prudence is fine as far as it goes, but it does not reach into the future in the same surefire way; "in its own nature, it is but presumption" (L 3.7). Hobbes uses an analogy from swordplay to display the superiority of sapience over prudence: "let us suppose one man endued with an excellent natural use and dexterity in handling his arms; and another to have added to that dexterity, an acquired science, of where he can offend, or be offended by his adversary, in every possible posture or guard: the ability of the former, would be to the ability of the latter, as prudence to sapience; both useful; but the latter infallible" (L 5.21).

It is because other animals lack language, and so a capacity for sapience, that their passions or desires are focused entirely on the present, and perhaps on the immediate, expected future. There "is no other felicity of beasts," Hobbes says, "but the enjoying of their quotidian food, ease, and lusts; as having little or no foresight of the time to come, for want of observation, and memory of the order, consequence, and dependence of the things they see" (L 12.4). But for human beings, of course, things are different: "man observeth how one event hath been

produced by another; and remembereth in them antecedence and consequence." And so a person may use reason to determine the future, or less
happily, may rely on fancy and testimony; "when he cannot assure himself of the true causes of things . . . he supposes causes of them, either
such as his own fancy suggesteth; or trusteth to the authority of other
men, such as he thinks to be his friends, and wiser than himself." As a result of this capacity to think about the future, human desires will naturally assume a different complexion from those of the beasts. People will
come to be as focused on what they think is likely to come about in the
future as on what they find pressing on their attention in the present.

This capacity to focus on the future may look like a release, freeing
human beings from what Hobbes calls "the short vehemence of any
carnal pleasure" (L 6.35). But the liberation has another side to it as
well, since the ability to reason about how things may be in the future
enables people to worry about what may yet transpire, and be para-
lyzed by fear and anxiety. This is the side of things that Hobbes emphasizes. He thinks concern for future evil is absolutely inevitable
among human beings: "it is impossible for a man, who continually en-
deavoureth to secure himself against the evil he fears, and procure the
good he desireth, not to be in a perpetual solicitude of the time to
come" (L 12.5). And so whereas "wolves, bears and snakes" are not "rapacious unless hungry," "man is famished even by future hunger" (DH
10. 3). As he puts it in *Leviathan*, the "object of man's desire is not to enjoy once only, and for one instant of time, but to assure forever the way
of his future desire" (L 11.1). Thus he posits as "a general inclination of
all mankind, a perpetual and restless desire of power after power, that
ceaseth only in death"; man "cannot assure the power and means to
live well, which he hath present, without the acquisition of more."

This anxiety for the future may have some good effects: it "disposeth
men to inquire into the causes of things: because the knowledge of
them, maketh men the better able to order the present to their best advantage" (L 11.24; EL 10.3). But it can also be a force for personal an-
guish and ill: "man, which looks too far before him, in the care of future
time, hath his heart all the day long, gnawed on by fear of death,
poverty, or other calamity; and has no repose, nor pause of his anxiety,
but in sleep" (L 12.5). On balance, the focus on the future makes human
life harder, not easier.

Beyond Life in the Private

As speech and reason enable human beings to learn about the ways in
which the future may transpire, thereby engaging their passions in a

new domain, so they also enable them to learn about the ways in which they differ from one another, expanding the range of their passions to this territory as well. The identification of differences presupposes an ability to compare objects against general categories, and take note of the classes in which they come together and in which they diverge. Hence, the identification of differences is only possible for a creature that has access to the words whereby classes are made available to thought and reason.[4] The identification may be registered in explicit comparison in respect to one or another category, or it may lead to the introduction of new comparative terms such as like, unlike, and equal (DCr 2.13).

Lacking the capacity to think in a classificatory way, other animals are insensitive to the ways in which they differ from or resemble their fellows, and so they live in the private as well as the present. But human beings can transcend the boundary of private concern as they can transcend the boundary of concern for the present. And transcend it they certainly will. It will be important for their welfare that they know how they compare with others and that they achieve a high relative standing.[5]

According to the Hobbesian picture, people's concern with returns to themselves—their own pleasure, or their avoidance of pain—will naturally lead them to want access to the resources or powers whereby such returns can be produced. If they are to satisfy their wants, they will need the "natural" resources represented by "the faculties of body and mind" as well as "instrumental" resources such as "riches, place of authority, friendship or favour, and good fortune" (EL 8.4). Bent on the pursuit of their own self-interest, then, they will seek the means of conducting that pursuit; moved by the love of self, they will look for a way of consummating that love. In this they will be no different from other animals, though they may be more adept at spotting the means whereby their ends can be realized.

But there is one aspect of the resources sought by human beings and other animals that only becomes clear on reflection and reasoning. This is that in a competitive world where the objects of desire are scarce, what will really matter to any creature is not the absolute level of its resources but their level relative to the resources of others. Where there is competition for resources, or competition in the use of resources, the important thing for each will be not the absolute quantity of resources commanded but the extent to which those resources enable the creature to outdo its competitors; "what all have equally is nothing" (DH 11.6). Letting the word *power* serve for resource, Hobbes finds a nicely turned way of putting the point. "And because the power of one man resisteth and hindereth the effects of the power of another: power simply is no more, but the excess of the power of one above that of another. For equal powers opposed, destroy one another" (EL 8.4).

These observations are true in some measure of all animals, but given their longer time horizons, it is particularly true of human beings. And it is only human beings, of course, who can become aware of the observations, since only they will be able to compare themselves with others for the resources they each command, and only they will be able to see that the important thing for each will be to have more resources than others—greater power. Under the pressure of this perceived need, the human being becomes a creature "whose joy consisteth in comparing himself with other men" (L 17.8).

Human beings must each be expected, then, to desire greater power than their fellows. More than that, they must be expected to want to be thought by their fellows to have such power, since this will serve in itself to inhibit and deter others from challenging them. According to Hobbes, "Reputation of power is power" (L 10.5; see also L 8.15). Indeed, reputation of power is in some contexts the most important source of power: "the power of the mighty hath no foundation but in the opinion and belief of the people" (B 16).

To be acknowledged in this way as having greater power than others is to be honored, Hobbes thinks; "to honour a man (inwardly in the mind) is to conceive or acknowledge, that that man hath the odds or excess of power above him that contendeth or compareth himself" (EL 8.5). So we must not only expect human beings to want greater power than others; we must also expect them to want to enjoy honor among their fellows.

A crucial effect of speech, then, is to focus people's concerns on power and honor. Hobbes acknowledges that human beings may be greatly troubled by pain or the expectation of pain, both of which involve appetites that we share with other animals. But he pays particular attention to another "sort of discontent which troubleth the mind of them who otherwise live at ease," which is found only among human beings. This is "a sense of their want of that power, and that honour and testimony thereof, which they think is due unto them. For all joy and grief of mind consisteth . . . in a contention for precedence to them with whom they compare themselves" (EL 27.3).

This is to say that human beings are moved not just by the private passions that dominate in other animals but by desires of a positional kind—in particular, desires for the enjoyment of a position of superiority in relation to others on matters involving power and the acknowledgment of power. He thinks that there is a characteristic joy taken by human beings in finding themselves honored, which he labels glory. "Sometimes the animal spirits are in concert transported by a certain joy that ariseth from their thinking themselves to be honoured; this elation of mind is called glory" (DH 12.6). He often suggests that the love of power, honor, and glory sums up all that is involved—all that proves on analysis to be involved—in the passions of the mind. He proposes in *The Elements of Law* (50) that the nature of the passions of the mind consists "in the pleasure men have, or displeasure from the signs of honour or dishonour done unto them." And in *De Cive* (1.2), he presents the proposal as an undoubted principle: "Every pleasure of the mind is either glory (or a good opinion of oneself), or ultimately relates to glory." But even if Hobbes does not stand fully by this suggestion—it is less prominent in *Leviathan*—he clearly thinks that human life is widely and deeply shaped by the love of power, honor, and glory that language makes possible.

This fact amplifies the contrast between human beings and other animals. Just as beasts are incapable of the focus on the future that mesmerizes our kind, so they are unmoved by the compulsion we experience to compare ourselves with others and look for comparative advantage. As Hobbes says, "Men compete for honour and dignity, animals do not" (DCv 5.5). The two respects in which we differ from other animals are not unrelated, of course. The concern for the future will become even more oppressive if it encompasses a concern for how one will stand in comparison with others. And the concern for how one stands in comparison with others will become even more dominant if it involves a concern for the future as well as the present. Indeed, the concern for relative standing would hardly get off the ground except in a creature who was capable of such a focus on the future for in general, if not inevitably, the "imaginations of honour and glory . . . have respect to the future" (EL 10.3).

The upshot is pretty bleak. When beasts pursue their private desires for food, water, and sex, they will naturally compete with one another for the resources available. But if sufficient resources are available, then they may each succeed in achieving full satisfaction. When human beings pursue their positional desires, however—in particular, their desires for superiority—no such benign outcome is possible. Power, honor, and glory are each essentially positional, and unlike equality, for example, they are asymmetrically positional. Where one succeeds in gaining such a good, therefore, others are bound to fail; it "is nothing if everybody has it, since it consists in comparison and pre-eminence" (DCv 1.2). Life among human beings looks destined to be a zero-sum game, then, by contrast with life among the animals. It is as if the advent of speech and the knowledge that came with it precipitated a secular fall: an expulsion from the tranquil world of private concern for the present into a turbulent existence where people sustain one another in frenzied anxiety about relative power—relative power not just now but into the indefinite future.

I noted at the end of my discussion of speech and the expression of desire that Hobbes would like to see people resolve the problem of interpersonal indexicality by setting up an arbitrator to whom they all defer; this arbitrator would determine common meanings for words like *good* and *bad*, much in the way common meanings for terms of measurement like *pint* and *yard* might be determined. What we can now see, though, is that the problem is much sharper than may have appeared earlier, and that the resolution looks to be much more difficult. For people do not just differ contingently in what they call good and bad. With their desires expanded under the influence of speech and reason, they come into necessary or inevitable conflict on such matters.

Human beings are not merely competitors, according to the emerging picture, but enemies. The problem they face is worse than the conventional issue of establishing a common metric, as they might establish a common measure for a pint or a yard; it reaches far more deeply into their souls. Since "men by natural passion are divers ways offensive one to another, every man thinking well of himself, and hating to see the same in others, they must needs provoke one another by words, and other signs of contempt and hatred, which are incident to all comparison; till at last they must determine the pre-eminence by strength and force of body" (EL 14.4).

In painting such a gloomy picture of the predicament of human beings once they come to be equipped with language, it must be said that Hobbes helps himself to a crucial, unargued assumption, as noted already in the introduction. This is that people can only be satisfied with superiority and the recognition of their superiority, and that they cannot settle for the positional good of equality in standing with others and the recognition of this equality. This is his most implausible move, I believe, for nothing in his argument precludes that possibility, and human experience testifies powerfully in its support.

The move is consequential. We shall see that the essentially competitive nature of human desire, as Hobbes thinks of it, is at the core of his argument for why an absolute state is necessary, and in particular for why the mixed constitution that republicans supported is impossible. In this connection, it is interesting to find a different perspective on human desire in Hobbes's republican contemporary, the poet John Milton. He writes with relish of the commonwealth where "they who are greatest . . . are not elevated above their brethren; live soberly in their families, walk the streets as other men, and may be spoken to freely, familiarly, friendly, without adoration" (Lovett 2005, 475). The tone is decidedly at odds with the note that Hobbes strikes.

We saw in earlier chapters that speech is a force for good on the cognitive and social front. It enables human beings to think in an active, general fashion, and it makes it possible for human beings to relate as individual persons and incorporate as group persons. But speech is not clearly a force for good on the motivational front. It prompts human passion to jump the barrier of the present, to stretch out in anxious solicitude for the future. And it downgrades the innocent, sensual concern with private satisfaction in favor of a concern for positional advantage over others. To anticipate a distinction to which Rousseau gave great importance, it replaces the natural love of self, *l'amour de soi*, with *l'amour propre*: the socially fostered love of enjoying precedence over others (Dent 1988). In doing this, it generates conflict and disorder among human beings. Language in Hobbes's picture is a mixed blessing. "By speech man is not made better," he says, "but only given greater possibilities" (DH 10.3).

CHAPTER SEVEN

The State of Second, Worded Nature

THE STATE OF SECOND NATURE

If the argument so far is reliable, then the message is clear. By words human beings are lifted out of the passive, particularistic mentality of animals, being given the capacity to reason, personate, and incorporate. But by words human beings are also cast out of the garden of animal innocence, and reduced to a life of quarrel and distrust, unknown among other living creatures. Hobbes refers to the "condition of men outside civil society" as "the state of nature" (DCv preface). What my argument shows is that the state of nature in his sense is not the precultural state in which human beings are as other animals but the state in which they have already mastered language. It is not the state of first nature, prior to language and the "kind of agreement" on the meanings of words that is "necessary for human society" (DCv 18.4). It is the state to which human beings are reduced, as language and the mixed blessings of language become second nature to them.

The recognition that this is what the state of nature means for Hobbes sets his story in contrast with Rousseau's account (1973) of the state of nature, presented most fully in his second discourse—the discourse on inequality. For it is crucial to Rousseau's way of thinking that the state of nature is the state of first nature, before human beings learn language and develop the capacity to think. The state of nature is the state of animals in general, he suggests, and in this state the human being can live an untroubled existence. "His soul, which nothing disturbs, is wrapped up in the feeling of its present existence, without any idea of the future, however near at hand; while his projects, as limited as his views, hardly extend to the close of the day" (Rousseau 1973, 56).

Hobbes need not have disagreed with any of this. For he also offers support for the idea that had human beings not come to the invention of language, then they might have lived in the relatively untroubled fashion of animals. Rousseau presents his account of the state of nature as an alternative to that of Hobbes, but for all he says, there need be no disagreement between them. What divides them is not a divergence in their conceptions of one and the same state of nature but rather a divergence in the state of nature that they were each meaning to characterize.

Under the reading of Hobbes that my argument supports, there are three possible modes of human existence: the state of first nature, when humans are as other animals; the state of second nature, when they leave community with beasts as a result of developing language; and the civil state in which they incorporate under a sovereign. Hobbes obviously thinks that the state of first nature is no longer attainable, with the irreversible effects that the invention of language has had. The claim he wants to defend is that the state of second nature is much inferior to the civil state, and that human beings should do everything possible to move from the one to the other.

When he casts things in this way, Hobbes inverts a widely established way of thinking. It had been customary since at least the time of Aristotle to think that the human being was a social or political animal, a *zoon politikon*, and to identify the great danger for social life with the possibility that human beings might fall to the level of the beasts, letting their lower desires, associated with *epithumia*, gain control of their actions. The unleashing of this beastly side of human nature is what Thucydides emphasized in his *History of the Peloponnesian War*, a translation of which Hobbes published in 1629. But whatever of Hobbes's ideas at that time, when he clearly thought that the book had an important lesson, he dropped the theme in his mature work.[1] The picture there is that other animals, driven by the simple appetites of the lower parts—if you like, epithumia—are fine. It is human beings who have a problem, insofar as they are moved by quite different, nonanimalistic motives, in particular the love of honor and the readiness to take offense that is associated in the Greek tradition with *thumos*: the sort of sentiment located in the breast rather than the belly. What produces social disorder is not the natural beast that erupts within but the unruliness of the word-made mind.[2]

Hobbes plays up this inversion of the tradition, particularly in *De Cive* (1.2), where he summarizes his picture of human beings. "The majority of previous writers on public Affairs," he says, "either assume or seek to prove or simply assert that man is an animal born fit for society—in the Greek phrase, *zoon politikon*" (DCv 1.2). But this proceeds from "a superficial view of human nature," he now insists. For the truth is that "every voluntary encounter is a product either of mutual need or of the pursuit of glory," and "all society, therefore, exists for the sake either of advantage or of glory." Yet "glorying, like honour, is nothing if everybody has it," and so we must say, contrary to received wisdom, that "man is not born fit for society" (DCv 1.2n1).

This, then, is the great human predicament. Simple animals may be fierce, like the wolf and the tiger, but even they have no great social problems; "they are not rapacious unless hungry" (DH 10.3). And things are even better in other parts of the animal world, since "certain living creatures (like bees and ants) live sociably one with another" (L 17.6). It would be bliss, Hobbes suggests, if human beings could be like these creatures; they "continually live in such good order and government, for their common benefit, and are so free from sedition and war amongst themselves, that for peace, profit, and defence, nothing more can be imaginable" (EL 19.5). But for reasons that we have now explored, this is impossible. For unlike simple creatures, and thanks to the mixed blessings of speech, human beings get into "strife about honor"; "aim at dominion, superiority, and private wealth"; "think themselves wiser than the rest"; "instigate one another to faction"; and contend with one another as "judges of right and wrong" (EL 19.5).

This takes us to the famous pronouncement that Hobbes makes on the state of nature in *Leviathan* (13.9).

> In such condition, there is no place for industry; because the fruit thereof is uncertain: and consequently no culture of the earth; no navigation, nor use of the commodities that may be imported by sea; no commodious building; no instruments of moving, and removing such things as require much force; no knowledge of the face of the earth; no account of time; no arts; no letters; no society; and which is worst of all, continual fear, and danger of violent death; and the life of man, solitary, poor, nasty, brutish, and short.

In the remainder of this chapter, I will look at Hobbes's account of how human beings may hope to escape this predicament. One question is whether it may be enough that they can use words to reason, finding a way out of the state of nature that is not particularly contractual. Another question is whether it may be enough that they can use words to form more or less regular contracts with one another, agreeing to live by the requirements of peace. Hobbes argues that neither mode of escape is possible and directs us to a Draconian solution, which involves a contract of more or less total submission to a sovereign individual or body. The ability that comes with words can serve to guide people out of the state of nature in which it drops them, but only at a severe cost to established preconceptions—particularly, the republican preconceptions that Hobbes abhorred—about the requirements of political order.

No Noncontractual Escape

In order to see why there is no noncontractual escape from the state of nature, we need to understand why that state inevitably involves conflict. Hobbes says in *Leviathan* (13.6) that in the state of nature there are "three principal causes of quarrel: first, competition; secondly, diffidence; thirdly, glory."

Competition stems from the desire for gain, which leads people to "use violence to make themselves masters of other men's persons, wives, children, and cattle" (L 13.8). This desire is targeted on objective, nonpositional goods, as are the desires of animals that seek the same piece of meat or the same resting place, but it is distinctively human insofar as it reaches into the future; people are satisfied only with the long-term appropriation of such goods, not with temporary use or possession.

The diffidence or lack of trust that Hobbes mentions is important at this point. Since people will be unsure of how in the future they may fare in competing with others, they are naturally led to be anxious about securing what they have against one another's power. "And from this diffidence of one another," as Hobbes says in *Leviathan* (13.4), "there is no way for any man to secure himself so reasonable as anticipation, that is, by force or wiles to master the persons of all men he can, so long till he see no other power great enough to endanger him."

The desire for reputation and glory, to turn to Hobbes's third cause of quarrel, springs from the desire for such power. It is a desire on people's part to have others recognize and acknowledge their power, presumably because this makes that power more effective: "all reputation of power is power" (L 10.5). And it serves as a hair trigger for violence. It can be loosed among people "for trifles, as a word, a smile, a different opinion, and any other sign of undervalue, either direct in their persons, or by reflection in their kindred, their friends, their nation, their profession, or their name" (L 13.7).

Consistently with people having desires of these kinds, it might still seem possible for one individual or one tightly knit coalition to impose peace on a society by subduing others. But Hobbes disallows the possibility of such a unilaterally driven equilibrium among human beings. It is axiomatic in his book that people enjoy a more or less basic equality of power. The point is made in *Elements of Law* (14.2) and *De Cive* (1.3), but the equal-power postulate is put particularly forcefully in *Leviathan* (13.1):

Nature hath made men so equal, in the faculties of body, and mind; as that though there be found one man sometimes manifestly stronger in body, or of quicker mind than another; yet when all is reckoned together, the difference between man, and man, is not so considerable, as that one man can thereupon claim to himself any benefit, to which another may not pretend, as well as he. For as to the strength of body, the weakest has strength enough to kill the strongest, either by secret machination, or by confederacy with others, that are in the same danger with himself.

If human beings are more or less equal in this sense, then none of them can hope to secure gain and power in relation to others, exercising an iron hand and imposing a unilateral equilibrium. But that now suggests that a different, multilateral equilibrium might emerge, as by an invisible rather than an iron hand.

We know that people are capable of learning from experience and reason. So won't it be obvious to all, and obvious to all that it is obvious to all, that no one can hope to attain supremacy in the state of nature? And won't that mean that people will rationally settle down in a peaceful stalemate, a common *modus vivendi*, however far this may frustrate their personal longing for gain and reputation? The possibility is that each person, having "a true estimate of his own capacities," "practices the equality of nature, and allows others everything which he allows himself" (DCv 1.4). As Hobbes puts it in *Elements of Law* (14.2), "Men considered in mere nature, ought to admit amongst themselves equality," and claiming no more than equality allows, prove themselves truly "moderate."

Hobbes thinks that this possibility is empty because people cannot be relied on to be moderate and rational in the manner described. This takes us back to the point emphasized in the discussion of personation and contract: that while rational people may be disposed to keep the contracts they find it rational to make, people are not always rational and cannot expect one another to be always rational; they are subject to *impotentia animi*, a weakness of the mind or soul (DCv 3.3). This theme assumes operatic proportions in Hobbes's account of the state of nature and why there is no easy path to the state.

Invoking the weakness of the human soul, or rather the power of the passions that hold sway there, he quickly dismisses the prospect of people's evolving a moderate, rational *modus vivendi*. Whatever the counsels of reason, Hobbes suggests, many people are likely to be moved by vainglory to think that they can achieve the superiority for which they yearn. They are "vainly glorious, and hope for precedency and superiority above their fellows, not only when they are equal in power, but also when they are inferior" (EL 14.3). Thus "the greatest part of men, upon no assurance of odds, do nevertheless, through vanity, or comparison, or appetite, provoke the rest, that otherwise would be contented with equality" (EL 14.5). The result is that the rest will also have to resort to force; they too will have "a will to do harm," though "not for the same reason or with equal culpability" (DCv 1.4).

Our discussion of desire revealed the extent to which people, shaped by the linguistically based capacity to compare themselves with others, become bent on power, honor, and glory. What Hobbes is now stressing is that they are also susceptible to a pathological form of the desire for glory.[3] They are capable of becoming vainglorious, with "every man thinking well of himself." This being so, they are easily led to "determine the pre-eminence by strength and force of body" (EL 14.4; see also DCv 1.4).

Hobbes is no adherent of rational choice theory, at least not as a descriptive theory of human nature, since it is crucial to his theory that people are subject to pathologies like vainglory. He sees the affliction everywhere. The "signs of vain glory" in people, he says, "are imitation of others, counterfeiting attention to things they understand not, affectation of fashions, captation of honour from their dreams, and other little stories of themselves" (EL 9.1). He offers a nice explanation in *Leviathan* (13.2) of the source of this:

> That which may perhaps make such equality incredible, is but a vain conceit of one's own wisdom, which almost all men think they have in a greater degree, than the vulgar; that is, than all men but themselves, and a few others, whom by fame, or for concurring with themselves, they approve. For such is the nature of men, that howsoever they may acknowledge many others to be more witty, or more eloquent, or more learned; yet they will hardly believe there be many so wise as themselves: For they see their own wit at hand, and other men's at a distance.[4]

He documents the destructive effect of vainglory in his account of the English Civil War (Holmes 1990), when he expands on what motivated "the Presbyterians and men of democratical principles" (B 193) to disturb the peace that reigned under the king:

> The chief leaders were ambitious ministers and ambitious gentlemen; the ministers envying the authority of bishops, whom they thought less learned; and the gentlemen envying the privy-council and principal courtiers, whom they thought less wise than themselves. For it is a hard matter for men, who do all think highly of their own wits, when they have also acquired the learning of the university, to be persuaded that they want any ability requisite for the government of a commonwealth, especially having read the glorious histories and the sententious politics of the Greeks and Romans, among whom kings were hated and branded with the name of tyrants. (B 23)

The upshot of these considerations is that there is no possibility of a noncontractual escape from the state of nature, whether by the imposition of a unilateral equilibrium or the emergence of an equilibrium of a multilateral kind. But is there a possibility that people might be able to escape this predicament by regular, contractual means? I turn next to that question.

No Regular Contractual Escape

A regular contractual solution to the problems of the state of nature might materialize in either of two ways. It might involve a recognitioin among the relevant parties that some alternative to the state of nature, by some agreed-on yardstick, is a superior dispensation. Or it might take the form of a bargain in which the parties each prove willing, in their own terms, to accept such an alternative instead. Either approach would constitute a regular contractual resolution, insofar as it puts the alternative in place without total abdication in favor of an absolute sovereign.

We know from earlier discussions that Hobbes takes *good*, *bad*, and cognate words to be wholly indexical, with people each calling good that which appeals to them personally and bad that which they find unappealing. In the absence of "a sovereign power to come up with rules or measures that will be common to all"—that is, in the state of nature—this creates a problem: "men's opinions differ about mine and yours, just and unjust, useful and useless, good and bad, honourable and dishonourable, and so on, and everyone decides them by his own judgement" (DCv 6.9).

Given that people's usage of these evaluative terms is bound to be at odds in this way in the state of nature, there will be no agreed-on yard-stick by reference to which people could recognize this or that alternative as better than the state of nature. There will be no common currency of evaluation such that people can each try to persuade others that the values given weight in that currency argue for the superiority of a certain alternative.

So much for the first way in which a regular contractual solution might materialize. What now of the second? Is there any chance that people might be able to bargain their way toward a solution that would appeal more to each than the state of nature? We know that there is a "necessity of nature," according to Hobbes, whereby people each "choose that which appeareth best for themselves" (L 27.8; EL 14.6; DCv 1.7), and equally, we know that unless they are mistaken or out of their minds, this will lead them to choose life and self-preservation over "that terrible enemy of nature, death" (EL 14.6). So the question is whether the dictates of self-concern might lead each to bargain with others for the achievement of some alternative.

The dictates of self-concern constitute a normative code, insofar as it requires each to look to their own life and good (Malcolm 2003). Hobbes identifies that code, like Hugo Grotius (2005) before him, with what he calls the natural law; in doing this, he reconstrues the ancient and medieval conception of the natural law as a moral law knowable by reason alone.[5] The natural law, according to Hobbes, offers people "conclusions or theorems concerning what conduceth to the conservation and defence of themselves" (L 15.41).[6] "A LAW OF NATURE is a precept, or general rule, found out by reason, by which a man is forbidden to do that, which is destructive of his life, or taketh away the means of preserving the same; and to omit that, by which he thinketh it may be best preserved" (L 15.3).

Hobbes takes the theorems of natural law to have two implications that bear on what each individual ought to do in the state of nature. The first is that since self-preservation is not a psychologically optional goal, there is no obligation on people in the state of nature to inhibit themselves about the means they adopt in the pursuit of that goal. In one sense of the term "liberty," then—that in which it is contrasted with obligation (L 14.3)—they are each at liberty to act for their self-preservation just as they judge to be best, just as they will. Each person has a "natural right," as Hobbes puts it, "to use his own power, as he will himself, for the preservation of his own nature; that is to say, of his own life; and consequently, of doing any thing, which in his own judgment, and reason, he shall conceive to be the aptest means thereunto" (L 14.1).[7]

This first implication of natural law is important for Hobbes because it means, as he sees things, that just as people have essentially conflicting desires—desires of an asymmetrically positional sort—so they have essentially conflicting rights. They each have a right to that which is needed for them to secure their preservation. But what is needed by one may also be needed by others. So the pursuit of their individual rights will lead them inevitably into conflict. As Hobbes says, "In such a condition every man has a right to everything, even to one another's body" (L 14.4).

The second implication of the natural law softens this result, however, identifying laws of nature—requirements dictated by sensible self-concern—and putting the focus on these laws rather than on the basic, conflictual right of nature. The first law of nature tells each person to seize on any safe opportunity that may arise for the achievement of peace and to resort to violence—that is, to exercise the right of nature—only in the absence of such an opportunity. "It is a precept, or general rule of reason, that every man, ought to endeavour peace, as far as he has hope of obtaining it; and when he cannot obtain it, that he may seek, and use, all helps, and advantages of war" (L 14.4).

The second law of nature spells out what it might mean to endeavor peace. Hobbes assumes that there will be peace only when people each give up the right of self-defense—including preemptive self-defense—that they have by nature. And so the law enjoins "that a man be willing, when others are so too, as far-forth, as for peace, and defence of himself he shall think it necessary, to lay down this right to all things; and be contented with so much liberty against other men, as he would allow other men against himself" (L 14.5).

This precept, like the first requirement of nature, is presented by Hobbes as a straightforward maxim of self-concern, in particular self-preservation. Granted that people cannot help but seek their self-preservation, the precept identifies the measure that they are best advised to agree to, should the opportunity for agreeing to it become available. Hobbes expects that those who exercise the power of reason, seeing what is good for them in the long run, will immediately see that this precept makes sense. And he expects equally that they will subscribe on the same basis to the third law of nature: "that men perform their covenants made" (L 15.1). Did they not accept this in tandem with the second law, then the second law would have no force.[8]

The discussion of natural law suggests that notwithstanding the indexical character of evaluative terms, there may be a basis on which people could each agree for their own reasons on the superiority of a certain alternative to the state of nature and could bargain their way toward its acceptance. Does this point us toward a regular contractual way, then, of resolving the predicament of people in the state of nature? Alas, no.

The problem is that natural law itself, as we saw in the discussion of contract in chapter 4, forbids people to enter a contract in which they depend on the future performance of others if there is even a "reasonable suspicion" (L 14.18) that others will let them down. In order for a contract to be valid under natural law, it is essential that "he that performeth first shall have no reasonable cause to doubt of the performance of the other" (EL 15.10). And given the weakness of mind, the *impotentia animi*, that manifestly affects human beings, no one can escape such doubt. Rationality might dictate to each that they ought to stick with the terms of any such contract, given the escape it guarantees from the state of nature. In other words, it might be that none of the parties would have a rational motive to free ride on the efforts of others and seek to benefit from the contract without assuming the contractual burden. It might even be, as Hobbes thinks, that only a fool would be otherwise disposed (L 15.4). But still there is going to be a problem. No one can be assured that others won't prove to be fools, allowing their rationality to give way under the pressure of irrational impulses.

The general danger, as we saw in the discussion of personation and contract, is that others may prove to be weak of mind. The particular danger, as we now know, is that contractual resolution may give way when people, out of vanity, believe that they can achieve superior power, honor, or glory, despite their basic equality with others. Spurred on by the passion for secure superiority, they may prove unable to keep to the terms of any contract that reduces them to a condition of equality with others. No one can be assured that others won't be moved in these ways; no one can be assured that others will remain faithful to any sort of regular contract for peace that they might try to establish.

The problem would not arise, as we know from earlier discussion, if there were a sanction that parties to the contract could each admit as a penalty hanging over their defection, so that by admitting that penalty they would each give credibility to their contractual words, and would each ascribe credibility to the words of others. But in the state of nature it is not clear how such penalties can be made available, except under special circumstances. That is why Hobbes himself suggests that "the connection of men by covenants" is unlikely to be a robust or reliable phenomenon in the state of nature, being "so long only valid as there ariseth no just cause of distrust" (L 22.29). As he says in *The Elements of Law* (19.1), "Till there be security amongst men for the keeping of the law of nature one towards another, men are still in the estate of war"; men still live in "the precincts of battle" (L 18.9).

THE DRACONIAN SOLUTION

The upshot, then, is that just as there is no noncontractual way out of the state-of-nature predicament, so there is no regular contractual mode of exit either. The problem is that "covenants without the sword are but words, and of no strength to secure a man at all," "notwithstanding the laws of nature" (L 17.2). But this diagnosis, which derives from his general line on contract, itself suggests a solution. Why not devise an arrangement under which a regulatory sword is established at one and the same time that people contract for peace? The Hobbesian solution is to adopt precisely that line.

Hobbes proposes that people in the state of nature can make a contract that ensures the fulfillment of the very condition that is necessary for its validity—namely, that there be a common, policing power. The idea is to have a bootstrapping, self-validating contract whereby people can extricate themselves from the state of nature. This contract will oblige them in the manner of any valid contract and will create the very power whose capacity to sanction defection is necessary for the validity of the contract.

How is this to be done? The answer is by having individuals contract to incorporate, and do so in a way that gives more or less absolute power to the individual or group that personates the incorporated individuals. This is the one and only contract that will create the very power—the corporate agency—that can hold them each to their word. It represents a Draconian solution to the predicament insofar as the parties subject themselves not to a limited representative but to an absolute sovereign. "The only way to create such a common power . . . is to confer all their power and strength upon one man, or upon one assembly of men, that may reduce all their wills, by plurality of voices, unto one will, which is as much as to say, to appoint one man or assembly of men to bear their person" (L 17.13).

Why does the sovereign have to be absolute, rather than being subject to certain conditions and limits? Very simply, because there would be no one available to sanction a sovereign who breached such limits (DCv 6.18; L 18.4). The one and only way of setting up a sovereign who can enforce the very contract in which sovereignty is established involves giving that sovereign absolute authority; I will return to the issue in the next chapter, when debating the extent of the sovereign's authority.

Hobbes's defense of his Draconian solution is found in *The Elements of Law*, *De Cive*, and *Leviathan*, though for reasons that are probably related to the rise of Parliament in England (Skinner 2005), the terms *personation* and *representation* are introduced only in the later book. In each text, Hobbes mentions how natural concord may work to ensure a degree of social life among certain animals, but that it is unavailable with human beings. And in each case he emphasizes that the clue to solving the human problem is union, not concord, where by union he means the incorporation of the multitude of contractors into a single corporate entity. "A union so made is called a commonwealth or civil society and also a civil person; for since there is one will of all of them, it is to be taken as one person; and is to be distinguished and differentiated by a unique name from all particular men" (DCv 5.9).

Hobbes's picture is that as they each contract to create a commonwealth, people know that should they later defect, then the sovereign, drawing on the strength of the rest, will be there to punish them. As they each know this in their own case, so they know that it applies to other contractors too, so that they can be assured of not being let down by others. The "public sword" that will police the contract is wielded by "the untied hands of that man or assembly of men that hath the sovereignty, and whose actions are avouched by them all, and performed by the strength of them all, in him united" (L 18.4).

The contractors who think about defecting later will each see that a lone defection will promise little profit, assuming the difficulty of duplicity (L 15.5). They will each see that they can all give their individual word not to defect and make that word stick—exposing themselves to the sanctions of the sovereign, they can put enough at stake to give their word credibility. This is true only of lone defection, of course, or defection involving a sufficiently small number for the strength of the rest to be able to prevail over them. As a commercial bank will go broke if all its customers seek to withdraw their savings at the same time, so Hobbes's commonwealth will dissolve if too many of its people defect at once from the contract that binds them to the sovereign. But this is not a weakness in Hobbes's theory, since he holds that the "obligation of subjects to the sovereign is understood to last as long, and no longer, than the power lasteth by which he is able to protect them," and this power may fail "through the ignorance and passions of men" leading to "intestine discord" (L 21.21).

We saw earlier that there are two modes in which people may contract into a regime whereby a sovereign is established—in particular, an individual sovereign—and incorporation achieved. One involves the acceptance by each of a would-be sovereign, perhaps on the basis of paternal dominion or military conquest; the other is the institution of a sovereign by a contract between subjects. I abstract from that difference in the current discussion, but will return to it again in the next chapter.

The incorporation that gives power to the sovereign, be the sovereign "a man or assembly of men," certainly creates an agent that will be capable of punishing any contractual defection. But how can Hobbes be sure that the sovereign thereby authorized will be motivated to penalize such defection? How can he be sure that the sovereign will prove to be a consistent and punctilious enforcer, not just a random force for contractual policing?

Were the sovereign not to enforce the contract whereby sovereign power is established, then that would be self-defeating: allowing others to challenge the sovereign's power with impunity, it would put the very preservation of the sovereign in doubt. Hence, we may certainly expect that the sovereign will enforce the original, self-abasing contract whereby individuals subject themselves to the sovereign.

The regime of collective incorporation under an untied sovereign power will be attractive to people in the state of nature, however, only so far as the sovereign may be expected not just to punish any challenge to sovereign power but also to establish and enforce laws whereby people may live in peace and indeed prosperity. These laws will have to protect people from one another and make it possible for them to enter more particular contracts, with defection attracting the penalty of the sovereign's sanction. And so the question is why parties in the state of nature would have reason to expect the untied, absolute sovereign to go to the trouble of ensuring peace under such a regime of law.

Hobbes's response to this problem is to assert that a sovereign who did not establish peace in this way would not last long, not delivering the goods sought in the contract. The idea is that it will be in the self-interest of the sovereign to look after the law and order of the realm; "the good of the sovereign and people, cannot be separated" (L 30.21; see also DCv 10.2; EL 28.1). The benefit for which the commonwealth is "instituted, namely, the peace and preservation of every particular man . . . extendeth equally both to the sovereign, and to the subjects" (EL 24.1). Thus he says of kings that "it concerns them in their own interest to make such laws as the people can endure, and may keep them without impatience, and live in strength and courage to defend their king and country, against their potent neighbours" (D 144).

Hobbes thinks that the identity between a sovereign's interest and that of the people is a contingent matter, but that it holds with particular strength when the sovereign is an individual monarch. This, indeed, is his principal argument for thinking that of the different sorts of commonwealth possible, monarchy is the best. "The riches, power, and honour of a monarch arise only from the riches, strength and reputation of his subjects," he says, since "no king can be rich, nor glorious, nor secure, whose subjects are either poor, or contemptible, or too weak (through want, or dissension) to maintain a war against their enemies" (L 19.4). But things are likely to be quite different in a democracy or an aristocracy, where self-seeking on the part of those in power can lead them into offering "perfidious advice," contemplating "treacherous action" or even waging "civil war" (L 19.4).

But won't kings, notoriously, seek to offer benefits to their particular favorites? Even Hobbes cannot deny that this is so. His line, however, is that when a number of people share in the sovereignty, as in aristocracy or democracy, there will be a larger number of potential favorites and a greater prospect of destructive competition (L 19.8). The limited favoritism of the individual monarch is less likely to make an impact on the country as a whole—it will not be "sensible to the kingdom"—and it promises to redound eventually, as in a trickle-down effect, to the welfare of the people. "As to the enriching of now and then a favourite, it is neither sensible to the Kingdom, nor is any treasure thereby conveyed out of the realm, but so spent as it falls down again upon the common people" (D 24).

Apart from the fact that it is going to be in the self-interest of the sovereign to look after subjects, ensuring that they live in peace and prosperity, there is a further consideration to put on the table. In Hobbes's view—and presumably as a consequence of this tie with the sovereign's self-interest—it is going to be incumbent on the sovereign as a matter of natural law to work for the welfare of the people. The "sovereign (be it a monarch or an assembly)" is "obliged by the law of nature" to procure "the safety of the people"; and this, in a rich sense of that goal: "by safety here is not meant a bare preservation, but also all other contentments of life, which every man by lawful industry, without danger or hurt to the commonwealth, shall acquire to himself" (L 30.1). This obligation on the sovereign is not contractually based, and involves an issue of what Hobbes calls equity, not justice (L 30.15, 30.20). It is for the sovereign to declare what is just and what is unjust, as we shall see in the next chapter, but the sovereign who breaches natural law in defining or implementing justice can be criticized for behaving inequitably (L 18.6)—ultimately, for acting against self-interest.

Why does Hobbes stress this aspect of things and not just rest with the assertion that it will be in the self-interest of the sovereign to look after the people? He thinks that it is important for stability that everyone have an understanding of how things stand between sovereign and subjects, and the formulation in terms of natural law allows of conveying this at large. Thus, he says that it is important that the "grounds" of the sovereign's rights in natural law—and by implication, the grounds of the sovereign's duties—"be diligently and truly taught." Otherwise subjects will not "know the right of any law the sovereign maketh." And if they do not know this, then they will take legal "punishment" only as "an act of hostility, which, when they think they have strength enough, they will endeavour by acts of hostility to avoid" (L 30.4). Hobbes is not content with discerning the sense that he finds in absolutist political arrangements. He also wishes that sense to be discernible by others—subjects and sovereign, presumably, alike. He fears that otherwise error or ignorance may make those arrangements unstable; they may collapse for want of being understood.

APPENDIX: HOBBES IN GAME THEORY

We saw in the discussion of contract that the problem for human beings who would like to benefit from contractual arrangements is not that they are each likely to have a rational temptation to defect from a suitable contract. Given the likelihood of being found out, defection in such a case is never going to be a rational option, according to Hobbes; only the fool could think otherwise. This point applies in particular to the contract whereby people are supposed to be able to exit the state of nature and set up a commonwealth.

The difficulty that requires the introduction of a sanctioning power, as we have just seen, is that even though people in general will have a rational motive for entering and complying with a contract for peace, giving power to the words that they exchange, they cannot be sure that others will always act on that rational motive: the fool is irrational, but not impossible. Knowing this, the issue they each face is how to give their words credibility, assuring others that they will be proof against the sort of weakness or vanity that might lead them, irrationally, not to live up to the words they exchange in contract. And that assurance problem is solved just so far as they are each exposed, in the case of defection, to the penalty threatened by the corporate agency they establish (Curley 1994, xxvi–xxviii; Martinich 2005, 217–18); only then will they have "sufficient security that others will observe the same laws" (L 15.36).

These observations are relevant to the question of how best to represent Hobbes's state of nature in game-theoretical terms. One common approach is to depict it as a prisoner's dilemma (Gauthier 1969). This approach is not faithful to Hobbes's texts, however useful it may have proved among contemporary theorists in generating varieties of what is sometimes described as Hobbesian contractarianism (Kraus 1993).

According to the simplest version of the prisoner's-dilemma representation of the state of nature, it is a two-party game in which each person confronts the others; we may ignore more complex variations (Pettit 1986). People would each prefer that they all stick to the contract than that no one does so, but the best outcome is to be able to break the contract while others keep it, and the worst is to keep the contract while others break it. The predicament can be described in the following matrix, with the higher numbers signifying better results, and the first number in each box describing the result from the point of view of the individual, and the second from the point of view of the others.

		The Others	
		Cooperate	Defect
	Cooperate	3, 3	1, 4
The Individual			
	Defect	4, 1	2, 2

Under the prisoner's-dilemma model of the state of nature, defecting dominates cooperation, since it is the best thing for the individual to do, no matter what choice others make; if others cooperate, it gives the individual 4 rather than 3, and if others defect, it gives the individual 2 rather than 1. The model does not give us an accurate view of Hobbes's state of nature, since he says that lone defection should only appeal to the fool; it does not represent the temptation with the greatest payoff, as in the prisoner's dilemma (Tuck 1989). Hobbes may be overly sanguine in thinking that detection is always so likely that only a fool would risk it. But plausibly or implausibly, that is what he thinks, so that his image of the state of nature cannot be properly represented as a prisoner's dilemma.

In the prisoner's dilemma, lone defection is more attractive than joint cooperation, joint cooperation is more attractive than joint defection, and joint defection is more attractive than lone cooperation. In the state of nature, lone defection may not be as bad as cooperating when others defect but it is no better than joint defection. The payoffs are roughly of the following character.

		The Others	
		Cooperate	Defect
The Individual	Cooperate	3, 3	1, 2
	Defect	2, 1	2, 2

Here, the best outcome on all sides is joint cooperation and the only problem is that the worst outcome of all is cooperating while others defect. The problem is one of assurance, not compliance. Everyone is disposed to cooperate, and benefit from the cooperation, but only if an assurance is available that others will be rational and cooperate too. The game is close to the stag hunt, as that has been analyzed recently by Bryan Skyrms (2003). Where the prisoner's dilemma is presented in a story of two prisoners who are given a hard choice by a canny prosecutor, the stag or deer hunt draws on a suggestion in Rousseau's discourse on inequality. "If a deer was to be taken, every one saw that, in order to succeed, he must abide faithfully by his post: but if a hare happened to come within the reach of any one of them, it is not to be doubted that he pursued it without scruple, and, having seized his prey, cared very little, if by so doing he caused his companions to miss theirs" (Rousseau 1973, 78).

The change from the prisoner's dilemma in the stag-hunt game is precisely that while lone cooperation remains the worst outcome, joint cooperation becomes more attractive than lone or joint defection. Thus while no one is tempted to defect on others, they will each want an assurance that others are going to cooperate before cooperating themselves; there is still a danger or risk of ending up in the worst position, as the lone cooperator. Rousseau's story casts the members of a team that is hunting a deer as the cooperators and defection as the act of leaving the team in order to chase a hare on one's own, where this may make the team too small to catch the deer. Getting a hare for sure is better than chasing a deer in a team that may not catch it; but being part of a team that successfully hunts a deer is better than managing to get a hare.

CHAPTER EIGHT

The Commonwealth of Ordered Words

AND SO WE COME TO THE COMMONWEALTH that Hobbes hails as the salvation of humankind. Although human beings are born in animal quietude, the invention of words leads them into inevitable strife, putting them at motivational loggerheads and making it impossible for them to agree on any common, normative currency for the regulation of their affairs. But the invention of words provides the solution for the very problem it creates, enabling human beings to enter into a contract for incorporation that creates a sovereign sufficiently powerful to embody the commonwealth: "that great Leviathan," "that Mortal God to which we owe, under the Immortal God, our peace and defence" (L 17.13).

Not only is access to the commonwealth made possible by the power of contract and incorporation that words introduce. The commonwealth itself is characterized in great part, as we shall see, by the order of words that it sets up. It is associated with the appearance of the words *just* and *unjust*, with the invention of property and the definition of the words *mine* and *yours*, and more generally with the ordering of words, such as *good* and *bad*, that typically drive people to blows. All such words come to have in every mouth the single, uncontentious meaning that is authorized by the sovereign: the arbiter, as the sovereign becomes, of all ambiguity and discord. In this way, it becomes possible for human beings to find the sure and common path in reasoning about civil affairs that is otherwise available only for those who reason about "the comparison of magnitudes, numbers, times, and motions" (EL 13.3).

But the ordering of words associated with the commonwealth bears on possibilities of personation and incorporation as well as ratiocination. The existence of a commonwealth under the common power of the sovereign not only establishes a currency for common understanding and coordination, it also creates a space in which people can give one another their word, exposing themselves to sanctions that make their words credible. Thus, as we have seen, it enables people to personate themselves and others, establishing a network of contract and covenant, and set up the private corporations that are exemplified for Hobbes by the company of merchants.

The commonwealth, then, is the great facilitator of the positive capacities that language confers on human beings. It enables them to overcome the warping of appetite that words engender and make the most of the cultural heritage by which they are distinguished from the animals. Transformed by the capacities associated with words, human beings may be denied the easy coexistence and community that some animals attain by nature. But they can go one better. They can achieve "not the concord, but the union of many men" (EL 27.7).

In this chapter, I look at how Hobbes's argument for the commonwealth should be understood, distinguishing it from traditional contractarian arguments. I then go on to explore a number of questions that naturally arise in light of that account. These bear on the unity, basis, and extent of the sovereign's authority, the goal of sovereign government, and the room that is left for the freedom of the commonwealth's subjects. The language theme will come into explicit focus at different points and in different ways, but it remains an important part of the background at every stage in the discussion.

Understanding the Commonwealth

In documenting the generation of the commonwealth Hobbes privileges the story in which it emerges by institution, rather than by the acquisition of power by one would-be sovereign. But this story about how the commonwealth can come about through the contract of everyone with everyone—a contract fully in accord with natural law—is not meant just to tell us how the commonwealth, independently understood, might be generated. It is designed at one and the same time to tell us how we should understand the entity thereby generated: how we should define or conceive of a commonwealth.

Think of one of Hobbes's favorite analogies, involving the circle. As we saw in the first chapter, he admits that though there is no telling whether a figure presented in perception be "a true circle or no," "nothing is more easy to be known to him that knows first the generation of the propounded figure" (DCr 6.5)—"perhaps not that by which it was made," as he explains elsewhere, "yet that by which it might have been made" (DCr 1.5). The reason is that to understand what is involved in being a circle, we only have to draw on our knowledge of how to make a circle and of what follows from that; "nothing more is required to know the phenomenon peculiar to any figure whatsoever, than that we consider everything that follows from the construction that we ourselves make in the figure to be described" (DH 10.5).

What is true in geometry is true, for Hobbes, in civil science, since here too the objects of study—contracts and commonwealths, laws and norms—are entities "whose generation depends on the will of men themselves" (DH 10.4). The story about how to construct a circle—by "the circumduction of a body whereof one end remained unmoved" (DCr 6.5)—tells us all we need to know about such a figure: that it is "a figure, from whose one middle point all the extreme points are reached unto by equal radii." Hobbes thinks that his story about how to construct a commonwealth, in particular how to construct it by institution, will do the same. It will enable us to understand a commonwealth, seeing how it should be defined; it will direct us, in the title of a chapter in *Leviathan*, to "the causes, generation, and definition of a commonwealth" (L 17).

The story will do this, moreover, for the commonwealth that is constructed by acquisition, not just by institution. Even if we construct a figure by other means than with a compass, it will still be a circle so long as it preserves the properties that construction with a compass would guarantee. The same is true of the commonwealth. Even if it is constructed other than by "the assembly and consent of a multitude"— say, "by compulsion" on the part of a would-be sovereign (EL 20.1)—it will be a commonwealth so long as it preserves the properties that construction in the canonical, institutional mode would ensure. That is why a conqueror can come to serve as a sovereign who truly personates the people (L 17.5).

When the sovereign acquires public power in this manner, people do not contract with one another to incorporate and have a sovereign. Nor do they each make a separate contract with the would-be sovereign, as with a private master.[1] Rather, they each contract to accept that individual or body as sovereign, perhaps under duress or coercion, on the assumption that others do so too. They submit to that individual or group not as a private master but as someone who can play the role of the sovereign, where the role is understood on the basis of the canonical generation. Thus, if it turns out that others do not contract to accept the individual or body as sovereign, then there will be no sovereign, and no one can submit to that person or group as to a sovereign.

It is not surprising, in view of this, that the generation of a commonwealth by acquisition can give it the same features as the canonical generation by institution would confer. The arrangement made by each individual with the would-be sovereign implicitly involves all other subjects as well. Here, as in the generation of a commonwealth by institution, the subjects combine with one another to "authorize all the actions of that man or assembly that hath their lives and liberty in his power" (L 20.2). Thus, no matter what the actual method of generation, "the rights and consequences of sovereignty are the same" (L 20.3).

Under generation by institution, we can distinguish the contract of each with each to have a sovereign, and the decision to have this or that individual or group as sovereign; this decision will go by default if the people assembled preserve sovereignty in themselves, as in a democracy, but otherwise will be determined by unanimous or perhaps majority vote (L 18.5). Under generation by acquisition, the focus is on the second decision, to have this individual or group as sovereign, and while it may involve each contracting with that individual or group, it presupposes an understanding on the part of each that others too will decide on the same individual or group as sovereign, and will by implication acquiesce in having some sovereign. The fact that they each hold and act on the understanding that others are similarly disposed means that there is something close to the multilateral contract that characterizes the generation of the commonwealth by institution. People will each submit to a particular individual or group as sovereign so far and only so far as they can assume that others will submit in the same way—that is, can assume that others will acquiesce both in having a sovereign and having this particular individual or group as sovereign.

It is now standard to distinguish two varieties of contractualism in political theory. In one, the contract is an allegedly historical event that serves to legitimate the treatment of parties according to the agreed-on terms. In the other, it is a hypothetical contract that people would supposedly have made in suitable circumstances, where the fact that they would have done so is meant to show that the arrangements agreed to are ethically attractive (Rawls 1971). Hobbes's contractualism, by the account sketched here, is of a third and different kind.[2] The contract described in the generation of the commonwealth by institution need not have occurred in history, he thinks, so it does not figure as a legitimating historical event. But neither does it figure primarily as an ethical heuristic, designed to show why the commonwealth is attractive. Its first job in Hobbes is to reveal to us the true nature of the commonwealth and demonstrate that any commonwealth worthy of the name will have certain characteristics. We may be ethically reconciled with the commonwealth as a result of understanding the Hobbesian story, but that is a by-product of the exercise, not its main purpose.

What are the characteristics of the commonwealth that we should come to understand and appreciate, then, as a result of its being capable of being generated in the canonical contract envisaged by Hobbes? I will give over the remainder of this final chapter to the discussion of that question. I focus on the authority enjoyed by the commonwealth and sovereign, addressing a number of topics in turn: the unity or indivisibility of that authority; its basis; its extent; the variety of its exercise; and its significance for people's liberty.

When we learn how to construct a circle, as we decide to name the construct, we build up a definition of the circle and its related elements that encodes the properties ensured by that mode of construction; I discussed this in the brief account of Hobbes's method in chapter 1. Thus, the elaboration of those properties can be seen as a priori demonstrable, on the basis of our understanding or definition of the terms involved (DH 10.4–5). The same, in Hobbes's view, will be true of the commonwealth. Identifying the generation by institution as canonical, we define a commonwealth and its related terms—sovereign, representation, law, and so on—in such a way that as a matter of a priori demonstration, it will have the required properties. Hence, the investigation to follow can be seen, in Hobbesian terms, as an exercise in deducing a priori the important features of the commonwealth.

Isn't there something arbitrary, however, in selecting a certain mode of generation as canonical, whether with the circle or the commonwealth, and then defining the object constructed so as to reinforce that decision? Hobbes's view may be that we start from a rough or ready idea of a circle or commonwealth, explore how we might reliably make or construct such an object, and then render that idea more precise in a definition that privileges the mode of construction we have identified. He therefore says in the circle case, "If there be set before us a plain figure, having, as near as may be, the figure of a circle, we cannot possibly perceive by sense whether it be a true circle or no; than which, nevertheless, nothing is more easy to be known to him that knows first the generation of the propounded figure" (DCr 6.5). In both the geometric and the political case, the suggestion has to be that there is a common meaning for the term we wish to define, since Hobbes lays great stress, as we saw at the end of chapter 2, on such commonality. The role of the constructive enterprise must be to make that common meaning precise, an exercise of clarification that according to Hobbes, "needs a keen judgment and intense labour" (DCv 18.3).[3]

THE INDIVISIBILITY OF SOVEREIGN AUTHORITY

The first feature of the commonwealth that is guaranteed by its canonical mode of generation—by institution—is that it should be guided by one will, having just one sovereign to speak in its name. This feature is of great importance for Hobbes, as it was for the originator of the idea, Jean Bodin (1992). It enables him, as it did Bodin, to make a strong case against the mixed constitution—"mixarchy," as he mischievously calls it (B 116). This is an idea of Greek provenance that had been a centerpiece in republican theory, from Polybius and Cicero in classical Rome, through Niccolò Machiavelli and other theorists of the Renaissance, down to his own day.

The mixed constitution would make a place for a king or a monarch, an assembly of the few, and an assembly of the many. Thus it would have elements of monarchy, aristocracy, and democracy, and the traditional hope was that this would give the state stability; it would stem the corruption of the constitution that was long thought to be inevitable with simple regimes. Hobbes complains, however, that such an arrangement supports "not one independent commonwealth, but three independent factions; nor one representative person, but three" (L 29.16). His argument is straightforward: "if the king bear the person of the people, and the general assembly bear also the person of the people, and another assembly bear the person of a part of the people, they are not one person, nor one sovereign, but three persons, and three sovereigns."

The reasoning that Hobbes deploys here derives directly from his view of the commonwealth as an incorporation of people in which each member takes the will of the sovereign for the will of them all. Incorporation requires artificial personation in which one individual or body bears the common person of the members, acting and speaking for the corporate entity with the authorization of members. Hence, there can only be a corporate entity if there is a single personator, a single voice, in which the corporate will is revealed. If there is more than one voice, more than one commanding personator—not "one representative person," as he says, "but three"—then there can be no pretense that a corporate body materializes (L 29.23). We cannot say of the people living under such an arrangement, as we should be able to say of a duly generated commonwealth, that there is "a real unity of them all, in one and the same person" (L 17.13). They will still be a plurality, not a unity, a multitude, not a people; in effect, they will still exist in the state of nature.

The thesis of the unity or indivisibility of the sovereign is used throughout Hobbes's work to combat the doctrine of the mixed constitution and thereby challenge the republican tradition (DCv 7.4; EL 20.15). But it also motivates him in another conflict that is just as significant from his point of view: the conflict with those who would have the church be independent of the sovereign, whether through allowing people to be ruled by the pope in Rome, the Presbyterian ministers, or private conscience (B 3).

Hobbes tries to argue with these opponents from religious premises, such arguments offering the best hope of convincing them. But perhaps his most important ground for objecting to the independence of the church or religion in any guise is that this would make for division within the commonwealth. He is convinced that just as sovereignty cannot be divided within itself, so it cannot coexist with an independent ecclesiastical authority. Thus he argues at length, on religious grounds, for the unlikely view that God speaks not via the conscience, and certainly not via an independent church, but "by his vicegods, or lieutenants here on earth, that is to say, by sovereign kings, or such as have sovereign authority as well as they" (EL 26.11).

The sovereign in civil matters, then, is to be the sovereign in all. Hobbes takes great pains to try to make this message palatable to Christians, but I will not follow him in his interesting, if convoluted, attempts at persuasion. What is crucial is the upshot, which is that there shall be no rule but that of the one and only sovereign possible in any land. This sovereign is to dictate not just what shall be done but also what opinions shall be expressed; "heretics are none but private men, that stubbornly defend some doctrine prohibited by their lawful sovereigns" (L 42.130). This message need not be as harsh as it sounds, for it applies only to "profession with the tongue," and so only to the opinions that are held in public, since "belief and unbelief never follow men's commands" (L 42.11; see B 62). But the thrust is still quite clear. People are expected in Hobbes's vision to disown the false sovereigns of church and conscience, and acknowledge the one and only power in any land: the sovereign, period. They can continue to constitute a unity, a corporate person, only if they have but one spokesperson.

For Hobbes, as I mentioned earlier, the sovereign who bears the person of the people or commonwealth may be a monarch, a small committee of aristocrats, or the people entire—the committee of the whole. He goes to some pains in all his works to argue that monarchy in his view is best, though this is not something that he treats as demonstrable in the same way as the other elements in his political theory (Ryan 1996). In *The Elements of Law* and *De Cive*, as I noted, he argues that when the commonwealth is formed by institution, democracy inevitably materializes at the moment of deciding to have a sovereign, as distinct from deciding who shall be sovereign; thus, "democracy is the beginning both of aristocracy and monarchy" (EL 21.6). But even then he thinks that it naturally evolves, under the familiar difficulties of contention, either into aristocracy or monarchy (EL 21; DCv 7). In *Leviathan*, he treats the three possible systems as coeval and is content to point out what he sees as the particular advantages of monarchy. One advantage on which he insists, as we saw in the previous chapter, is that the interests of a monarch will tend to go more closely with those of the commonwealth than will the interests of any committee (L 19.4).

This argument for monarchy is decidedly subsidiary in Hobbes's work, however, and we need not give it much attention. He may have been happy for the claim to assume a subsidiary position, wanting to make room for the possibility of a legitimate democracy. Something approaching democracy must have seemed to be on the cards in England right through the 1640s, especially after the execution of Charles I in 1649. The possibility would only have begun to fade with the emergence of Oliver Cromwell's protectorate, and the restoration of the monarchy when Charles II returned from France in 1660.[4]

The Basis of Sovereign Authority

There were two salient stories prominent in Hobbes's time as to what gave a sovereign authority over others. One was the story according to which kings, if not sovereigns in general, ruled by divine right. In an old medieval phrase (Canning 1996), it had commonly been granted that kings ruled *Dei gratia*, by the grace of God. But this was now interpreted to mean not that the rule of an individual monarch or monarchical line was allowed by God, as the rule of a republic might be allowed by God, but that it was prescribed by the divinity; it alone had divine license. Hobbes gave no credence whatsoever to this view, not even bothering to counter it directly. He holds, as we saw, that there is "no obligation on any man which ariseth not from some act of his own; for all men equally are by nature free" (L 21.10). It follows from this claim, a basic axiom of his system, that kings and sovereigns more generally can have no natural authority. Not even a parent has "dominion over his child because he begat him"; such authority derives from "the child's consent, either express or by other sufficient arguments declared" (L 20.4).[5]

The other story about sovereign authority that was prominent in Hobbes's time was associated with a group known as the monarchomachs; this group worried him a lot, as it worried other absolutists like Bodin. Conscious of medieval corporate theory and versed in biblical stories about the people of God, the monarchomachs spoke on behalf of religious minorities like the Huguenots in France who were subject to governmental persecution—a persecution exemplified for all by the St. Bartholomew's Day massacre in 1572. Monarchomach doctrine was given an early well-known formulation in a 1579 tract issued anonymously in France under the title *Vindiciae contra Tyrannos* (Garnett 1994).

The monarchomachs argued that a people like the Huguenots were a corporate person or body, represented by their more or less local spokespersons; that such a people must be presumed to have made a contract with their king whereby the monarch would rule them justly in return for their obedience; that this presumptive contract had clearly been broken in the practice of persecution; and so that they had the right to rise up and reject that king—to kill the king, as suggested in the Greek etymology of the word *monarchomach*. The appearance of monarchomachian tracts and ideas was the main spur for Bodin's (1992) defense in 1576 of more or less absolute sovereignty, and it remained a powerful stimulus in Hobbes's writing, not least because of the monarchomachian character of many parliamentary tracts (Skinner 2005). The thesis that sovereigns rule as a result of a contract with their people is given absolutely no credibility under Hobbes's theory; it is so directly ruled out, indeed, that the theory might have been constructed specifically in order to undermine it.

Drawing on the medieval theory of the corporation, as they themselves had done, Hobbes agrees with the monarchomachs that for a people to exist as a group agent or person, it must be personated or spoken for. But insisting that if it is to be truly a single agent, it must have but one spokesperson or spokesbody, he maintains that the people does not come into existence as such until a single sovereign has been instituted and recognized; a diversity of spokespersons—say, local magistrates or elders—will not serve the purpose, contrary to monarchomachian assumptions. Thus, Hobbes holds that it is impossible for a people as a single entity to have made a contract with a sovereign. For before the sovereign was established, there was no people there to enter such a contract. The sovereign cannot make a contract with "the whole, as one party," Hobbes says, "because as yet they are not one person" (L 18.4). And the sovereign cannot make a contract with the multitude, since no action, let alone the making of a contract, can be "truly called the action of the multitude"; there can be no such collective action "unless every man's hand, and every man's will, (not so much as one excepted) have concurred thereto" (EL 20.2).

Hobbes's position on the formation of the people means that it is false, contrary to a well-known medieval doctrine, that the sovereign is superior to the people considered as individuals or *singuli*, but subordinate to them, considered as parts of a whole—as *universi*. This is because, as he says, the whole is not distinct from the sovereign and "the power of all together is the same with the sovereign's power" (L 18.18). The claim "that the people is a distinct body from him or them that have the sovereignty over them," he insists, "is an error" (EL 27.9).

The fact that the people exist as a body only in and through the sovereign also has a related implication, bearing on rebellion. It means that should the people rise up and kill a sovereign king, as might make sense under monarchomachian thinking, then by that very stroke they would cease to exist as a people, dissolving instead into a multitude. Regicide on the part of a people would amount to corporate suicide.

So much for the doctrines about the basis of sovereign authority that are ruled out by Hobbes's canonical generation of the commonwealth. What doctrine, then, is ruled in?

Hobbes's reconstruction of the commonwealth shows, he thinks, that when there is a sovereign recognized by each, then the people in that commonwealth are incorporated into a corporate entity, all implicitly acquiescing in an arrangement whereby the sovereign speaks and acts for the whole. This acquiescence, this implicit contract with others, is entirely voluntary, even if it is coerced or pressured; the presence of fear or intimidation, after all, is consistent with the exercise of will. Moreover, it is a form of acquiescence or contract that makes perfect sense, and enjoys perfect validity, under the natural law of self-preservation and self-concern, since it enables each to live in peace and avoid "a war of all men against all men" (DCv preface). And so it obligates each to go along with the will expressed by the sovereign—that is what political incorporation requires—save in the extreme case where that is to his or her own detriment.

How much of a detriment must the sovereign threaten if the obligation is not to hold? Although Hobbes does not always speak clearly on the question, the one unambiguous case is where there is a danger to life—say, a threat of "death, wounds, and imprisonment (the avoiding whereof is the only end of laying down any right)" (L 14.29). It is only in matters involving such a degree of danger to oneself that it is impossible to contract away one's right of self-defense. And it may only be in cases where the sovereign represents that degree of danger that Hobbes thinks one is not obliged to submit.

On this account, the basis for sovereign authority is made manifest in the nature of the commonwealth and the role of the sovereign. The commonwealth is a corporation, implicitly accepted by all, that is designed for the self-preservation and self-concern of each member. Unless the sovereign is granted suitable authority, however, the commonwealth is going to be impossible. So those who voluntarily accept the commonwealth, embracing its fruits, are obliged by that act to grant the sovereign the authority needed.

Hobbes is inviting us to look on the commonwealth in this incorporating, contractual light, and seeing it in that way, to recognize that we are obligated as members of the commonwealth to obey those laws that are laid down by the sovereign in the corporate name—"you shall not do it"—and that are supported by attendant sanctions: "anyone who does, shall pay the penalty" (DCv 14.23). The laws do not oblige us because of the sanctions—say, because it would be foolhardy to risk attracting those sanctions. The laws oblige us because of our implicit acquiescence in the encompassing contractual regime, and the sanctions serve only to guard us against the urge—irrational though it may be—to try and defect; we are "compelled to performance by fear of the penalty laid down in the law" (DCv 14.2n; cf. DCv 13.16).

This might best be described as a doctrine of political incorporation, starting as it does from an insight that, according to Hobbes (EL 27.7), "hath not been taken notice of." This is the insight that as people incorporate in a private body like a company of merchants, so they can be said to incorporate in the commonwealth. By Hobbes's analysis, the political incorporation found in the commonwealth is implicit, voluntary, and valid under natural law, and the source of an absolute obligation of obedience to the sovereign.

The theory of divine right denies a basis of sovereign authority to usurpers, and the theory of popular contract denies it to rulers rejected by the people or in breach of their presumptive contract with the people. When is political incorporation not satisfied by a ruler? When is the basis for sovereign authority lacking, under Hobbes's theory? Precisely when the ruler is not capable of commanding general obedience, and so not able to protect people from each other or foreign dangers. "The obligation of subjects to the sovereign is understood to last as long, and no longer, than the power lasteth by which he is able to protect them. For the right men have by nature to protect themselves, when none else can protect them, can by no covenant be relinquished" (L 21.21).

The Extent of Sovereign Authority

Perhaps the most troubling question in political theory throughout the Middle Ages and the early modern period was how far the rights of a ruler ran, and in particular whether the ruler was *legibus solutus*, above the laws (Skinner 1978). The long republican tradition had insisted, of course, that the ruler was not above the law, arguing that the ideal dispensation involved an empire of laws, not of men; this theme was taken up with particular vehemence by Hobbes's republican opponent, James Harrington (1992). But on this claim, as on so many others, Hobbes took issue with the republicans; together with the monarchomachs, they were the opponents that he was most keen to discredit.

The practical reason for his quarrel with republicans is that he thought there would be little chance of securing the peace under a regime where no one was the final, more or less absolute authority; the doctrine of the rule of law, like that of the mixed constitution, would dangerously weaken the claims of the sovereign. Yet the quarrel was not fought on practical grounds. For the theory of the commonwealth that Hobbes developed made the doctrine of the rule of law—the doctrine that the sovereign was subject to the law—seem quite incredible.

For Hobbes, as for contemporary legal theory, no laws, no matter how carefully formulated, are proof against rival construals. "All laws, written and unwritten, have need of interpretation" (L 26.21). This means that law cannot rule over human beings, strictly speaking, since in order to do so it would have to be self-interpreting. We have to give up the idea of a rule of law, then, in favor of recognizing that legislation involves legal interpretation as crucially as it does legal imposition. But if the sovereign is to impose the law, as all sides will agree that the sovereign should, who is to interpret it? For Hobbes, it has to be the individual or body in the sovereign position, or those appointed by the sovereign who act under the sovereign will (D 44, 68). "For else, by the craft of an interpreter the law may be made to bear a sense contrary to that of the sovereign, by which means the interpreter becomes the legislator" (L 21.20).

But even were the law self-interpreting, Hobbes thinks that we should still treat the sovereign as above the law. By definition, the sovereign is the one who makes the law, even if some of the laws preexist the person or body in question; having the capacity to change such laws, the sovereign's silence in such a case is "an argument of consent" (L 26.7). If the sovereign can make or change the law, though, that means that the "sovereign of a commonwealth, be it an assembly, or one man, is not subject to the civil laws. For having power to make, and repeal laws, he may when he pleaseth, free himself from that subjection, by repealing those laws that trouble him, and making of new; and consequently he was free before" (L 26.6; see also EL 27.6; DCv 6.14).[6]

Not only does Hobbes extend the authority of the sovereign to the point where that individual or body is above the law. He even goes so far as to say that the sovereign holds power without being subject to a contractual condition of any kind. Provided that the sovereign is powerful enough to fulfill the role required, there can be no grounds on the part of subjects for saying that there has been a breach of trust or contract, and that the sovereign's authority is forfeit (L 18.4).

The reason for this is that by Hobbes's lights, the contract whereby the commonwealth is established cannot give the sovereign authority subject to certain limiting conditions. A contract is valid, as we know, only to the extent that its clauses are ones that can be enforced, so that parties are guarded against suspicion that others may defect. But who would be able to enforce a limiting condition in the contract whereby the commonwealth is established? The only power available to police that contract is the power of the sovereign—say, that of a king "whose actions are avouched by them all, and performed by the strength of them all, in him united" (L 18.4; see also DCv 6.18). But no monarch, no sovereign of any kind, could be expected to enforce the terms of a contract under which their own sphere of action would be curtailed.

The theme emerging here is of the greatest interest. We know from the discussion in the last chapter that the contract that establishes the commonwealth is special because it meets the need for a sanctioner of defection by bringing precisely that sort of force into existence: the corporate person, as represented by the sovereign. What we now see is that in Hobbes's view, this contract will work only insofar far as it is a contract that in no way binds the sovereign. So far as it limited the sovereign's power it would not be valid, since no one could expect the sovereign to enforce such a limitation. Hobbes observes, as elsewhere, that "covenants, being but words and breath, have no force to oblige, contain, constrain, or protect any man, but what it has from the public sword" (L 18.4). And from this observation he concludes that no covenant that is policed by the sovereign, the public sword, can put conditions on how that sword is used (for a reconstruction, see Hampton 1986, chapter 4).

This conclusion is meant to hold whether the commonwealth is set up by institution or acquisition: by the contract of each with each to have a sovereign, or by the contract of each with a certain individual or group to recognize that person or group as sovereign. This illustrates the general claim that whether a commonwealth is set up by institution or acquisition, "the rights and consequences of sovereignty are the same" (L 20.3).

Hobbes is conscious that this doctrine of more or less absolute sovereign authority may seem incredible when applied to individual monarchs. He thinks it is more palatable, however, in the case of popular, democratic sovereignty: "no man is so dull as to say, for example, the people of Rome made a covenant with the Romans, to hold the sovereignty on such or such conditions; which not performed, the Romans might lawfully depose the Roman people" (L 18.4). He therefore tries to make a general case for the absolute extent of sovereignty by insisting that the rights that seem natural in the case of a wholly democratic sovereign—if indeed they do seem natural—must be ascribed on parallel grounds to a sovereign of any kind.

Hobbes does not deny, of course, that the sovereign may behave toward subjects in a way that breaches natural law. But such a breach of natural law does not entail a breach of the terms of any contract, nor does it entail an act of injustice in any independent sense; as we shall see, the sovereign is the one who defines what is just and unjust, setting up the laws that identify what shall and shall not be in breach of the founding contract. Using "iniquity" to designate a violation of natural law, Hobbes says that "they that have sovereign power may commit iniquity, but not injustice, or injury in the proper signification" (L 18.6). "There may indeed in a statute law, made by men be found iniquity, but not injustice" (D 30).

Not only is it impossible for the sovereign to breach the founding contract or do anything unjust. Hobbes really drives home the unlimited authority of the sovereign when he identifies a further reason why the sovereign is beyond the reach of any legitimate complaint on the part of subjects. When they embrace the sovereign as their corporate voice and agent, those subjects accept that what is done by the sovereign qua sovereign is done in the name of the commonwealth and so in their own names.[7] Thus, "he that complaineth of injury from his sovereign complaineth of that whereof he himself is author, and therefore ought not to accuse any man but himself" (L 18.6). For as Hobbes puts it elsewhere, when a subject "hath once transferred his right of judging to another, that which shall be commanded, is no less his judgment, than the judgment of that other" (EL 25.12).

The upshot of all of this is that the sovereign has a truly extraordinary range of authority in Hobbes's theory. The rights assigned "make the sovereign power no less absolute in the commonwealth, than before commonwealth every man was absolute in himself to do, or not to do, what he thought good" (EL 20.13). The considerations rehearsed mean that the sovereign, whether set up by institution or acquisition, has a power "as great as possibly men can be imagined to make it" (L 20.18). The array is dazzling, as Hobbes illustrated with a monarch in mind.

> His power cannot, without his consent, be transferred to another: he cannot forfeit it: he cannot be accused by any of his subjects, of injury: he cannot be punished by them: he is judge of what is necessary for peace; and judge of doctrines: he is sole legislator; and supreme judge of controversies; and of the times, and occasions of war, and peace. (L 20.3)

Does the enjoyment of absolute power mean that a sovereign will be likely to abuse the subjects of the realm? No, it does not, since the sovereign's own interests are supposed, as we have seen, to coincide pretty well with those of the people as a whole. A sovereign individual or body will have reason not to abuse subjects because such abuse will generally be against the sovereign's own interests. People cannot be contractually bound to compromise their own safety and preservation— this would be contrary to natural law—and so they will not be obliged by the founding contract to allow the sovereign to do them harm. This means that the sovereign who abuses subjects will thereby make their resistance legitimate.

Not being bound by a contract to the contrary, of course, the sovereign will certainly have a right to kill me. But it is entirely consistent with this, according to Hobbes, that "I am not bound to kill myself when he commands me" (L 21.14).[8] More generally, he thinks that people who are threatened by their sovereign, even people on the gallows, are entitled to do all that they can to preserve their own lives. Such resistance does not frustrate "the end for which the sovereignty was ordained" (L 21.15): "the safety of the people" (L 27.3; DCv 13.2). It is sourced in a necessity of nature and so is permitted, even required, under natural law. "For man by nature chooseth the lesser evil, which is danger of death in resisting, rather than the greater, which is certain and present death in not resisting" (L 14.29).

This theme shows that while Hobbes is an absolutist, his theory does make room for limits on sovereign power. Those who live under government give up all the rights they can give up, but this means, crucially, that they retain a right of resistance against any threat to their lives from the sovereign. That being the case, the sovereign would do well not to trigger the exercise of that right on the part of subjects; the sovereign is naturally motivated to rule with a velvet rather than an iron hand. This legitimation of resistance led Hobbes's contemporary, Bishop Bramhall, to describe *Leviathan* as a "rebel's catechism" (Curley 1994, 142n22). While this is surely an overstatement, the right of resistance retained in Hobbes's theory does mean that the sovereign has a serious motive for respecting the interests of subjects. However absolute sovereign authority, the bearer will still have reason to be cautious in the exercise of it (Ryan 1996, 41).[9]

THE EXERCISE OF SOVEREIGN AUTHORITY

What form does the exercise of sovereign authority take in Hobbes's theory? Perhaps because of believing that administration and adjudication can be more or less safely put in the hands of deputies—he probably thinks that such deputies are easily monitored and controlled—Hobbes tends to focus on legislation as the main function of the sovereign. The laws issued by the sovereign are commands that administrative deputies can put into effect and judicial deputies adjudicate. Unlike administrative and judicial functions, legislation cannot be alienated; laws represent "the will of the sovereign" (L 26.7), and only the sovereign is in a position to say what that will is.

Why describe laws as commands of the sovereign, and legislation as an exercise of command? The answer, according to Hobbes, is that the reason for complying with a command, unlike the reason for complying with someone's counsel, is that it represents the will of the person issuing it (L 25.2), and this is the sort of reason, he thinks, that applies with the law. We comply with counsel on the grounds that it is sound or wise, so the lesson goes; we comply with law on the grounds that it is what the sovereign wills. We do this because the founding contract obliges each of us to obey the commands of the sovereign, whatever they may be. When entering that contract, we do not make an agreement in which "we must settle what is to be done before we are obligated"; here "the obligation to do comes first, and we determine afterwards what is to be done" (DCv 14.2). More specifically, we determine what is to be done by reference to what the sovereign has commanded.

Legislation should meet various conditions, in Hobbes's view, if it is to conform to natural law (L 26), but the laws enacted will be laws, whether or not they meet those conditions; indeed, it will still be the case that "obedience to the civil law" is required by "the law of nature" (L 26.8; see also B 51). In this respect, Hobbes is a positivist about law. He rejects the view that only laws that conform to the natural law count as laws—a view that had been associated with the older natural law tradition that he and Grotius had overturned.

According to Hobbes, uncontroversially, a great deal of legislation will be regulative of activities and institutions that are independently well-defined and understood. Laws prohibiting different forms of violence against others would provide an example of purely regulative legislation. But one aspect of his theory that is particularly worth noting, given the theme of this book, is that much legislation will have a constitutive as well as regulative character. It will not draw on preexisting terms to describe the sorts of behavior that are mandatory or forbidden for the populace. It will first introduce new terms or concepts, and so new possibilities of behavior, and then regulate for how these should materialize in social life.

The best example of constitutive legislation is that whereby, as Hobbes thinks, the sovereign will introduce the notion of property and identify at the same time the activities of buying and selling, bestowing and inheriting, owning and of course stealing. Before the erection of a sovereign power and the establishment of a commonwealth, there is just the free-for-all of the state of nature. While people may possess and make use of different things in that scenario, they do not have property or "propriety" in anything, since the titles and rights required for property will not exist; there is "no propriety, no dominion, no *mine* and *thine* distinct; but only that to be every man's, that he can get; and for so long, as he can keep it" (L 13.13; see also EL 18.10; D 34, 136).[10] So those who live in the state of nature will be unable to buy or sell, own or steal, in any strict sense of those terms. It is only when the titles and rights of property are established under the sovereign that such activities become possible. The sovereign will put in place "the rules, whereby every man may know, what goods he may enjoy, and what actions he may do, without being molested by any of his fellow-subjects; and this is it men call propriety" (L 18.10).

In some matters, as we saw earlier, Hobbes thinks that there is a measure given by nature, so that people may all be mistaken in what they say about those things; "no one man's reason, nor the reason of any one number of men, makes the certainty" (L 5.3). But in other matters, there is "want of a right reason constituted by nature" and so want of a common measure. Hobbes stipulates that in order to avoid trouble, such as coming to blows, people should "set up for right reason the reason of some arbitrator or judge." This is precisely what happens in the case of property. Lacking an objective measure of what belongs to anyone, people set up a sovereign to pronounce on the matter; the sovereign will mark out the bases on which they can each make claim to anything, and in doing so will set up the institution of property.

The constitutive role of the sovereign in establishing terms with common meanings, thereby giving people new categories by which to orient themselves, is of the first importance for Hobbes. Not only will the sovereign do this with the words that institute property, the sovereign will also do it with the words that institute morality: "it is the responsibility of the same sovereign power to come up with rules or measures that will be common to all, and to publish them openly, so that each man may know by them what he should call his own and what another's, what he should call just and unjust, honourable and dishonourable, good and bad; in summary, what he should do and what he should avoid doing in social life" (DCv 6.9).[11] Indeed, the sovereign is to establish the conventional meanings of a range of terms: not just "what is to be called right, what good, what virtue," but also "what much, what little . . . what a pound, what a quart," what even in deformed or premature births is to be called "a man"; in all these matters, as in matters of ownership, "private judgments may differ, and beget controversy" (EL 29.8).

There is no measure given in nature on such questions, according to Hobbes: no objectively right reason. "But this is certain, seeing right reason is not existent, the reason of some man, or men, must supply the place thereof; and that man, or men, is he or they, that have the sovereign power" (EL 29.8; see also D 26). The upshot from the point of view of the subjects of a commonwealth is that they gain new coordinates under the rule of the sovereign, having new concepts by which to navigate. The "civil laws are to all subjects the measures of their actions, whereby to determine, whether they be right or wrong, profitable or unprofitable, virtuous or vicious; and by them the use and definition of all names not agreed upon, and tending to controversy, shall be established."

The regulative and constitutive roles of sovereign authority explain why, for Hobbes, Leviathan is such a great boon to humankind. The constitutive role means that the sovereign saves ratiocination from the problems deriving from the indexical, perspective-relative character of words like *good* and *bad*, and *mine* and *yours*. It establishes an order of public meanings in an area where such an order is not spontaneously available, restoring the power of words to provide people with common bearings and shared reasons.

The regulative role of sovereign authority supports this new order of common meanings and also ensures a further, even more important benefit. With a common, regulative power in place, sufficient "to keep them all in awe" (L 13.8), people are now able to give their words to others, confident of having them accepted, and develop the capacity to achieve all the wonders of life in social and political union. They will escape the state of nature, that wasteland where words are hollow and contract is next to impossible. They will have entered a realm, to judge by Hobbes's encomiums, that falls only a little short of the attractions of the promised land: "outside the commonwealth is the empire of the passions, war, fear, poverty, nastiness, solitude, barbarity, ignorance, savagery; within the commonwealth is the empire of reason, peace, security, wealth, splendour, society, good taste, the sciences and goodwill" (DCv 10.1).

The achievements of sovereign authority on the constitutive and regulative fronts make good sense within the perspective adopted here. Words enable people to reason, but only where nature supplies a common measure; they enable people to personate and incorporate, but only up to the limit where mutual assurance fails. The institution of the commonwealth and the authorization of a sovereign solve both problems. The words that waver too much to facilitate ratiocination are regimented appropriately, releasing the capacity of reason to bring people to a common mind. And the words that lack the backing to make them tokens of credible contract are given a power that unblocks people's potential to personate and incorporate to mutually beneficial, even transformative, effect. The appearance of sovereign authority, so understood, is a liberating event that enables people to achieve the destiny held out by the invention of speech.

LIBERTY AND THE AUTHORITY OF THE SOVEREIGN

But is the event liberating in the strict sense of enhancing the liberty or freedom of ordinary people? This is the final, crucial question that we must address.

The first thing to say in response is that by the understanding of liberty that prevailed in the long republican tradition—and perhaps more broadly—subjection to an absolute sovereign would have been in direct conflict with freedom. And so unsurprisingly, republicanism was rejected by Hobbes not just for its championing of institutions like mixed government and the rule of law but above all for its embrace of this conception of freedom. In response to the claim that freedom is only available to a person under institutions like mixed government and the rule of law, he asserts, "I think I may truly say, there was never any thing so dearly bought, as these western parts have bought the learning of the Greek and Latin tongues" (L 21.9). That learning, as he says elsewhere, was taken from "Cicero, Seneca, Cato, and other politicians of Rome, and Aristotle of Athens" (B 158).

In the republican tradition, to be free is to be no one's servant, slave, or dependent. It is to be more or less proof, by cultural standards, against interference by others, or at least against arbitrary interference: roughly, the sort of interference that is not governed by one's more or less explicitly avowed interests (Pettit 1997; Skinner 1998, 2007; Viroli 2002). To the extent that it is forced to track the interests one is ready to avow, nonarbitrary interference will be subject to one's control. Republicans thought that government interference would be nonarbitrary in roughly this sense, insofar as citizens had important interests in common and the prevailing institutions ensured that government would have to track these.

If people's freedom requires this independent standing in relation to others, then it will be put in question by any power of arbitrary interference on the part of another individual or group. Even if the power of interference is not actually exercised against the them, its existence will mean that what they are able to do in this or that domain, they are only able to do *cum permissu*: by the implicit leave of the power holder. In effect, it will mean that they are under the control of that individual or group, whether totally or to a certain degree, comprehensively or in a certain domain. In the language of Hobbes's time, they will not be "freemen" but rather "bondsmen."

According to this conception of freedom as nondomination or nonsubjection, living under Hobbes's image of the commonwealth is bound to mean living as a servant or slave. Even if the sovereign does not exercise the absolute power available against some individuals, the sovereign will have the unlimited power of doing so. Thus whatever they do, they will do by the grace and favor of that power in their life. They will live under the sovereign's control.

Hobbes responded to the threat of having his work derided on this count by arguing that freedom had never been properly defined prior to him—"no writer has explained what liberty and servitude are" (DCv 9.9)—and that properly construed, a great deal of freedom remains in place under his vision of the commonwealth. In order to understand the line he takes, we must first look at how he defines freedom and then see how far freedom remains consistent, in his view, with life within the commonwealth, under a dispensation of absolute sovereignty.

Although he does not make the point explicitly, Hobbes distinguishes quite clearly and consistently between two sorts of freedom (Pettit 2005). The first is the freedom of decision: the freedom to decide one way or another, forming one's will as between a set of alternatives; he describes this as the freedom to do or not to do (EL 12.1; DCv 13.15), to do or forbear (L 14.3), or to do or omit (L 27.20; DCv 3.3). For reasons that will appear shortly, we may call this "contractual freedom." The other is the freedom of action, as we might call it: the freedom to enact a decision already made, a will already formed. He generally refers to this as "corporal freedom" (DCv 8.30; L 20.12), casting it as a condition in which the person's body—and so the person's action—is left "at liberty" (EL 22.3).

The freedom of decision in a particular matter looks like it is going to be lost as soon as a decision on that matter is made—and made irrevocably. Broaching this theme, Hobbes says that "deliberation . . . is a putting an end to the liberty we had of doing or omitting, according to our own appetite or aversion" (L 6.50). He offers spurious support for this claim when he explains that etymologically, to deliberate is to deliberate or make unfree (L 6.52); actually, the word comes from *librare*, to weigh, not from *liberare*, to liberate. But Hobbes's claim that deliberation takes away the freedom of decision does not come to much. For the agent who hasn't yet acted can always reopen deliberation, and so long as someone remains able "to change his mind," they should still be "taken to be deliberating" (DCv 2.8). While it is true that deliberation takes away a person's freedom to do or not do something, then, no one can say that deliberation is complete before the moment of action (Brett 1998, 212). Deliberation only takes away freedom, it turns out, once it has issued in action.

Is there any other means whereby the freedom of decision might be lost? For Hobbes the answer is clear. Freedom is not forfeited in deliberation, because the possibility of second thoughts means that "he that can bind, can release," so that "he that is bound to himself only, is not bound" (L 26.6). But where it is impossible that one "be obligated to oneself" (DCv 6.14) in this way, it is possible, as we know from our discussion of contract, to be obligated to another. Hobbes therefore insists that the obligation one incurs in contracting with another takes away one's freedom of decision. Here there is no going back to reopen deliberation so that such covenants "consequently are obligatory" (EL 15.9). And that means that the freedom to decide a different way from how one has bound oneself to act is now gone. At this point "liberty ceaseth" (EL 15.9), since "obligation and liberty . . . in one and the same matter are inconsistent" (L 14.3). It is because of the connection with contract that I propose to describe the freedom we have to decide one way or another on a certain issue as contractual freedom; it is the freedom one enjoys by virtue of not being contractually bound in the matter.

This line of thought means for Hobbes that living in the commonwealth involves a serious loss of liberty. It implies acquiescence in an arrangement with others to recognize a sovereign, acknowledging an obligation to obey whatever the sovereign declares to be law. That acquiescence or contract means that one has effectively given one's word, tied up one's will, and lost one's freedom of decision—one's contractual freedom to obey or not obey, just as one wills.[12] So there can be no question of retaining discretion with respect to any set of options on which the law rules, enjoining the choice of one particular alternative or subset of alternatives. Hobbes is quite explicit on the topic: "a subject may no more govern his own actions according to his own discretion and judgment, or, (which is all one) conscience, as the present occasion from time to time shall dictate to him; but must be tied to do according to that will only, which once for all he had long ago laid up, and involved in the wills of the major part of an assembly, or in the will of some one man" (EL 24.2).

Apart from the freedom to decide one way or another, which is taken away by contractual obligation, Hobbes also acknowledges the freedom to enact a decision already made. This is not taken away by obligation, since there need be no block to enacting a decision that breaches a contract. Obligations will be enforced by sanctions, as we know, but while sanctions may induce fear and inhibition, they will not put a block or obstruction in the way of an agent's action (L 21.3). Freedom of action disappears only when people are "restrained with natural impediments" (EL 22.3) and are unable to do that which they are of a will to do, whether consistently or inconsistently with their obligations. Where freedom of decision is equivalent in Hobbes's accounting to contractual freedom—the freedom that consists in not being obligated— freedom of action is equivalent to corporal freedom—the freedom that consists in not being obstructed.

Hobbes illustrates the difference between the two sorts of freedom, and the two ways in which freedom may be lost, via an analogy with two modes of slavery (EL 22; DCv 8). Though the Romans did not make the distinction in the ambiguous name of *servus*, Hobbes says that they recognized two different ways in which a slave might be bound: one, by a verbal bond, involving a contract with the master; and other, by a physical bond, whereby the master keeps the servant under "forcible custody" (EL 22.3). In the one case the slave is bound by "verbal bonds of covenant," and in the other by "natural bonds, as chains, and the like, or in prison."

Hobbes elaborates the notion of freedom of action, freedom as nonobstruction, with a model from the natural world (L 21.1):

> Liberty, or freedom, signifieth properly the absence of opposition (by opposition, I mean external impediments of motion); and may be applied no less to irrational and inanimate creatures than to rational. For whatsoever is so tied, or environed, as it cannot move but within a certain space, which space is determined by the opposition of some external body, we say it hath not liberty to go further. And so of all living creatures, whilst they are imprisoned, or restrained with walls or chains; and of the water whilst it is kept in by banks or vessels that otherwise would spread itself into a larger space; we use to say they are not at liberty to move in such manner as without those external impediments they would.

This model, in particular the analogy with water, supports three important points that Hobbes wants to make about liberty as nonobstruction (see also DCv 9.9, 13.15). One is that freedom in this sense presupposes the inherent ability, external impediments permitting, to act in the relevant manner. He argues for this point by explicit analogy with natural things: "when the impediment of motion is in the constitution of the thing itself, we use not to say it wants the liberty, but the power to move" (L 21.1). That an agent is said to be free or unfree to do something presupposes an ability to do it, then, and if this ability is lacking then the question of freedom simply does not arise (Skinner 2002, 215). It will not be the case that the agent is free, and it will not be the case that the agent is unfree. We might say that the agent will be nonfree: not available for being described in this sense as free or unfree.

A second point that Hobbes's natural analogy supports is perhaps counterintuitive. If the water in his example had no disposition to spread itself, then the banks described are no impediment to it; "that which is not subject to motion is not subject to impediment" (L 21.2). In an inescapable analogy, Hobbes wants to say that if an external impediment is to take away an agent's freedom as nonobstruction, then the agent must already be disposed to act in the manner obstructed, having already made a decision on what to do. The agent confronts a "stop, in doing what he has the will, desire, or inclination to do." I am not deprived of my freedom as nonobstruction, then, by obstacles to options I might come to will, only by obstacles to my actual will. If I choose to do A and there are no obstacles to my doing so, for instance, then I will be free in doing A—even if there are obstacles to every alternative.[13]

The third point that the analogy with natural things supports is that freedom as nonobstruction can only be removed by physical obstacles—including, no doubt, the obstacles deployed in forcing the agent, against their will, to take a particular course of action or inaction (Skinner 2002, 213). Freedom as nonobstruction is not lost as a result of psychological states such as fear or duress, or the coercive threats that rouse fear or distress. "Fear and liberty are consistent: as when a man throweth his goods into the sea for fear the ship should sink, he doth it nevertheless very willingly, and may refuse to do it if he will" (L 21.3). The physical obstacles that remove freedom will do so by rendering it impossible to enact one's choices.[14]

Hobbes sums up his view of freedom as nonobstruction in his famous definition of a free-man. This is found only in *Leviathan*, and while contractual freedom is emphasized elsewhere in that work, the definition clearly puts corporal freedom center stage: "a free-man is he that in those things which by his strength and wit he is able to do is not hindered to do what he has a will to" (L 21.2).[15] The three points signaled are all encoded in this definition. Freedom or unfreedom is predicated only of the agent who is able to do the action in question; that agent has the "strength and wit" required. Freedom or unfreedom is predicated only of the agent who has decided on a certain action; that agent "has a will to" perform it. And whether the agent is free or unfree turns simply on whether he is "hindered" or obstructed in the attempt to perform it; psychological inhibition, such as that which danger or threat induces, does not count.

This account of things makes it relatively easy to have freedom of action, freedom as corporal nonobstruction. Such freedom is distinct from ability, though it can only be predicated of people with the relevant ability to act. It does not require an absence of obstruction to any of the things one might decide to do, only to that which one has actually decided to do. And it is not compromised by threat or coercion, fear or inhibition. Freedom of action is taken away only when the option affected is rendered impossible; it is not affected in any way by the fact that the option is made difficult, dangerous, or unappetizing.

Hobbes's picture of freedom, unfreedom, and what I have called nonfreedom can be summed up in this list of scenarios, with their implications for freedom.

1. A cannot and wills not X; can but wills not Y; can and wills Z
   $\longrightarrow$ A is "nonfree" to X and to Y; freedom is at issue only with Z
2. A is obstructed in doing Z
   $\longrightarrow$ A is corporally unfree to Z
3. A is not obstructed in doing Z, though is perhaps threatened and penalized
   $\longrightarrow$ A is free to Z
4. A is not obligated not to Z
   $\longrightarrow$ A is contractually as well as corporally free to Z
5. A is obligated not to do Z
   $\longrightarrow$ A is corporally but not contractually free to Z

We saw earlier that contractual freedom is severely reduced in the commonwealth insofar as every subject is bound by the implicit social contract to accept whatever the sovereign declares to be law and obey it. How is corporal freedom affected? Given that it is so easily enjoyed, Hobbes's answer, unsurprisingly, is that for those who obey the law and avoid punishment it is hardly affected at all. Let people not be able to do something, or not actually have decided on doing it, and the question of their freedom of action will not even arise. If it does arise then, notwithstanding the inhibition induced by the threat of sanction, a person will be corporally free to do it, whether or not it is contrary to law and obligation. As Hobbes says, "If we take liberty in the proper sense, for corporal liberty; that is to say, freedom from chains, and prison, it were very absurd for men to clamour as they do, for the liberty they so manifestly enjoy" (L 21.6).

Hobbes's line on freedom within the commonwealth should now be crystallizing. People under the commonwealth are deprived of their freedom as contractual nonobligation, their freedom of decision, insofar as they are already contractually committed to obey whatever laws are enacted. But this unfreedom is perfectly consistent with their enjoying full corporal freedom, freedom in the sense of nonobstruction—that is, freedom "in the proper sense," freedom in the sense associated in *Leviathan* with being "a free-man." In any case, as he observes in a number of places, the loss to their freedom of decision need not be extensive. As subjects they will retain liberty in this dimension—they will enjoy "the liberty of subjects" (L 21.6; DCv 13.15)—as long as the law does not cover every choice they face, only a subset of them. They will enjoy freedom as contractual nonobligation "in the silence of the law" (L 21.18). This sort of liberty is significant, Hobbes suggests, since "the things that are neither commanded nor forbidden must be almost infinite; and each man can do them or not at his own discretion" (DCv 13.15).

There is no doubt that Hobbes is trying here to sugar the pill. For though he insists on these grounds that the subjects of the commonwealth can have unbounded corporal freedom and a high degree of contractual freedom, the sort of freedom countenanced is a variety that he thinks slaves may also enjoy. When he distinguishes the two sorts of slavery, he claims that the slave in verbal bonds is just as much the property of the master as the slave in natural bonds. A master, he asserts, has "no less right over those, whose bodies he leaveth at liberty, than over those he keepeth in bonds and imprisonment; and hath absolute dominion over both" (EL 22.4). The lesson is that however far the sovereign leaves them physically unrestrained, and whatever range of discretion the law accords them, the subjects in a commonwealth are still nothing more than the slaves or servants of the sovereign. The "absolute power" of a monarchical sovereign means, as Hobbes puts it in the words of Scripture, that they "shall be his servants" (L 20.16). Those who live under a commonwealth may be free-men in the sense of Hobbes's definition—retaining corporal freedom—but they are not free-men in the intuitive sense of not being anyone's servant or subject.

It is not surprising, in view of this, that Hobbes's line did little to assuage his republican opponents. They would have seen the properly constituted, republican commonwealth as a power that gave people freedom under the nonarbitrary protection of the law: under a form of protection dictated by the interests that citizens are disposed to avow in common (Pettit 2007a). But they would have seen the commonwealth of Hobbes's absolute sovereign as a regime in which the law fails to give anyone such freedom as nondomination in relation to the sovereign. After all, Hobbes's sovereign is not bound to act on any particular matter in the perceived interests of the subjects; sovereignty permits quite arbitrary behavior. Hobbes freely admitted the point, saying of the subjects of a commonwealth that "they are governed, not as every one of them would himself, but as the public representant, be it one man, or an assembly of men thinks fit; that is, by an arbitrary government" (L 46.35). By its very nature, a commonwealth, whether it is monarchical, aristocratic, or democratic, ensures that people are made servants of the sovereign's will and law (B 157).

The most prominent, distinctively republican reaction to Hobbes came in James Harrington's *Oceana*, published a few years after *Leviathan*. Harrington (1992, 20) argued that failing to appreciate the value of freedom under a nonarbitrary law—freedom "by the law"— Hobbes had confused it with the freedom that people may have "from the law": the freedom they may have in the silence of law; thus he was guilty of "a little equivocation." For Harrington, as for all his republican compatriots, freedom was the status that people enjoyed under the protection of a nonarbitrary law. It was not something essentially compromised by law.[16]

The shift that Hobbes consciously made in his thinking about liberty looks, in retrospect, to have been a rigged job. He did not give any credence to the received notion of the free citizen: the person protected with and against others, under a republic of nonarbitrary law. Rather he took the word "freedom" and, sensitive to the demands of his political ontology, gave it a content that would allow the best possible gloss on the absolutist regime he recommended. The free person ceases to be someone with a secure status in relation to power—no one has such a standing before the sovereign—and is recast, in the words from *Leviathan*, as the person who happens not to be obstructed in the pursuit of those things "he has a will to" do among actions that by "his wit and strength he is able to do."

People can no longer be said to be free, then, as a matter of their personal standing. It is actions that are free or unfree in the first place, and persons, no matter how subjected, are said to be free just so far as their actions happen not to be obstructed (Pettit 2007e). Freedom in this very thin sense—freedom, as Hobbes would have it, in the "proper and generally received meaning" (L 21.2)—is consistent with the legal sanctions imposed by an arbitrary sovereign, since they do not make action impossible, just more difficult or demanding. Such sanctions affect freedom only in the secondary, contractual sense, and then only indirectly: only when they are signs of ways in which subjects are obligated under the social contract.

Few if any contemporaries or immediate successors followed Hobbes in the shift from identifying freedom with the protected standing of a republican citizen to casting it as a property of those actions that happen not to be impeded, and to allow for the second sense of freedom, that happen not to be sanctioned and forbidden.[17] This shift proved to be of immense importance, however, in the later development of political theory. From the end of the eighteenth century, freedom came to be cast as a property of actions in the first place, not persons, and more specifically, as the property of not being interfered with intentionally by others—not being blocked by their stops or burdened by their sanctions (Pettit 1997, chapter 1). This twist, most prominent in the work of early utilitarians like Jeremy Bentham (1843) and William Paley (1825), shaped our contemporary understanding of freedom, transmitting Hobbes's influence right down to the present day. It is ironic that the notion of freedom deployed in most contemporary liberal circles is one that was shaped in the first place by the most prominent of all absolutist thinkers.

Summary

THE ITINERARY WE HAVE FOLLOWED in tracking Hobbes's ideas is built around some clear landmarks. The theory of the natural mind marks out Hobbes as a convert to the new science who thinks that the motions of matter found in human and nonhuman animals give rise to a passive, particularistic sort of mentality. But what of the complex mentality that distinguishes human beings, giving them a capacity for active, general thought? Where Descartes thinks that this is the only sort of mentality, and that it is due to the presence of a nonmaterial *res cogitans*—a thinking thing—Hobbes's theory of the transformative invention of language offers a materialistic explanation of how it emerges. But the invention-of-language hypothesis does more than vindicate Hobbes's materialism in relation to the dualism of his great, French contemporary. It also provides the basis for a general account of human psychology and an argument, derived from that account, for an absolutist politics.

According to the psychology that the hypothesis supports, there are three great capacities that the invention of language has elicited in human beings and one pathology to which it has subjected them. The first capacity is their ability to reason on the basis of the meanings of words to the connections that must obtain among the realities that the words denote. The second is their ability to personate, dealing with one another as spokespersons for themselves, and establishing thereby a novel network of contract and obligation. And the third is the ability to incorporate, rallying individually behind the words of a collective spokesperson—this may be an individual or a group—and contracting to behave as the words of that spokesperson require.

The pathology to which language has subjected human beings is as dark in its implications, however, as the capacities are bright. With words available, human beings become able to reason about the future and invest their desires in the future. And with words available, they become able to compare themselves with others and invest their desires in having greater power than others. Unlike other animals, they become essentially antagonistic in their relations to one another, living as much for the future as for the present and living in permanent anxiety about their long-term security. They get locked into a zero-sum game where no one gains without another losing.

The scene is set at this point for Hobbes's politics. The structure of desires, once warped by words, makes for the predicament that he describes as the state of nature. And from this predicament, according to the Hobbesian logic, there is no exit on the basis of individual reasoning or regular, provisoed contract. Fully rational parties, aware in common of their rationality, might achieve such a solution, but ordinary people cannot. The problem is that ordinary people are not reliably rational, and that even rational individuals must lack assurance, therefore, that others will behave as reason or contract requires—in particular, that they will renounce the search for superiority.

The only solution for this predicament, as Hobbes trumpets, is to have a special, Draconian form of contract that establishes an absolute sovereign: an individual or group with unprovisoed rights over others. Under this solution, individuals become a unity, incorporating as a commonwealth behind the authorized words of the sovereign. That sovereign will have absolute rights in the large domain where subjects are able to cede their rights—that is, in any area where their lives are not thereby put at greater risk—but will not be motivated to harm others unnecessarily, since that would justify and perhaps prompt rebellion. The sovereign will ensure the peace and prosperity of all, giving common, binding meanings to words like *mine* and *thine*, *just* and *unjust*, and enabling people to speak credibly for themselves in personating and incorporating on the private front; the credibility will derive from acceptance of the sanction that the sovereign can impose on nonperformance. Yet in doing all of this, the sovereign need not greatly reduce people's liberty, in Hobbes's novel sense of that term. People may be contractually unfree to break the law, but the law will often be silent. People may be corporally unfree to avoid the legal sanctions imposed on them, but those sanctions will only fall on the disobedient.

So much for the landmarks on the itinerary we have pursued. Since it may also be useful to have a reference list for the more detailed points argued in the text, I offer the following summary of the main claims made.

CHAPTER ONE: MIND IN NATURE

1. The medieval picture of the natural universe suggested that the senses faithfully reproduce the accidental properties of things—including, for example, their texture, color, and sound—and that the intellect faithfully reproduces the universal natures that different classes of things supposedly share—their essences as instances of this or that type or kind.

2. This picture was rejected by those like Hobbes who learned from the new sciences that the earth moves and the world in itself is not as it seems to be, either to the senses or the intellect. For Hobbes the world in itself is just matter in motion, devoid of texture, color, or sound, with matter parceled out in particular bodies that lack any universal nature.

3. The natural mind of beasts and humans, according to Hobbes, is just a formation in matter, not anything nonmaterial of the kind envisaged by his contemporary, Descartes. Hobbes gave a speculative account of how the mind that beasts and humans share is constituted out of matter, distinguishing between its cognitive and motive abilities. Its activity involves nothing more than the internal motions of matter.

4. Bodies in the world give rise to such internal motions in the mind, and these are the building blocks of cognitive competence. They constitute perceptions, memories, or imaginings, depending first on whether they are subject to the control of external bodies, and second on whether the controlling bodies are currently encountered or were encountered in the past. Such conceptions, as Hobbes also calls them, may be more or less organized in the way they materialize, whether at a time or in temporal succession. Cognitive competence or prudence consists in reliable expectation, and develops naturally in humans and animals as experience accumulates.

5. These same internal motions are the stuff of motivation as well as cognition. They move to the heart, and depending on whether they help or hinder the flow of blood, they give pleasure or pain. Learning about what gives pleasure and pain, beasts and humans form appetites or passions, and these combine with their cognitions, opinions, or beliefs to guide them in animal motion—that is, intentional action. The process in which they form their last appetite or will about what to do is called deliberation, and what is done is the issue of will and therefore counts as voluntary, no matter what the appetites involved—no matter, for example, whether the action is done out of fear.

6. By contrast with this more or less speculative account of the natural mind, Hobbes believes that science can give us a firmer, a priori account of the natural, geometrically figured bodies that we can construct with a compass and the social, conventionally structured bodies that we have to create in setting up commonwealths. In each case, we can have a maker's knowledge of the phenomena. His civil science is devoted to an investigation of how meanings and morals, sovereigns and states, are and can be constructed among human beings, and thus how they are best defined and understood.

7. Appendix. Hobbes's use of the word *cause* encompasses both the components of phenomena and the antecedent events that trigger

phenomena: the events we would normally describe as causes. This is important to understanding his discussion of the causes whereby phenomena like circles and commonwealths are generated; he does not mean to discuss causes in the contemporary sense of antecedents.

CHAPTER TWO: MINDS WITH WORDS

1. Hobbes presents the natural mind that is common to beasts and humans as limited in two ways. First, it only represents the world in a wholly particularistic, body-by-body way; it does not abstract or generalize. And second, it only develops its beliefs and forms its desires in an unregulated, nonintentional manner; those internal motions come and go without any intentional, desire-driven control. But the human mind transcends both limitations, being capable of classificatory and intentionally directed thought.

2. Where Descartes explains this human capacity by positing a non-material mind of divine origin, Hobbes puts forward a dramatically different and entirely original view. He argues that the capacity for active, general thought derives from the invention of words. This culturally transmitted invention, sourced in our somewhat greater curiosity, transforms the natural mind and marks off human beings from beasts.

3. This theory was first put forward by Hobbes in 1640 and must have been consciously aimed at Descartes, who had maintained in 1637 that the ability to speak is a sure sign of the presence of a special, nonmaterial human mind. In holding that speech was the source of what made the human mind special, not just a sign of that special character, Hobbes rejected the Cartesian view. Indeed, he also rejected the closely related views that had been part of the long tradition of Western philosophy. He struck a decidedly novel, iconoclastic note.

4. How does language make it possible for human beings to think in a general, classificatory way? The learning of common names, itself a process that materializes on the basis of subliminal sensitivity to similarities and differences between things, enables people to think of a single object under different names, each associated with a different conception, and to think of different objects under the same name and the same conception. It enables them to focus not on this or that particular triangle, for example, but on triangles as such, and develop a body of knowledge about them.

5. How does language make it possible for human beings to think in an active way—to think in an intentional manner, directed by a desire for truth? Language is designed to serve communication, for which purpose names are put together in affirmation and negation, for instance.

Thinking actively is just pursuing this sort of activity in the internal forum; it means raising various questions with oneself and rehearsing the answers that are found compelling.

6. Language operates with common meanings. These are available because of the similarity of constitution among human beings, particularly their similarity in classificatory dispositions, and they are established by the implicit agreement of speakers among themselves.

CHAPTER THREE: USING WORDS TO RATIOCINATE

1. Reason is the ability to think inferentially about what follows from what and it is made possible by language. It consists in working out the relations between the classes denoted by various words, trying to determine, for example, whether one named class plus another, or minus another, makes a third named class. It is an exercise in something like addition and subtraction.

2. This model demystifies reasoning, making it look like humdrum reckoning with counters; it connects reasoning with science, as that is exemplified in mathematical calculation; and it emphasizes the fact that reason is a skill that is learned on the basis of language, not an innate faculty that comes on stream, ready-made, at a certain point of development. It may presuppose a basic, perhaps distinctively human computational ability, and Hobbes may have been original in supporting a computational model. But a computational ability does not ensure a capacity to reason any more than a musical sensitivity ensures a capacity to play the piano; such skills require a cultural practice and individual training.

3. Reasoning proceeds reliably only when certain conditions are satisfied. The words employed must be given constant meanings, starting from strict definition; they must be used coherently, with words being joined in affirmation or negation only when the kinds of thing they denote can go together in a corresponding way; and the process of explicating the connections between the denoted classes must be conducted with care.

4. In order to guard against the abuse of reason, it is necessary to take particular care about avoiding incoherence and inconstancy. Incoherence springs from the thoughtless parroting of words that is typical of scholastic philosophy and avoiding it requires attention to what one's words mean. Inconstancy is sourced in a lack of definition and overcoming it requires the use of strict, scientific method: words have to be precisely defined, and then deductions made on the basis of their precise meanings.

5. The avoidance of inconstancy requires particular attention to the dangers of metaphor, rhetorical redescription, and the indexical character of evaluative words: the character exemplified in my using *good* of what appeals to me, and your using it of what appeals to you. The only remedy, again, is strict method and definition. In the case of indexicality, this will require setting up a neutral arbiter to define problematic terms.

6. Although strict definition is presented as a requirement of science, it is often used by Hobbes with the same effect as rhetorical, self-serving redescription. As his opponents frequently complained, he routinely defines words with substantial adjustment to their common meanings—against his own strictures—and in a way that serves his polemical purposes.

CHAPTER FOUR: USING WORDS TO PERSONATE

1. The concept of a person is a role concept in Hobbes's work, not the concept of a metaphysical kind of entity. To be a natural person is not to be an agent who is necessarily constituted in any particular way but rather to be an agent who can perform in a certain manner. It is to be able to communicate one's attitudes intentionally, when the communicative words or actions can be "considered as one's own" by others.

2. One's words or actions can be considered as one's own insofar as one can be taken, as a matter of common awareness, to authorize them as tokens of one's mind. One will authorize them in the sense of providing a guarantee that they are appropriate tokens: they are rightly used in making up one's mind—in forming one's judgment or will—and manifesting that mind to others.

3. Authorizing one's words and actions in that sense means representing oneself to others as a spokesperson for oneself, not as someone with the inside knowledge of a good reporter. Hobbes describes the activity as personating oneself: identifying a *persona* or system of attitudes, and vouching for it as one's own.

4. Personation, like reasoning, is a skill that human beings develop only by virtue of being able to speak; it involves the capacity to give one's word and stick to it. Where nonhuman animals can only interact on the basis of a passive knowledge of one another's dispositions, human beings can interact on the basis of a form of knowledge that has the authorization of those known. This capacity makes community possible.

5. Why expect people to be faithful to their authorized words and actions? They will have reason to be faithful to self-representations that

they have not withdrawn because infidelity would amount to incoherence. To hold by a certain account of one's will or judgment and not to display that will or judgment in action would be to show oneself to be absurd, and hence expose oneself to being reduced to absurdity.

6. Why expect people not just to be faithful to unwithdrawn words but not to withdraw those words that they give in making promises and contracts? Despite the fact that everyone must will their own good, people will each have a rational motive to conform to any contracts rationally made, at least when there have been no unforeseen developments; conformity promises far more benefits than defection, especially given that defection will usually be detectable. But the parties to any contract need to be assured that others will prove to be contractually rational—human beings are subject to weakness of mind and soul—and this condition can only be met when there is a system of sanctions, feared penalties, in place.

7. This account of contract means that a contract formed under conditions of duress, pressure, or coercion may still be valid and binding. Thus, the slave who is bound by words rather than chains is contractually obligated to the master, and so are the vanquished who submit to the conqueror. The fact that the contract was entered out of fear does not make it involuntary, for the reasons we saw earlier, and so it does not remove the obligation to conform to the contractual terms.

CHAPTER FIVE: USING WORDS TO INCORPORATE

1. The self-representation or self-personation of the natural person is paired nicely, in Hobbes's theory, with the possibility of representing or personating something other than oneself. One may personate other individuals, if they authorize one to do so; one may personate inanimate objects, if the owners authorize one to do so; and one may personate a multitude of individuals, if the members individually authorize one to personate them as a whole.

2. When a multitude is represented or personated by a single individual, then that spokesperson or personator speaks and acts for it—or directs what is said and done in its name—so that it ceases to be many and becomes one. Its unity derives from the unity of the representer, and the appearance of that unity transforms the multitude, giving it a new character as a personatee—a passive, corporate person—that is bound, on the basis of member authorization, by whatever is said or done in its name.

3. The incorporation of individuals may give rise to a private or public corporate body. With the private body, such as a company of

merchants, the personator is given only limited authority, being licensed to speak or act for the group on just a certain range of matters. The personator of the public group person is given unlimited authority, up to the point where people's lives are jeopardized and they are not able in rational self-concern—not able under what Hobbes sees as natural law—to accept that jeopardy. Private corporate bodies only form in any abundance when there is a public corporate body available to regulate them.

4. The public corporate body is the commonwealth or people, and the personator is the sovereign. The commonwealth may come into existence in either of two broad ways. The members of the multitude may contract with one another to recognize a sovereign, so that the commonwealth is established by institution. Or they may individually contract to accept a would-be sovereign—say, a conqueror—as sovereign, provided others do so; here, the commonwealth is established not by institution but by the private acquisition of public power.

5. The personation of a multitude may be enacted by a group or committee, not just by an individual, natural person. And that personating group, whether in a private company or the commonwealth, may be a subcommittee or a committee of the whole. This means that groups may actively form as personators without themselves being passively personated by some individual. Hobbes does not emphasize the difference between the active and passive corporate body, perhaps because doing so would sharpen the contrast between the active personation associated with democracy—here, the multitude rule as a committee of the whole—and the passive personation achieved in his preferred, monarchical form of government.

6. Appendix. Hobbes thinks that the active group can form its will and judgment about different questions, on the basis of majority rule. But this is a mistake. As recent results demonstrate, individually consistent voters may generate inconsistent group judgments under a range of voting systems. Neither majority rule nor any plausible variation on it can serve as a reliable recipe for the creation of a suitably rational group person.

CHAPTER SIX: WORDS AND THE WARPING OF APPETITE

1. The three benefits conferred by the invention of speech—the ability to reason, personate, and incorporate—are offset by a disadvantage that it also imposes. This appears in the effect on people's desires of having words available. Speech enables people to express their desires, leading to difficulties in reaching reasoned agreement. But much more

drastically, it expands the range of human desires, pitting people against one another in inextricable conflict.

2. Desires are expressed, as we saw, in indexical words like *good* and *bad*, which are used to name what is found attractive or aversive. While those words invite people to reason about what to do, they introduce equivocation and controversy insofar as people differ across time and among themselves in what appeals to or repels them. The solution to intertemporal inconstancy is to privilege what is good from the point of view of the agent across time—by this test, for example, self-preservation is really good. The solution to interpersonal inconstancy is to privilege what is good from the point of view of a neutral arbitrator. But neither solution is easily implemented.

3. The desires or appetites of the natural mind, which are shared among beasts and humans, have two characteristics. First, they are focused more or less exclusively on the present or immediate future. And second, they concern only the private welfare of the subject, not how that subject fares in relation to others. The effect of speech is to expand human desires beyond the present and the private, with dire results.

4. Speech gives people the ability to reason about what the current state of things indicates for how things will be in the future, even the far future. This means that people can form desires about things that in the far future and can be moved in anxiety for that future to take precautionary action against various dangers. It primes them to worry about the range of future possibilities.

5. Speech also gives people the ability to compare the resources of desire satisfaction at their disposal and those available to others. Thus, since they will be competing with others in seeking to satisfy their desires, it prompts them to worry about their position relative to others. This leads them to seek greater power than others; honor, which is the recognition of that greater power; and glory, which is the satisfaction of having such power and honor.

6. The pursuit of such positional goods, combined with an anxiety over the possession of those goods into the far future, means that human beings become locked into a pattern of inevitable conflict. They are caught in a zero-sum game where no one can win without others losing. Unlike the beasts who fight with one another only when they chance to want the same thing, human beings are caught up in inextricable conflicts. They are not just competitors but enemies.

7. Hobbes ignores the possibility, marked among republican writers in his own time as well as traditionally, that people might be content with enjoying equality with others, and being recognized as equal. He insists that people will strive for superiority, using this as a crucial step in his own argument for absolutism. Yet he never explains why they

should not be content with having manifestly equal status. This is a gaping weakness in his argument, as suggested in the introduction.

CHAPTER SEVEN: THE STATE OF SECOND, WORDED NATURE

1. The disorder of human desires means that without suitable arrangements for peace, human beings will exist in a permanent state of mutual hostility. This is what Hobbes calls the state of nature. It is a state of second nature because it presupposes the impact of words on minds, not the state of first nature, prior to the invention of speech. The state of first nature would not have held out possibilities of reasoning, personating, and incorporating but it would have been decidedly more tranquil, with human desires having the less conflictual cast exemplified by the passions of beasts.

2. There is no noncontractual way out of the predicament represented by the state of nature—that is, the state of second nature. No one person will be powerful enough to be able to impose a unilateral equilibrium of peace. And people in general will not be rational enough to accept the fact of equality and acquiesce in a multilateral equilibrium. There will always be some who are vain enough—weak of mind enough—to believe that they can make themselves superior, and this will mean that no one can afford to be complacent about the intentions of others.

3. Neither is there a regular, contractual way out of the predicament. The indexicality of values means that there is no common normative currency that people might invoke in agreeing on an alternative to the state of nature. And while the requirements of the natural law—imperatives of self-concern and self-preservation—might argue for seizing on any contract that is capable of achieving the peace, no one will have the assurance about the intentions of others that is required for them to be able validly to enter such a contract. The required contractual assurance, as we saw, is only going to be available if those who would otherwise be irrational enough to defect—moved as they may be by weakness or vanity—can be manifestly exposed to inhibiting sanctions. The state of nature is not going to have any arrangement in place for imposing such sanctions.

4. But there is a third, more political way out of the state of nature; indeed, this is the only form of exit that Hobbes contemplates. Given the difficulty of having sanctions available to impose on defectors, people must make the sort of contract that will not only open the way toward peace but also set up an agent that is powerful enough to be able to punish defection. The contract required is the sort that would set up a

sovereign to personate the multitude as a whole, giving that sovereign unlimited power to punish potential defectors; the power will have to be unlimited since there will be no one able to impose a limitation. This power will derive from the ability of the sovereign, under the terms of the contract, to use the power of the compliant majority against any defectors.

5. But won't the sovereign, thereby empowered, be free to act on whim? In theory, yes; in practice, no. The sovereign will have reason in self-interest to punish any defection from the contract that establishes sovereign power. The sovereign also will have the same sort of reason, though perhaps not a reason of the same salience, to issue and enforce laws that make peace possible among the subjects of the commonwealth. Otherwise those subjects might withdraw their allegiance in sufficient numbers to undermine the sovereign's power. In short, there is going to be an identity or at least a substantial convergence of interest between sovereign and subjects. Hobbes thinks that this convergence is particularly marked when the sovereign is a single individual, and that is one reason why he favors a monarchical regime.

6. Appendix. Hobbes's state of nature is often represented as a game-theoretical predicament. But the predicament involved, contrary to a number of interpretations, is not a prisoner's dilemma, in which the problem is that participants have a rational motive to defect on one another. It is rather the stag-hunt predicament, in which the problem is one of achieving assurance about the rationality of others.

Chapter Eight: The Commonwealth of Ordered Words

1. The creation of a commonwealth by institution, like the drawing of a circle by means of a compass, is a canonical mode of generation on the basis of which we can properly understand what a commonwealth is. What emerges is that the commonwealth is a voluntary incorporation of subjects under the personation of the sovereign, with the sovereign having more or less unlimited authority to speak and act for the whole. In particular, it is the sort of incorporation whereby society is made possible among agents who, by virtue of their linguistically disordered desires, are incapable of otherwise living at peace with one another. This story is meant to explain the indivisibility of sovereign authority, its basis, its extent, the variety of its exercise, and its significance for people's liberty.

2. The authority of the sovereign is indivisible or one, since the person of the people or commonwealth will only have unity if it is represented by a single voice. This means, as Hobbes sees things, that the republican

idea of mixed government is confused, reflecting a failure to understand what a commonwealth is. And it means that any proposal to give independent authority to a pope, a minister, or even conscience is also deeply mistaken; it will undermine the status that the sovereign is required to have if the people are to have the unity of a group person.

3. The basis for political authority in this story is the fact that implicitly or explicitly, the subjects of any commonwealth will always have voluntarily acquiesced in an arrangement for their representation as a whole by the sovereign. The voluntariness and validity of this agreement or contract will not be compromised by its having been elicited by fear. And it is their agreement that obliges subjects to obey, not the sanctions attendant on defecting from the agreement; these serve only to regulate people's performance and provide an assurance to each that others will play their part too. This novel account of the basis of authority is an alternative to the royalist theory of divine right as well as the monarchomachian theory that authority rests in a contract between the sovereign and the people as a whole; the people as a whole cannot have made a contract with the sovereign since they do not exist as a whole until they are personated by the sovereign.

4. The authority of the sovereign under this account is of more or less unlimited extent. It is bounded only by those limits that people, under the natural law of self-concern and self-preservation, cannot have contracted away; people, for example, cannot have contracted not to resist the sovereign's decision to kill them. The sovereign's authority has to be unlimited in this way, according to Hobbes, because of the requirements for the validity of the founding contract. In the state of nature, people can validly contract to incorporate under a sovereign only when they can be sure that the sovereign thereby recognized will have the power and inclination to punish any defection from that contract. But this condition means that the contract cannot contain any clauses that limit the sovereign, since there will be no one to enforce those limits. The only valid contract whereby people might escape the state of nature will give the sovereign—the monarchical, aristocratic, or democratic sovereign—more or less unlimited authority.

5. Sovereignty is paradigmatically exercised in legislation, with the sovereign being free to create whatever laws appeal and enjoying full immunity from the constraints that the laws impose. There are two aspects to this exercise: one constitutive, and the other regulative. The sovereign uses the law to establish constitutive rules that determine the meanings of *just* and *unjust*, *mine* and *yours*, thereby enabling subjects to reason unequivocally and profitably about what should or should not obtain in relevant areas. But equally, the sovereign uses the law to establish regulative rules that impose sanctions on the breach of private

contracts, making it possible for subjects to give their words to one another and make them stick. The rule of the sovereign delivers people
out of the wasteland in which words have restricted ratiocinative
power, on the one hand, and little or no power of personation or incorporation, on the other.

6. What of the liberty of subjects under the commonwealth? Hobbes
distinguishes between the liberty to make decisions for or against an
option, which is removed by contractual obligation, and the liberty to
enact a decision made, which is removed by corporal obstruction. Contractual obligation reduces people's freedom of decision in the commonwealth, but only up to the point where the laws speak; where the
laws are silent, this freedom remains intact. And corporal obstruction
need not be any more conspicuously present within the commonwealth
than without; on the contrary, the sovereign's law will presumably inhibit others from imposing such obstruction on a person. Hence the
commonwealth, as envisaged by Hobbes, is supposed to make room
for considerable liberty among the subjects. Rejecting the republican
notion that freedom requires not having a master in one's life, his
analysis is supposed to reconcile us to the rule of an absolute sovereign;
under the republican approach, the rule of such a sovereign would represent the antithesis of a free state.

Notes

INTRODUCTION

1. I am not the first to notice Hobbes's view that human thought is shaped by language. As Yves Charles Zarka (1995, 20) paraphrases the Hobbesian position, for example: "l'homme n'est pas simplement un etre qui parle, c'est un etre qui devient ce qu'il est par la parole." But while others have emphasized this component in Hobbes's views, I don't find any who give it the degree or kind of significance, historical or philosophical, that I propose in this book. Many writers have focused on the importance of the linguistic turn in Hobbes's general philosophy, without particularly emphasizing the way he thinks that language shapes thought. See, for example, Watkins 1973, chapter 8; Whelan 1981; Ball 1994, chapter 4. The theory of language and mind, I suspect, is of great importance to understanding not just Hobbes's political philosophy but also the theories of many other classical authors. The point is routinely made about Jean-Jacques Rousseau, but surely it applies more widely. For a discussion of John Locke on language, for instance, and the connections with his political philosophy, see Dawson 2005.

2. Sometimes it is linked with the suggestion that once language was in place, it would have created a natural as distinct from a cultural selection pressure in favor of brain changes that facilitated linguistic performance. See Deacon 1997. The core Hobbesian claim can be reconciled with a variety of such elaborations about the role of natural selection in improving people's capacity to make use of their cultural creation.

3. The full quotation from act 2, scene 1, is: "He gave man speech and speech created thought, Which is the measure of the universe." The second, characteristically romantic line would have been deeply anathema to Hobbes. Despite his nominalism, as I argue in chapter 1, he clearly believed that the world dictated to the mind, not the mind to the world.

4. Hobbes's detailed philosophy of language and logic is also of historical interest and influence, but does not have the same contemporary relevance. For a range of studies, see Martin 1953; Toernebohm 1960; Hungerland and Vick 1981; de Jong 1990; Soles 1996.

CHAPTER ONE

1. Richard Tuck (1988a) argues that the acceptance of a disjuncture between appearance and reality—rather, for example, than a belief in a mechanistic explanation—was the hallmark of the new philosophy.

2. Occupying space, by Hobbes's account, comes down to nothing more than "existing without the mind" (DCr 7.2), so that on this definition there cannot be

anything mind-independent that does not count as matter; "that which is not body, is no part of the universe" (L 46.15). Although this materialism would seem to entail atheism, Hobbes is always careful to guard himself against such a charge, not least because he wants to argue in religious terms for the political vision he defends. And so, following this assertion of materialism, he adds, "Nor does it follow from hence, that spirits are *nothing*: for they have dimensions, and are therefore really *bodies*; though that name in common speech be given to such bodies only, as are visible, or palpable; that is, that have some degree of opacity" (L 46.15).

3. He takes the reduction of all change to motion to be obvious to anyone bent on discovering truth who is not "corrupted with former opinions"—with the opinions of the Aristotelians and scholastics (DCr 6.5). The argument he offers for the reduction is that we predicate change only on the basis of a difference between how something now appears to sense and how it appeared previously; that this difference means there must be a change in the causation of appearance, given that like causes bring about like effects; and that this causal difference can only "consist in the motion of the parts, either of the body which is perceived, or of the sentient body, or of both" (DCr 9.9).

4. Richard Rorty (1980) is wrong, I believe, to suggest that contemporary philosophy is almost entirely focused on the epistemological predicament that emerged in this period. I think it has been just as robustly focused on the naturalistic predicament; see Pettit 2004. For a contrasting perspective on the assessment of this aspect of Hobbes's work, see Sorell 1986. To a contemporary eye, one of the surprising aspects of Hobbes's response to the naturalistic predicament is that he gave no attention whatsoever to consciousness—to the fact that there is something it is like, for example, to perceive things.

5. This interaction will yield a sensitivity to the similarity or difference between the bodies as a by-product of the process, but despite the view of scholastics (L 2.9), it will do so without a further judgment or "perception made by a common organ of sense" (DCr 25.8).

6. This anticipates Hume's more famous discussion of how we come to have the concept of cause and effect.

7. See Hobbes's account in *De Cive* (18.4) as to why "2+3=5" is a priori knowable, though he doesn't use that phrase there: "those who made the decision and the rule of language that the number ** is called *Two*, *** *Three*, and **** *Four*, are also responsible for the fact that the proposition, *Two* and *Three* taken together make *Five* is true."

8. Such definitions, unlike the definition of a nonbasic figure like a circle, cannot decompose their target but will highlight connections that "raise in the mind of the hearer perfect and clear ideas or conceptions of the things named" (DCr 6.13).

9. Notice a contrast with the sense in which natural psychology tells us how mental phenomena could have come about: that is, could have come about, for all we know. With a given circle, we may only be able to speculate in the same way that it could have been made by the use of a compass. But we also know in an extra, distinct sense that it could have been made in that way. We know, and know a priori, that it is objectively possible to make a circle with a compass,

whereas we do not know the counterpart claim with a natural psychological phenomenon in the same a priori way. The common possibility claim that we know in each case is this: it is epistemically possible, possible for all we know, that this particular circle or phenomenon came about in such and such a manner. The possibility claim that we know only in the geometric case, and know a priori, is this: it is objectively or ontologically possible to construct a circle in such and such a manner.

10. In this account of how Hobbes sees geometry, I have left it indeterminate whether Hobbes thinks that definitions come first, as if from an exogenous source—say, from ordinary usage—and insight into the a priori connections second; or whether he thinks that as we learn how to make geometric figures reliably, we will introduce definitions of the sort that reflect what we learn and ensure that the connections involved are a priori derivable. See the discussion of common meaning at the end of chapter 2.

11. The notion of a *scientia civilis*, a civil science, had emerged in the previous century, as Daniel Lee has made me aware, and was strongly associated with Hobbes's fellow absolutist Jean Bodin. See Kelley 1976.

CHAPTER TWO

1. Hobbes admits, sincerely or otherwise, that God may have communicated supernaturally with Adam when he gave him his initial instructions, including the direction to name the things around him. But he sets this aside as a special case (DH 10.2). While this discussion in *De Homine* gives us some idea of how Hobbes thought about the beginnings of language, elaborating on the theory set out earlier in *Elements of Law* and *Leviathan*, it bears at the same time on a contemporary but philosophically less interesting issue—one that engaged his friend, Marin Mersenne, for example (Lenoble 1971, 514–17)—as to whether there was an original Adamic language or whether all language is conventional (Aarsleff 1976; Murphy 2005). Hobbes connects with that debate when he denies "that names are imposed on things according to the nature of those things" (DH 10.2). Words might be conventional or arbitrary, as Hobbes argues that they are, without speech being in any sense at the origin of thought. Such conventionalism was adopted by many who would have rejected Hobbes's more radical thesis.

2. He does not say that this passion is also necessary for the mastery of language, though he might be taken to imply that this is so, since he nowhere suggests that animals could be inducted into our language; the parrot remains the exemplar of a mind that uses words without the capacity for thinking that words make possible (EL 6.3). See the discussion in the following chapter of the computational model of mind, to which Hobbes appears to be committed.

3. Hobbes would have been familiar with Epicurean thought through the neo-Epicureanism of his French friend, the priest Pierre Gassendi, and this would certainly have sat easily with his materialism. But it is worth noticing that in the great Epicurean poem by Lucretius (2004, 182–83), the idea of an individual invention of language is positively mocked:

Thus, to think
That in those days some man apportioned round
To things their names, and that from him men learned
Their first nomenclature, is foolery.
For why could he mark everything by words
And utter the various sounds of tongue, what time
The rest may be supposed powerless
To do the same?

4. This is the burden of the scholarly work to which I refer, though some re-
marks by Isocrates certainly suggest that he came close to the Hobbesian view.
He claims to find "that none of the things which are done with intelligence take
place without the help of speech, but that in all our actions as well as in all our
thoughts speech is our guide, and is most employed by those who have the
most wisdom" (Norlin 1961, 81). I am indebted to Victor Casson for directing
me to the classical sources on the issue of thought and language, and to Chris
Karpowicz for helping me to research them.

5. In this respect, he broke not just with the later romantics but with the emphasis in the French Renaissance figure, Michel de Montaigne (1991), on the
variety of human cultures.

6. Unsurprisingly, the account does not address the problems of rule following that became dominant in light of Ludwig Wittgenstein's work. These bear
on how human beings can master rules of thought—say, the rule governing
how a basic predicate is to be used across an indefinite range of cases—and
they are at the center of a contemporary philosophical controversy (Wittgenstein 1958; Kripke 1982; Miller and Wright 2002; Pettit 2002, part 1).

7. Words denote things, in Hobbes's usage, and signify the conceptions that
we form of those things (DCr 2.5), as recent commentators on his philosophy of
language have rightly emphasized (Hungerland and Vick 1981; Soles 1996;
Murphy 2005, chapter 3). But the conceptions signified by general terms may
still be available only by virtue of a mastery of those terms.

8. Rousseau is the one most often associated with the focus on how language is essential to the development of general, classificatory ideas and the
release of human beings from particularistic thinking. But not only does
Hobbes anticipate Rousseau in this matter; he may even be the source of some
of Rousseau's reflections. It is perhaps significant that in making the point
about the necessity of language for abstract thought, Rousseau should have
used Hobbes's core example. "The definition of a triangle alone gives you the
true idea of it. As soon as you behold one in your mind, it is a particular triangle and not some other one, and you cannot avoid making its lines to be per-
ceptible or its plane to have color. It is therefore necessary to utter sentences,
and thus to speak, in order to have general ideas" (Rousseau 1973, Second Discourse, 1.30).

9. A passage in *De Corpore* 1.3 talks of reasoning "in our silent thought, without the use of words," and illustrates what is involved by pointing out that seeing a man at a distance, I may recognize him as just a body, nearer up as an
animate body, and only at some proximity as a human being. It is not clear

whether Hobbes is thinking here of reasoning by a human being capable of using language but not actually using it, or more problematically, of reasoning of a kind that does not presuppose any linguistic capacity. But even in the second case, the passage need not give us difficulty. What Hobbes has in mind would make sense in light of his comment in *Leviathan* 5.5, where he indicates that reckoning "without the use of words" may only "be done in particular things (as when upon the sight of any one thing, we conjecture what was likely to have preceded, or is likely to follow upon it)." Such conjecturing, as Hobbes makes clear, would consist in forming expectations and need only involve the prudence of which any animal is capable; in the example given, it would consist in seeing the body at a distance and, despite not registering anything more particular about it, forming the expectation that it will prove to be a man.

10. Hobbes says in one place that "it is not necessary to dispute whether definitions are to be admitted or no" (DCr 6.15). But what he means, as that context suggests, is that if a student refuses to accept a definition, having been brought to "understand all the parts of the thing defined," then there is no point in debating; it is as if the student "refused to be taught."

11. Hobbes's claim about common meanings may also seem to be at odds with the idea, broached in the discussion of method in the previous chapter, that philosophers and scientists will generally frame their definitions of certain terms, like the geometric term *circle*, so as to fit with the practical knowledge of how to construct the referents of such terms—circles and the like. Perhaps his thought there is that while most ordinary terms will retain in science the meanings that are fixed for them in common usage—or at least in unwarped common usage—there are some limited adjustments that are permissible for the sake of scientific precision and clarity. His complaint against the Oxford professors may be not that they make adjustments but that their adjustments are too widespread or radical to be acceptable.

CHAPTER THREE

1. But only broadly. See Hungerland and Vick 1981; Soles 1996. One important break with Aristotle that Hobbes inaugurates is an understanding of the universal proposition "All As are Bs" in such a way that it does not presuppose the existence of any As; here he anticipates the developments in logic after Gottlob Frege.

2. I was led to appreciate the force of this view by a discussion with Jim Moor.

3. Leibniz was aware of Hobbes's work, expressing enthusiasm in some correspondence from 1670; we do not know whether Hobbes ever received those letters. For an illuminating discussion of Hobbes and Leibniz on these topics, see Hungerland and Vick 1981, 105–26. For evidence of Hobbes's influence on Leibniz's natural philosophy and ultimately on the foundations of calculus, see Jesseph 1998.

4. Here I take a different line from the more theoretical view of reason and natural law that is developed by John Deigh (1996). On that issue I side with

Kinch Hoekstra (2003). One other issue dividing Deigh and Hoekstra is whether the word reason is used unambiguously by Hobbes for an artificial skill, or as Hoekstra maintains, it sometimes refers to a natural faculty. When he speaks of natural reason, Hobbes sometimes means to distinguish "what proceeds from natural reason, what from supernatural inspiration" (DCv 17.14), and in that sense of "natural," reason may still be an artificial skill. But elsewhere he does use "natural reason" to refer to the capacity to learn and master that artificial skill (e.g., EL 1.4, 15.1; L 47.20); this capacity might be equated with the computational capacity discussed in the text.

5. The connection between language and the epistemology of natural law is emphasized strongly among successors of Hobbes in the tradition of modern or Protestant natural law, as it is often called (Tuck 1987; Haakonssen 2004), especially in the work of Samuel Pufendorf (Hochstrasser 2000). Notice that there is also a second important connection between language and natural law that is marked in that tradition, and is crucial to Hobbes. This, as we shall see, is that entering contracts and incurring obligations presuppose access to language, and involves discharging recognizable social roles or offices (Haakonssen 2004, 101).

6. For useful and intriguing discussions of Hobbes's ambivalent and shifting relation to rhetoric, see Johnston 1986; Skinner 1996.

CHAPTER FOUR

1. I reject Jean Hampton's (1986) downplaying of the role of contract in Hobbes's theory; I think it is absolutely at the core of his claims.

2. The standard view is that it was only in medieval times that the notion of a corporate entity, fit to play the role of a legal person, evolved. But Ulrike Malmendier (2005) has recently argued that in republican Rome, commercial corporations were recognized in case law; they were hired to discharge public offices like tax collecting, maintaining public property, and constructing public works.

3. This is the logical order in which to consider the topics, but it raises a difficulty for anyone expounding Hobbes's ideas. The reason is that much of what he has to say about persons is said about artificial persons and the corporate entities they constitute, and in reconstructing his view of natural persons it is necessary to draw on the implications of this commentary. There are three implications that are particularly important to me in my reconstruction of Hobbes's view of natural persons. The first is that natural persons speak for themselves, as we have just seen. The second is that in speaking for themselves, they do more than give an involuntary, evidential sign of their mental states, as simple animals may do—or as they themselves may do in yawning or laughing. And the third is that in speaking for themselves, as authors of their words—and indeed their actions—they authorize those words and invite others to rely on them; that, I take it, is what it means for others to consider the words as theirs. Hobbes does not himself speak of individuals authorizing their own words, only of their authorizing the words of others who speak for them, but his general position seems to me to underwrite this possibility.

4. Not only does the authorization of my words or actions involve me in the role of being a spokesperson for myself, not just a self-reporter. The guarantee provided when I authorize my words or actions is not given on the basis of a reporter's knowledge of the will and judgment I manifest. Rather, it is given on the basis of a maker's knowledge, as we might describe it, of the will and judgment I form—a sort of knowledge to which, as we saw, Hobbes assigns a certain priority. This is the knowledge I have by virtue of being able to make up my own mind appropriately—to form my own will and judgment—and make it the case—say, by efforts of self-regulation—that unless a new consideration appears, the will and judgment formed will remain steadfastly on display. The idea has a certain currency in contemporary philosophy (cf. McGeer 1996; Moran 2001), and it is intriguing to find it already present in Hobbes.

5. Because of the centrality of this theme in Hobbes, I treat him as a psychological egoist. For arguments that he was not an egoist, or at least not a consistent or wholehearted one, see Gert 1967; Kavka 1986; Lloyd 1992.

6. What certainly looks likely to be true is that the expected cost of defecting is high—that is, the cost that would attend defecting times the chance of detection. In particular, the expected cost is likely to be higher than the expected benefit. This is the theme emphasized in the gloss offered by Edwin Curley (1994, xxvii).

7. There is a large literature on why exactly Hobbes thinks of the person who tries to free ride as a fool, and I take a rather brisk line on the issue here, anchoring my interpretation in the claim that such a person "declareth that he may with reason do so" (L 15.5) and agreeing with Kinch Hoekstra (1997) that Hobbes is focused on this sort of case. For an exchange on Hoekstra's line, see Hayes 1999; Hoekstra 1999. For a brief review of other approaches to the problem, see Tuck 1996, 193–95.

8. Thus, Hobbes says, "it is not reasonable that people who are full of good-will to others should be put under an obligation by every promise reflecting their momentary feelings" (DCv 2.8).

9. Notice that Hobbes leaves much implicit. It will not be enough to solve the problem he raises that each is subject to a penalty in the event of defecting from a contract. Each must know that this is true of each, each must know that each knows this, each must know that each knows that each knows this, and so on. In other words, the penalty must hang over defection as a matter of common awareness; there must be nothing hidden about it.

10. We may wonder how it could have been rational, and therefore valid under natural law, for those demanding the ransom to allow the prisoner of war to go free; they would apparently have had no assurance that the person would pay the ransom. Hobbes does not comment on this problem.

11. This should help to explain why for Hobbes, the just person will not only perform the just action—the action that the contract requires (L 15.2)—but will perform it because it is required, not because it is subject to sanction; he will "delight in doing justice" and will do "just things because the law so instructs," whereas the unjust will do them "because of the penalty attached" (DCv 3.5; see also L 15.10; D 72).

CHAPTER FIVE

1. There has been an ongoing debate between Quentin Skinner, David Runciman, and Richard Tuck about the proper interpretation of Hobbes on the matters discussed in this chapter. See Runciman 1997, 2000, 2003, 2006; Tuck 1998, 2006b; Skinner 1999, 2005. The questions that arise in that debate bear on how Hobbes thinks about the people, the person of the people, the state in relation to the people, and the representation of the people—in particular, how he thinks about them in the case of a monarchy as distinct from a democracy. Does the multitude that is personated by a single monarch constitute the people, or is the monarch the people, as Hobbes once suggests (DCv 12.8)? If the multitude is the people in such a case, does it constitute a corporate person, distinct from the person of the monarch? If the people is a corporate person, does it constitute the commonwealth or state? And does the sovereign represent the state or the multitude? The answers for which I argue in the text and notes, based primarily on *Leviathan* and later works, are that the personated multitude does constitute a people; that it is a corporate person, in Hobbes's usage, but only in a passive sense that contrasts with the active sense in which the people is a corporate person under a democratic constitution; that the people qua person just is the commonwealth or state; and that Hobbes is easy about saying either that the state, the people, or the multitude are represented by the sovereign. One background, metaphysical issue to the debate is whether the people has to count as a new entity over and beyond the multitude. I see no problem there. Seen as personated, the multitude merits the new name of "people," and sorted under that name, it deserves to be tracked over time and possibility in a different way from how the multitude is tracked; thus, it may remain the same people while the multitude changes as a result of a change of membership. But I think that even Hobbes, despite his nominalism, can make sense of this metaphysical possibility.

2. As Quentin Skinner (2002, 195n96) notes, Hobbes rewrites one passage on personation in the Latin translation of *Leviathan* as: "Paucae res sunt, quarum non possunt esse personae"; "there are few things of which there cannot be persons." Clearly this means that there are few things that cannot be personated; Skinner's own translation is somewhat misleading on this point, for he renders it as: "there are few things incapable of being persons."

3. In making that remark he refers back to his original discussion of personation in *Leviathan*, chapter 16, although in that chapter the explicit claim is that a person is someone who represents, not someone who is represented (L 16.1). See Martinich 2005, 228.

4. The metaphysics in terms of which transubstantiation is understood involves the Aristotelian idea that matter may assume a new form so that a new entity comes into existence. Despite his rejection of Aristotelianism, I think that Hobbes thinks in quite Aristotelian terms—however unwittingly (Strauss 1952)—when he speaks of how the multitude come to be a people, through being personated. He cannot treat the transformation as a process in which a new entity is created, of course—this would be inconsistent with his nominalism—

but he can treat it as a process in which the multitude are changed so as to deserve to be put in a new class.

5. For a rich account of the ways in which Hobbes's views on the representation of the people go beyond the model of the juridical spokesperson, see Vieira 2005.

6. I benefited from discussion with Brookes Brown on this matter. Not a lot need turn on it, however. Even if the line I take is rejected, and the submission is the same as with a private master, there will be a group formed by virtue of the fact—the presumptively manifest fact—that everyone in the relevant multitude has made such a contract.

7. I side with Kinch Hoekstra and Quentin Skinner, against Richard Tuck, in downplaying Hobbes's commitment to anything that might deserve to be described as democracy. See Hoekstra 2006; Skinner 2006, 271–76; Tuck 2006a.

8. The reasoning behind Hobbes's early position turns on the distinction between two issues: that of determining that there shall be a sovereign, and that of fixing the identity of the sovereign (see Hampton 1986, chapter 6). In a democracy, those issues are solved at once, with the collective people being identified as sovereign at the very moment that sovereign rule is accepted. But they are naturally taken to come apart with a monarchy and an aristocracy, at least if these are set up by institution. First, the people will agree that there shall be representative rule, in which case they appear for the moment to make themselves a sovereign, democratic collectivity. And then that collectivity will transfer its sovereignty to the individual who is to be the monarch or the body of individuals that is to rule as an aristocracy.

9. A possible explanation for the line that Hobbes takes here is this. He is anxious in both his earlier and later works to insist that the people cannot rebel against the sovereign; as soon as they reject the sovereign, they cease to be a people and become a multitude again. In *Leviathan* he can easily maintain this point of view, since the multitude becomes a people in the case of monarchy by directly adopting an individual as sovereign, and in the case of aristocracy and democracy by adopting a committee as sovereign; thus if the people rejects its sovereign, be that an individual or a body, it loses its unity. But in the earlier works there is room for the thought that if the people constitute themselves as a democratic sovereign prior to going over to a monarchical sovereign, then they can resume that self-sovereignty in rejecting the monarch. Perhaps it is for fear of that thought that Hobbes insists on his peculiar line in two passages from *De Cive* (7.8, 12.8), arguing that under a monarchy the people is the monarch, under an aristocracy the council of aristocrats, and under a democracy the multitude.

Chapter Six

1. What might be worse than death? Hobbes acknowledges that "eternal torture is more terrible than death" (B 14–15), a fact he thinks that "the Roman clergy" exploit in suggesting that they can hold out worse penalties than regular

sovereigns. For an argument that Hobbes thinks the fear of such religious sanctions is important to the stability of a political order, not just the fear of death, see Lloyd 1992.

2. My reading of the passage in *De Homine* is not uncontroversial. On another reading, more tightly connected with his hedonism, Hobbes might be taken to say that life is always good except in the presence of awful pains, the suggestion being that such pains are not common.

3. Since Hobbes allows that animals may develop prudence, which is the habit of forming more or less reliable expectations about the future on the basis of past experience (L 3.10), he must presumably allow that animals can feel pleasure and pain in such immediate expectation as well as in present experience.

4. The preface to Marin Mersenne's *Ballistica*, published in 1644, which summarizes Hobbes's thought, and is generally thought to have been drafted by Hobbes, contains the following paragraph:

> When we imagine the difference between two things perceived in sensation, this comparison is the beginning of discourse. But this cannot happen with the clarity we usually need for reasoning, unless we attach fixed marks to them, which enable us to connect present things to past things. These marks we call *names*, and they help us to examine and investigate the causes of things. For how could we compare things or their phantasms, without being able to bring them back into our memory by means of various words functioning as labels? Since brute animals do not have them, they are far inferior to us. Indeed, they cannot even distinguish things from phantasms, and enjoy no pleasures other than sensual ones.

This translation is by George MacDonald Ross, and is available at http://www.philosophy.leeds.ac.uk/GMR/hmp/texts/modern/hobbes/ballistic/ballistic.html.

5. Hobbes thinks that not only does this sort of comparison have such instrumental value; the activity of comparison in general is inherently attractive for human beings. In "comparing the things that come into his mind one with another," he says, "a man delighteth himself either with finding unexpected similitude in things, otherwise much unlike . . . ; or else in discerning suddenly dissimilitude in things that otherwise appear the same" (EL 10.4). This activity of comparing and distinguishing, which may be applied in any domain—for example, to "persons, places and seasons"—is "commonly termed by the name of judgment: for, to judge is nothing else, but to distinguish or discern" (EL 10.4).

Chapter Seven

1. He does highlight the problem of competition in his later work, as we shall see in the next chapter, and he says in *De Cive* (1.6) that "the most frequent cause of why men want to hurt each other arises when many want the same

thing at the same time, without being able to enjoy it in common or to divide it." But competition among human beings is going to be different from competition among animals, since it is going to be shaped by mutual perception of the dangers people represent for one another and anxiety on that account. The sense of danger will be amplified by an awareness of the nature of competition and the problems of relative power that it makes salient.

2. Hobbes's later political theory is forged on the basis of his theory of language and mind—a theory that he only developed as a by-product of thinking about the place of mind in the nature described by the new science. Since he only became familiar with the new science in the 1630s, it should be no surprise to find that his views in 1629 are somewhat different from those of 1640, when he penned *The Elements of Law*. For an intriguing statement of Hobbes's earlier views, at least if the editors Noel Reynolds and Arlene Saxonhouse are correct to ascribe the text to him, see Hobbes 1995.

3. If this is right, then it is not sufficient for Hobbes's argument that people pursue superiority in relation to one another. But that they pursue superiority will still be necessary for his argument, and so the error ascribed to Hobbes in the introduction and at the end of the previous chapter will remain crucial to his case for the absolute state.

4. Hobbes goes on to make the nice point that "this proveth rather that men are in that point equal, than unequal. For there is not ordinarily a greater sign of the equal distribution of anything than that every man is contented with his share" (L 13.2).

5. Here I depart from the moralistic view of Hobbesian natural law that is associated with a number of people, most prominently Howard Warrender (1957). My view is much closer to the prudential view of natural law ascribed to Hobbes by John W. N. Watkins (1973). Debate continues on this issue, but the Watkins stance is now more or less accepted as the "orthodox" one; see the comments of John Deigh (1996), a dissenter on the issue. For discussions of Deigh's own view, according to which Hobbes's ethics is logically distinct from his psychology—contrary to the line taken here—see Murphy 2000; Deigh 2003; Hoekstra 2003. For a brief overview of different positions on Hobbes's view of natural law, see Tuck 1996, 190–93.

6. Some commentators in the moralistic tradition of interpretation have suggested that Hobbes's appeal to natural law is grounded in a belief in God, even in an allegiance to Christianity, and this may seem to be supported by the comment in *Leviathan* (15.41) that "the same theorems, as delivered in the word of God, that by right commandeth all things, then are properly called laws." As noted by Edwin Curley in an editorial footnote, however, this sentence is omitted from the Latin edition, published in 1668. References to God in Hobbes can generally be understood on the assumption that he didn't wish to proclaim himself an atheist—who would have in that period?—and that he very much wanted to persuade Christians that their religion supported or was at least consistent with his doctrines. Hobbes takes a different view of natural law, then, from someone like Samuel Pufendorf. Although an adherent of Protestant natural law, like Hobbes, Pufendorf held, in Stephen Darwall's words (2006, 23), "that genuine obligations can result only from an address"—in this case, an address from God.

7. There may be "external impediments" that block people doing all they are at liberty to do, given the absence of obligation, in pursuit of their self-preservation. These obstacles will mean that people's liberty is reduced in the distinct, "proper signification of the word"—that is, in the sense in which liberty is opposed to impediment rather than obligation. But this does not affect "the right of nature" postulated by Hobbes. It remains the case that when it comes to securing self-preservation, a person may use "the power left him, according as his judgment and reason shall dictate to him" (L 14.2); there is no obligation in the state of nature to reject such a path. These comments should be more intelligible in light of the discussion of freedom or liberty in the next chapter; they suggest a reading of *Leviathan* (14.1–3) under which both conceptions of liberty are put in play.

8. Let the first three laws of nature be satisfied, so that a dispensation of peace emerges, and Hobbes thinks that people will also be bound by a rich tapestry of supplementary laws. These are precepts of sensible self-concern that apply in the external forum, becoming more than mere desiderata (L 15.36) from the moment when people act on the more basic laws and peace begins to reign (Kavka 1986, 344). These supplementary precepts will rule out not only the injustice of breaking a covenant but also a host of other vices ranging from ingratitude to revenge, to pride and inequity (L 15.16–33).

CHAPTER EIGHT

1. This claim fits reasonably well, though not perfectly, with Hobbes's other discussions of the topic (EL 22, 23; DCv 8, 9; L 20). As suggested in an earlier footnote (chapter 5, note 6) the argument that follows can go through, at least with some amendment, even if the contract with the would-be sovereign is thought to involve only the sort of submission demanded by a private master. A commonwealth will emerge insofar as everyone proves to have made such a contract, and this is manifest to all; in such a situation, the individual empowered by those contracts should able to play the protective role of sovereign, calling on others to put down any lone defector or small group of defectors.

2. I have benefited from exchanges with Jim Wilson on this issue.

3. We might model the exercise of Hobbesian clarification with the help of John Rawls's (1971) method of reflective equilibrium. The idea would be that we start from a vague common idea of a circle or a commonwealth, but are prepared to revise it somewhat in order to achieve a coherence or equilibrium with the practical knowledge we gain of how to construct such an object.

4. By Hobbes's reading, sovereign authority became more or less democratic, certainly nonmonarchical, in the 1640s and 1650s: "it moved from King Charles I. to the Long Parliament; from thence to the Rump; from the Rump to Oliver Cromwell; and then back again from Richard Cromwell to the Rump; thence to the Long Parliament; and thence to King Charles II., where long may it remain" (B 204). For a reading of Hobbes that maintains he was more sympathetic to the revolutionaries than this would suggest, see Collins 2005; for a contrasting view, see Hoekstra 2004.

5. For a fascinating account of other de facto strains in Hobbes's thinking on these matters, see Hoekstra 2004.

6. This conception of absolute, lawmaking sovereignty had only emerged in the previous century, with the humanist debunking—in particular, by Bodin—of what had been taken to be the authoritative, relatively unalterable corpus of Roman law. Previously, the *princeps* or ruler had been said to be *legibus solutus*, free of the law, but that just meant free from the penalties of the law, not free to make and unmake the law. See Gilmore 1941; Franklin 1973.

7. Hobbes recognizes a distinction between cases where the sovereign artificially personates the people, acting qua sovereign, and cases where the sovereign self-personates and acts in a private capacity: here he bears not "the person of the people" but "his own natural person" (L 19.4; see also D 162).

8. More surprisingly, Hobbes also says in *Leviathan* (21.14–15) that I am not bound, on the sovereign's say-so, to kill a fellow or compatriot. The reasoning may be that were I to try to do this, I would be putting my own life at risk and so acting contrary to natural law. Hobbes suggests that because of the danger—or even the dishonor—of the act, I can refuse to kill another person except when this refusal "frustrates the end for which the sovereignty was ordained.

9. Jean Hampton (1986, chapter 7) raises difficulties for Hobbes's argument on the grounds that it is unclear how the limitations on the obligations of the citizen are to be determined. My sense is that Hobbes envisages a contract for the acceptance of an absolute sovereign, where it goes without saying—as a default condition—that while people may be generally obligated by that contract, they will not be obligated with respect to situations involving an imminent danger of death.

10. The line taken here is in tension with the interpretation of Hobbes as a "possessive individualist." See Macpherson 1962. My line is close to that of Keith Thomas (1965).

11. Does talk of what each person should call good or bad, just or unjust, suggest that Hobbes has some contrast in mind between what is good or bad, just or unjust, and what comes to be called so? I do not think so, since the evaluative categories in question will only be revealed, from Hobbes's perspective, as the corresponding words are given extensions according to commonly accepted rules.

12. For a more generous perspective on Hobbes, see Ivison 1999.

13. Hobbes vividly expresses the point to which he is committing himself here in an exchange with Bramhall. His opponent had argued that if the door to the tennis court is closed, perhaps unbeknownst to someone, then that person is unfree to play tennis, whether or not they have any wish to do so. Hobbes responds, "It is no impediment to him that the door is shut till he have a will to play, which he has not till he has done deliberating whether he shall play or not" (Hobbes and Bramhill 1999, 91). The lack of ability to perform a certain action, as we saw, may mean that the question of whether the agent is free or unfree to do it does not arise. Equally, we now see, the fact that an agent has not made a decision to perform a certain action means that the question of their freedom to do it does not arise. It will not be free or unfree, merely nonfree.

14. The obstacles may affect what the agent can do on a narrower or wider front. This latter point too is suggested by the analogy. "Water . . . when it is

open on all sides spreads; and the more outlets it finds the freer it is" (DCv 13.15).

15. Quentin Skinner (2002) argues that there was a serious development in Hobbes's views on liberty between 1640, when he wrote *The Elements of Law*, and 1651, when he offered this definition in *Leviathan*. In the later work, this freedom as nonobstruction is given primacy for the first time, as Skinner usefully observes, insofar as it is the only freedom mentioned in the definition of a free-man. But I think that this is a shift in Hobbes's use of the word "free-man"—a word he may have wanted to expropriate from parliamentary writers of the 1640s—not a shift in his underlying picture of how subjects relate to one another and their sovereign. It represents a semantic adjustment, not a development in his political ontology. In support of his more radical claim, Skinner quotes the reference in *Elements of Law* to something that "Aristotle saith well"—namely, "that no man can partake of liberty, but only in a popular commonwealth" (EL 27.3). Taken at face value, I find this remark utterly at odds with the main theses of that book, however, and I think that it must refer not to liberty as Hobbes understands it but to what is generally taken for liberty: to "liberty-so-called," as we might say. That interpretation fits with the view he adopts elsewhere in the book when, clearly speaking of liberty-so-called, he says that "freedom . . . in commonwealths is nothing but the honour of equality of favour with other subjects" (EL 23.9). This view is explicitly adopted in *De Cive* (9.9) when Hobbes suggests that in relation to a sovereign, slaves are on a par with their masters—both are subject to the sovereign—but that masters are called "free citizens" because "they perform more honorable services . . . and enjoy more luxuries."

16. There is one aspect of Hobbes's view that might be expected to have recommended itself to his republican contemporaries. This is the claim that to complain of injury at the hands of the sovereign is to complain of injury at one's own hand; "he that complaineth of injury from his sovereign complaineth of that whereof he himself is author" (L 18.6). In this theme Hobbes comes quite close to the proposition, familiar from Rousseau's *Social Contract* (1973), that what the sovereign does is done by the public, general will of the subjects, if not always in accordance with their particular, private wills. Hobbes approaches that very formulation in *The Elements of Law* (25.12) in a discussion of judgment or conscience: "For the conscience being nothing else but a man's settled judgment and opinion, when he hath once transferred his right of judging to another, that which shall be commanded, is no less his judgment, than the judgment of that other; so that in obedience to laws, a man doth still according to his conscience, but not his private conscience."

17. Not that Hobbes lacked influence in that period. One thinker on whom he made a particularly large impact, of course, is Benedict de Spinoza. For an illuminating study, see Lazzeri 1998.

References

Aarsleff, H. 1976. An Outline of Language-Origins Theory since the Renaissance. *Annals of the New York Academy of Sciences* 280:4–14.

Aubrey, J. 1994. The Brief Life. In *Thomas Hobbes: The Elements of Law, Natural and Politic*, ed. J.C.A. Gaskin. Oxford: Oxford University Press.

Bacon, F. 2000. *The New Organon*. Ed. L. Jardine and M. Silverthorne. Cambridge: Cambridge University Press.

Ball, T. 1994. *Reappraising Political Theory*. Oxford: Oxford University Press.

Bentham, J. 1843. *The Works of Jeremy Bentham*. Edinburgh: William Tait.

Bodin, J. 1992. *On Sovereignty*. Cambridge: Cambridge University Press.

Brennan, G., and P. Pettit. 2004. *The Economy of Esteem: An Essay on Civil and Political Society*. Oxford: Oxford University Press.

Brett, A. 1998. *Liberty, Right, and Nature*. Cambridge: Cambridge University Press.

Broome, J. 2004. Reasons. In *Essays in Honour of Joseph Raz*, ed. J. Wallace, M. Smith, S. Scheffler, and P. Pettit. Oxford: Oxford University Press.

Canning, J. P. 1980. The Corporation in the Political Thought of the Italian Jurists of the Thirteenth and Fourteenth Century. *History of Political Thought* 1:9–32.

Canning, J. P. 1983. Ideas of the State in Thirteenth and Fourteenth Century Commentators on the Roman Law. *Transactions of the Royal Historical Society* 33:1–27.

Canning, J. P. 1996. *A History of Medieval Political Thought, 300–1450*. London: Routledge.

Carey, S. 2007. *The Origin of Concepts*. Cambridge, MA: MIT Press.

Chomsky, N. 1965. *Cartesian Linguistics*. New York: Harper and Row.

Cicero, M. T. 1888. *The Orations of Marcus Tullius Cicero*. London: George Bell.

Clark, M. T. 1972. *An Aquinas Reader*. London: Hodder and Stoughton.

Cole, T. 1990. *Democritus and the Sources of Greek Anthropology*. Atlanta, GA: Scholars Press.

Collins, J. R. 2005. *The Allegiance of Thomas Hobbes*. Oxford: Oxford University Press.

Cowell, J. 1607. *The Interpreter or Booke Containing the Signification of Words*. Cambridge, UK: John Legate.

Curley, E. 1994. Introduction and Notes. In *Hobbes Leviathan*, ed. E. Curley. Indianapolis, IN: Hackett.

Darwall, S. 2006. *The Second-Person Standpoint: Morality, Respect, and Accountability*. Cambridge, MA: Harvard University Press.

Dascal, M. 1996. Hobbes's Challenge. In *The Prehistory of Cognitive Science*, ed. A. Brook. London: Palgrave Macmillan.

Dawson, H. 2005. Locke on Language in (Civil) Society. *History of Political Thought* 26:397–425.

de Jong, W. R. 1990. Did Hobbes Have a Semantic Theory of Truth? *Journal of the History of Philosophy* 28:63–88.

Deacon, T. 1997. *The Symbolic Species: The Co-evolution of Language and the Human Brain.* London: Penguin.

Deigh, J. 1996. Reason and Ethics in Hobbes's Leviathan. *Journal of the History of Philosophy* 34:33–60.

Deigh, J. 2003. Reply to Mark Murphy. *Journal of the History of Philosophy* 41:91–109

Dent, N.J.H. 1988. *Rousseau.* Oxford, UK: Blackwell.

Descartes, R. 1985a. *The Philosophical Writings, Vol. 1.* Trans. J. Cottingham, R. Stoothoff, and D. Murdoch. Cambridge: Cambridge University Press.

Descartes, R. 1985b. *The Philosophical Writings, Vol. 2.* Trans. J. Cottingham, R. Stoothoff, and D. Murdoch. Cambridge: Cambridge University Press.

Eschmann, T. 1944. Studies on the Notion of Society in St Thomas Aquinas: St Thomas and the Decretal of Innocent IV Romana Ecclesia, Ceterum. *Medieval Studies*: 1–42.

Fodor, J. 1975. *The Language of Thought.* Cambridge: Cambridge University Press.

Franklin, J. 1973. *Jean Bodin and the Rise of Absolutist Theory.* Cambridge: Cambridge University Press.

Frede, D., and B. Inwood, eds. 2005. *Language and Learning: Philosophy of Language in the Hellenistic Age.* Cambridge: Cambridge University Press.

Garnett, G., ed. 1994. *Vindiciae contra Tyrannos.* Cambridge: Cambridge University Press.

Gaskin, J.C.A. 1994. Introduction and Notes. In *Thomas Hobbes, Human Nature, and De Corpore Politico*, ed. J.C.A. Gaskin. Oxford: Oxford University Press.

Gauthier, D. 1969. *The Logic of Leviathan.* Oxford: Oxford University Press.

Gazzaniga, M. S., R. B. Ivry, and G. R. Mangun. 1998. *Cognitive Neuroscience.* New York: W. W. Norton.

Gert, B. 1967. Hobbes and Psychological Egoism. *Journal of the History of Ideas* 28:503–20.

Gilmore, M. P. 1941. *Argument from Roman Law in Political Thought, 1200–1600.* Cambridge, MA: Harvard University Press.

Gordon, P. 2004. Numerical Cognition without Words: Evidence from Amazonia. *Science* 306 (5695): 496–99.

Grotius, H. 2005. *The Rights of War and Peace, Vols. 1–3.* Ed. R. Tuck. Indianapolis, IN: Liberty Fund.

Haakonssen, K. 2004. Protestant Natural Law Theory. In *New Essays on the History of Autonomy*, ed. N. Brender and L. Krasnoff. Cambridge: Cambridge University Press.

Hampton, J. 1986. *Hobbes and the Social Contract Tradition.* Cambridge: Cambridge University Press.

Harrington, J. 1992. *The Commonwealth of Oceana and a System of Politics.* Cambridge: Cambridge University Press.

Hayes, P. 1999. Hobbes's Silent Fool: A Response to Hoekstra. *Political Theory* 27:225–29.

Hobbes, T. 1839a. *The English Works of Thomas Hobbes*. Ed. W. Molesworth. Vol. 1. Oxford: Oxford University Press.

Hobbes, T. 1839b. *The English Works of Thomas Hobbes*. Ed. W. Molesworth. Vol. 7. Oxford: Oxford University Press.

Hobbes, T. 1990. *Behemoth or the Long Parliament*. Ed. F. Toennies. Chicago: University of Chicago Press.

Hobbes, T. 1994a. *Human Nature and De Corpore Politico: The Elements of Law, Natural and Politic*. Oxford: Oxford University Press.

Hobbes, T. 1994b. *Leviathan*. Ed. E. Curley. Indianapolis, IN: Hackett.

Hobbes, T. 1994c. The Prose Life. In *Thomas Hobbes: The Elements of Law, Natural and Politic*, ed. J.C.A. Gaskin. Oxford: Oxford University Press.

Hobbes, T. 1995. *Three Discourses: A Critical Modern Edition of Newly Identified Work of the Young Hobbes*. Ed. N. B. Reynolds and A. W. Saxonhouse. Chicago: University of Chicago Press.

Hobbes, T. 1998a. *Man and Citizen*. Ed. and trans. B. Gert. Indianapolis, IN: Hackett.

Hobbes, T. 1998b. *On the Citizen*. Ed. and trans. R. Tuck and M. Silverthorne. Cambridge: Cambridge University Press.

Hobbes, T. 2005. *A Dialogue between a Philosopher, and a Student of the Common Laws of England*. Ed. A. Cromartie. Oxford: Oxford University Press.

Hobbes, T., and J. Bramhall. 1999. *Hobbes and Bramhall on Freedom and Necessity*. Ed. Vere Chappell. Cambridge: Cambridge University Press.

Hochstrasser, T. J. 2000. *Natural Law Theories in the Early Enlightenment*. Cambridge: Cambridge University Press.

Hoekstra, K. 1997. Hobbes and the Foole. *Political Theory* 25:620–54.

Hoekstra, K. 1999. Nothing to Declare? Hobbes and the Advocate of Injustice. *Political Theory* 27:230–35.

Hoekstra, K. 2003. Hobbes on Law, Nature, and Reason. *Journal of the History of Philosophy* 41:111–20.

Hoekstra, K. 2004. Hobbes De Facto? A Review and Conclusion. In *Leviathan after 350 Years*, ed. T. Sorell and L. Foisneau. Oxford: Oxford University Press.

Hoekstra, K. 2005. The End of Philosophy: The Case of Hobbes. *Proceedings of the Aristotelian Society* 105:22–60.

Hoekstra, K. 2006. A Lion in the House: Hobbes and Democracy. In *Rethinking the Foundations of Modern Political Thought*, ed. A. S. Brett and J. Tully. Cambridge: Cambridge University Press.

Holmes, S. 1990. Political Psychology in Hobbes's Behemoth. In *Thomas Hobbes and Political Theory*, M. G. Dietz. Lawrence: University Press of Kansas.

Hungerland, I. C., and G. R. Vick. 1981. Hobbes's Theory of Language, Speech, and Reasoning. In *Thomas Hobbes: Part 1 of De Corpore*, ed. I. C. Hungerland and G. R. Vick. New York: Arbaris Books.

Ivison, D. 1999. Pluralism and the Hobbesian Logic of Negative Constitutionalism. *Political Studies* 47:83–90.

Jesseph, D. M. 1998. Leibniz on the Foundations of the Calculus: The Question of the Reality of Infinitesimal Magnitudes. *Perspectives on Science* 6:6–40.

Johnston, D. 1986. *The Rhetoric of Leviathan: Thomas Hobbes and the Politics of Cultural Transformation*. Princeton, NJ: Princeton University Press.

Kantorowicz, E. H. 1997. *The King's Two Bodies: A Study in Mediaeval Political Theology*. Princeton, NJ: Princeton University Press.

Kavka, G. 1986. *Hobbesian Moral and Political Theory*. Princeton, NJ: Princeton University Press.

Kelley, D. R. 1976. Vera Philosophia: The Philosophical Significance of Renaissance Jurisprudence. *Journal of the History of Philosophy* 14:267–79.

Kerferd, G. B. 1981. *The Sophistic Movement*. Cambridge: Cambridge University Press.

Kraus, J. S. 1993. *The Limits of Hobbesian Contractarianism*. Cambridge: Cambridge University Press.

Kripke, S. A. 1982. *Wittgenstein on Rules and Private Language*. Oxford: Blackwell.

Lazzeri, C. 1998. *Droit, pouvoir et liberte: Spinoza critique de Hobbes*. Paris: PUF.

Lenoble, R. 1971. *Mersenne sur La Naissance du Mecanisme*. 2nd ed. Paris: Vrin.

List, C., and P. Pettit. 2002. Aggregating Sets of Judgments: An Impossibility Result. *Economics and Philosophy* 18:89–110.

List, C., and P. Pettit. 2004. Aggregating Sets of Judgments: Two Impossibility Results Compared. *Synthese* 140:207–35.

Lloyd, S. A. 1992. *Ideals as Interests in Hobbes's Leviathan: The Power of Mind over Matter*. Cambridge: Cambridge University Press.

Locke, J. 1960. *Two Treatises of Government*. Cambridge: Cambridge University Press.

Locke, J. 1975. *An Essay concerning Human Understanding*. Oxford: Oxford University Press.

Lovett, F. 2005. Milton's Case for a Free Commonwealth. *American Journal of Political Science* 49:466–78.

Lucretius. 2004. *On the Nature of Things*. Trans. W. E. Leonard. Mineola, NY: Dover Publications.

Macpherson, C. B. 1962. *The Political Theory of Possessive Individualism*. Oxford: Oxford University Press.

Malcolm, N. 2003. *Aspects of Hobbes*. Oxford: Oxford University Press.

Malmendier, U. 2005. Roman Shares. In *The Origins of Value: The Financial Innovations That Created Modern Capital Markets*, ed. W. Goetzman and G. Rouwenhorst. Oxford: Oxford University Press.

Martin, R. M. 1953. On the Semantics of Hobbes. *Philosophy and Phenomenological Research* 14:205–11.

Martinich, A. P. 1999. *Hobbes: A Biography*. Cambridge: Cambridge University Press.

Martinich, A. P. 2005. *Hobbes*. London: Routledge.

McGeer, V. 1996. Is "Self-Knowledge" an Empirical Problem? Renegotiating the Space of Philosophical Explanation. *Journal of Philosophy* 93:483–515.

Miller, A., and C. Wright, eds. 2002. *Rule-Following and Meaning*. Chesham, UK: Acumen.

Montaigne, M. d. 1991. *The Complete Essays*. Harmondsworth, UK: Penguin.

Moran, R. 2001. *Authority and Estrangement: An Essay on Self-Knowledge*. Princeton, NJ: Princeton University Press.

Morgan, E. S. 1988. *Inventing the People: The Rise of Popular Sovereignty in England and America*. New York: W. W. Norton.

Murphy, J. B. 2005. *The Philosophy of Positive Law: Foundations of Jurisprudence*. New Haven, CT: Yale University Press.

Murphy, M. C. 2000. Desire and Ethics in Hobbes's Leviathan: A Response to Professor Deigh. *Journal of the History of Philosophy* 38:259–68.

Norlin, G. 1961. *Isocrates*. London: William Heinemann.

Paley, W. 1825. *The Principles of Moral and Political Philosophy, Vol. 4, Collected Works*. London: C. and J. Rivington.

Pettit, P. 1986. Free Riding and Foul Dealing. *Journal of Philosophy* 83:361–79.

Pettit, P. 1997. *Republicanism: A Theory of Freedom and Government*. Oxford: Oxford University Press.

Pettit, P. 2001. *A Theory of Freedom: From the Psychology to the Politics of Agency*. Cambridge, UK: Polity.

Pettit, P. 2002. *Rules, Reasons, and Norms: Selected Essays*. Oxford: Oxford University Press.

Pettit, P. 2003. Groups with Minds of Their Own. In *Socializing Metaphysics*, ed. F. Schmitt. New York: Rowan and Littlefield.

Pettit, P. 2004. Existentialism, Quietism, and Philosophy. In *The Future for Philosophy*, ed. B. Leiter. Oxford: Oxford University Press.

Pettit, P. 2005. Liberty and Leviathan. *Politics, Philosophy, and Economics* 4:131–51.

Pettit, P. 2007a. Joining the Dots. In *Common Minds: Themes from the Philosophy of Philip Pettit*, ed. H. G. Brennan, R. E. Goodin, F. C. Jackson, and M. Smith. Oxford: Oxford University Press.

Pettit, P. 2007b. Neuroscience and Agent-Control. In *Distributed Cognition and the Will: Individual Volition and Social Context*, ed. D. Spurrett, D. Ross, H. Kincaid, and L. Stephens. Cambridge, MA: MIT Press.

Pettit, P. 2007c. Republican Liberty: Three Axioms, Four Theorems. In *Republicanism and Political Theory*, ed. C. Laborde and J. Manor. Oxford, UK: Blackwells.

Pettit, P. 2007d. Participation, Deliberation, and We-Thinking. In *The Illusion of Consent: Essays in Honor of Carole Pateman*, ed. D. O'Neill, M. Shanley, and I. Young. Philadelphia: Pennsylvania State University Press.

Pettit, P. 2007e. Free Persons and Free Choices. *History of Political Thought* 28.

Rawls, J. 1971. *A Theory of Justice*. Oxford: Oxford University Press.

Rorty, R. 1980. *Philosophy and the Mirror of Nature*. Oxford, UK: Basil Blackwell.

Rousseau, J.-J. 1973. *The Social Contract and Discourses*. London: J. M. Dent and Sons Ltd.

Runciman, D. 1997. *Pluralism and the Personality of the State*. Cambridge: Cambridge University Press.

Runciman, D. 2000. What Kind of Person Is Hobbes's State? A Reply to Skinner. *Journal of Political Philosophy* 8:268–78.

Runciman, D. 2003. Moral Responsibility and the Problem of Representing the State. In *Can Institutions Have Responsibilities?* ed. T. Erskine. London: Palgrave.

Runciman, D. 2006. Hobbes's Theory of Representation: Anti-Democratic or Proto-Democratic. Cambridge Social and Political Sciences Department, Cambridge, UK.

Ryan, A. 1996. Hobbes's Political Philosophy. In *Cambridge Companion to Hobbes*, ed. T. Sorell. Cambridge: Cambridge University Press.

Ryan, M. 1999. Bartolus of Sassoferrato and Free Cities. *Transactions of the Royal Historical Society* 6:65–89.

Schuhmann, K. 1998. *Hobbes: Une Chronique*. Paris: Vrin.

Schuhmann, K. 2004. Leviathan and De Cive. In *Leviathan after 350 Years*, ed. T. Sorell and L. Foisneau. Oxford: Oxford University Press.

Shapin, S., and S. Schaffer. 1985. *Leviathan and the Air-Pump*. Princeton, NJ: Princeton University Press.

Skinner, Q. 1978. *The Foundations of Modern Political Thought*. Cambridge: Cambridge University Press.

Skinner, Q. 1988. A Reply to My Critics. In *Meaning and Context: Quentin Skinner and His Critics*, ed. J. Tully. Cambridge, UK: Polity.

Skinner, Q. 1996. *Reason and Rhetoric in the Philosophy of Hobbes*. Cambridge: Cambridge University Press.

Skinner, Q. 1998. *Liberty before Liberalism*. Cambridge: Cambridge University Press.

Skinner, Q. 1999. Hobbes and the Artificial Person of the State. *Journal of Political Philosophy* 7:1–29 (reprinted with revisions in Skinner 2002).

Skinner, Q. 2002. *Visions of Politics: Vol. 3, Hobbes and Civil Science*. Cambridge: Cambridge University Press.

Skinner, Q. 2005. Hobbes on Representation. *European Journal of Philosophy* 13:155–84.

Skinner, Q. 2006. Surveying the Foundations: A Retrospect and Reassessment. In *Rethinking the Foundations of Modern Political Thought*, ed. A. Brett and J. Tully. Cambridge: Cambridge University Press.

Skyrms, B. 2003. *The Stag Hunt and the Evolution of Social Structure*. Cambridge: Cambridge University Press.

Soles, D. H. 1996. *Strong Wits and Spider Webs: A Study in Hobbes's Philosophy of Language*. Aldershot: Avebury.

Sorell, T. 1986. *Hobbes*. London: Routledge.

Strauss, L. 1952. *The Political Philosophy of Thomas Hobbes*. Chicago: University of Chicago Press.

Tattersall, I. 2002. *The Monkey in the Mirror: Essays on the Science of What Makes Us Human*. New York: Harcourt.

Thomas, K. 1965. The Social Origins of Hobbes's Political Thought. In *Hobbes Studies*, ed. K. C. Brown. Cambridge, MA: Harvard University Press.

Toernebohm, H. 1960. A Study in Hobbes' Theory of Denotation and Truth. *Theoria* 26:53–70.

Tuck, R. 1987. The "Modern" Theory of Natural Law. In *The Languages of Political Theory in Early Modern Europe*, ed. A. Pagden. Cambridge: Cambridge University Press.

Tuck, R. 1988a. Hobbes and Descartes. In *Perspectives on Thomas Hobbes*, ed. G.A.J. Rogers and A. Ryan. Oxford: Oxford University Press.

Tuck, R. 1988b. Optics and Skeptics: The Philosophical Foundations of Hobbes's Political Thought. In *Conscience and Casuistry in Early Modern Europe*, ed. E. Leites. Cambridge: Cambridge University Press.

Tuck, R. 1989. *Hobbes*. Oxford: Oxford University Press.

Tuck, R. 1996. Hobbes's Moral Philosophy. In *The Cambridge Companion to Hobbes*, ed. T. Sorell. Cambridge: Cambridge University Press.

Tuck, R. 1998. Hobbes and the Body Politic. Harvard Government Department, Cambridge, MA.

Tuck, R. 2006a. Hobbes and Democracy. In *Rethinking the Foundations of Modern Political Thought*, ed. A. S. Brett and J. Tully. Cambridge: Cambridge University Press.

Tuck, R. 2006b. Hobbes on Civil Persons and Representation. Harvard Government Department, Cambridge, MA.

Vico, G. 1982. *Selected Writings*. Ed. and trans. L. Pompa. Cambridge: Cambridge University Press.

Vieira, M. A. 2005. *The Elements of Representation in Hobbes: Aesthetics, Theatre, Law, and Theology in the Construction of Hobbes's Theory of the State*. Cambridge: Cambridge University Press.

Viroli, M. 2002. *Republicanism*. New York: Hill and Wang.

Warrender, H. 1957. *The Political Philosophy of Hobbes*. Oxford: Oxford University Press.

Watkins, J.W.N. 1973. *Hobbes's System of Ideas*. London: Hutchinson.

Wells, G. A. 1987. *The Origin of Language*. La Salle, IL: Open Court.

Whelan, F. G. 1981. Language and Its Abuses in Hobbes' Political Philosophy. *American Political Science Review* 75:59–75.

Wittgenstein, L. 1958. *Philosophical Investigations*. Oxford: Blackwell.

Woolf, C.N.S. 1913. *Bartolus of Sassoferrato*. Cambridge: Cambridge University Press.

Zarka, Y. C. 1995. *Hobbes et la pensee politique moderne*. Paris: Presses Universitaires de France.

Index

absolute state, 4, 96, 125–29

absurdity, self-contradiction as, 61–63, 66, 147

action, freedom of, 134–40, 153

active thought, 37–39, 144–45

Adam, 26, 157n1

addition, 43–44

affirmations, 39, 48, 50, 52, 144

amour de soi, 3, 97

amour propre, 3, 97

analytic knowledge, 21

animal motion, 16–18, 143

animals: curiosity in, 27; desires of, 89–91; humans versus, 2, 4, 10, 13, 25–27, 36, 39, 46, 60, 91, 95, 99–100, 116, 164n4; relations of, to one another, 59; sociable living of, 100, 108; and state of nature, 98. *See also* natural mind

anxiety, 92

a posteriori knowledge, 19–20

appearances, 10

appetite: animal and human, 90; definition of, 17. *See also* desire

a priori demonstration, 19–22, 119, 143, 156n9

Aquinas, Thomas, 29, 55

arbitrator: evaluative judgments and, 88–89; property determination and, 131

aristocracy: drawbacks of, 110; emergence of, 71, 80, 121

Aristotelianism, 29, 43, 162n4

Aristotle, 99, 159n1

artificial persons, 56, 70, 71

assurance, contracts and, 64–66, 113

atheism, 156n2, 165n6

attention, 15

Aubrey, John, 50

authority: basis of, 161n4; of multitudes, 72, 75; over children, 122; persons and, 58–59, 146; sovereign, 119–40, 151–53

aversion, 17, 85

Bacon, Francis, 5, 49

Baldus de Ubaldis, 76

Ballistica (Mersenne), 164n4

Bartolus of Sassoferrato, 76

beasts. *See* animals

being, hierarchy of, 12

belief: desire and, 17; language and, 4–5

Bentham, Jeremy, 140

blood, 16, 143

Bodin, Jean, 119, 122–23, 157n11, 167n6

Boethius, Anicius Manlius Severinus, 55

Boyle, Robert, 6, 54

Bramhall, John, 129

causes, 22–23, 27, 143–44

Cavendish family, 51

change, 10, 156n3

Charles I, 122

Charles II, 122

children, authority over, 122

Chomsky, Noam, 28

Cicero, Marcus Tullius, 29–30, 74

circle, 21, 116–19

civil law, 130, 131

civil persons, 76, 108

civil science, 21–22, 46, 116, 143, 157n11

civil society. *See* commonwealth

civil state, as development from second nature, 99

Civil War, English, 103

classes, 42–43, 145

classificatory thought, 26, 30–36, 39, 158n8

coercion: and commonwealth foundation, 124; contracts and, 66, 147; freedom and, 137; volition and, 67

cognition, natural mind and, 13–16

color, 10–11, 36

commitments, 61–62. *See also* contracts

committee-of-the-whole, 79, 80, 148

commodious living, 63–64

common meanings, 40–41, 89, 131, 145

commonwealth: by acquisition, 77–78, 117–18, 148; benefits of, 115–16, 132; conditions for, 115; contracts and, 77–78; as corporation, 77; generation of, 77–78, 108, 116–19, 142, 148, 151; by institution,